D1087730

HUMAN RIGHTS
IN
JEWISH LAW

HUMAN RIGHTS
IN
JEWISH LAW

By
Haim H. Cohn

Published for
THE INSTITUTE OF JEWISH AFFAIRS, LONDON
by
KTAV PUBLISHING HOUSE,INC.
NEW YORK
1984

The Institute of Jewish Affairs gratefully acknowledges
the assistance of The Memorial Foundation for Jewish
Culture in the preparation of this volume.

Library of Congress Cataloging in Publication Data

Cohn, Haim Hermann, 1911-
  Human rights in Jewish law.

  Bibliography: p.
  Includes index.
  1. Civil rights (Jewish law) I. Title.
LAW   342'.085'088296   83-14846
ISBN 0-88125-036-8   342.85088296

MANUFACTURED IN THE UNITED STATES OF AMERICA

CONTENTS

PREFACE

The suggestion to restate the attitudes of Jewish legal and religious traditions to human rights was first made to me by my good friend, Dr. Stephen J. Roth, the Director of the Institute of Jewish Affairs of the World Jewish Congress in London, and this book was commissioned by the Institute of Jewish Affairs. I am deeply beholden to Stephen Roth for his initiative and constant encouragement.

I have tried to state the law as it developed from the earliest periods of Jewish legal history until after the last codification in the sixteenth century, leaning on the texts of the sources and quoting from them *in extenso.* In the Introduction I have given a short survey of the various sources of Jewish law, and in the Abbreviations and References the reader will find some basic information about their terminology and chronology. Translations of biblical texts are—unless otherwise indicated—taken from the King James Version; translations of all other sources are my own.

I have chosen twenty-five of the human rights (including non-discriminations) enumerated in the Universal Declaration of Human Rights. The choice was predicated by the fact that Jewish law does not take cognizance of all "human rights" therein provided for: rights to social security and rights to participate in government, for instance, are outside the realm of traditional Jewish law. Such "cognizance" as Jewish law may take of "human rights" as presently understood may, of course, reflect wholly negative attitudes. I have stated the law as I found it, endeavoring to explain its origins and its reasons, and refraining from embellishments and apologetics.

At the risk of being unduly repetitious I have at times described the same legal phenomenon and quoted the same sources under each of the various headings to which they are relevant, in order to avoid too many cross-references.

Much of the material reproduced here was published by me before. In particular, I have drawn on my contributions to the

vii

Encyclopaedia Judaica (Jerusalem, 1972), reprinted in M. Elon, ed., *The Principles of Jewish Law* (Jerusalem, 1975), and on the Introduction to, and some of my papers reprinted in, H. Cohn, ed., *Jewish Law in Ancient and Modern Israel* (New York: Ktav, 1971).

Some of the material in the Introduction was first published in my "Ancient Jewish Equity," in R. Newman, ed., *Equity in the World's Legal Systems* (Brussels: Bruylant, 1973), in my "The Methodology of Jewish Law—A Secularist View," in B. S. Jackson, ed., *Modern Research in Jewish Law, Jewish Law Annual,* supplement one, (Leiden: Brill, 1980), and in my "Legal Change in Unchangeable Law," in A. Blackshield, ed., *Legal Change* (Sydney: Butterworths, 1983). The chapters on "Equality before the Law," "Judicial Standards," and "Procedural Safeguards" contain some of the mterial presented by me to a Symposium on the Jewish Tradition and Its Relevance to Modern Life, held at the Center for the Study of Democratic Institutions at Santa Barbara, California, in 1973, and later incorporated into my article on "Some Aspects of Justice in Ancient Jewish Law," published in the *Revista Juridica de la Universidad de Puerto Rico* (vol. 46, 1977). My indebtedness to all those distinguished *fora* is gratefully acknowledged.

INTRODUCTION:
Rights and Duties

"Jewish Law" is the collective term for the system of religious law which comprises Scriptural or Written Law, said to emanate from direct or indirect divine revelation, and Oral Law, first expounded in the talmudical sources and later developed by the rabbis. Some customary law must have prevailed long before the children of Israel were molded into nationhood; but no law antedating the scriptural is recognized as "Jewish law." In view of the dogmatic divinity of the law it is well nigh self-evident that there is not "any nation so great that hath statutes and judgments so righteous as all this law" (Deut. 4:8). The immutability and perfection implied in the divinity of the law led to the strong repudiation of any addition to or detraction from God's law (Deut. 4:2, 13:1), the most flagrantly transgressed of all God's injunctions. God's law was given forevermore and is binding on all generations to come (Exod. 28:43, Lev. 26:46, Num. 15:15, Deut. 29:28, et al.), a tenet often reiterated both in Scripture (e.g., Isa. 24:5, Ezek. 46:15, Ps. 119:120, 160) and in apocryphal texts (Ben Sira 24:10, En. 99:2, Tob. 1:6, Jub. 23:16).

Philo Judaeus commented adversely on the laws of other nations, which had to be changed and revised time and again. He praised the Mosaic law as the only one which had really proved durable: it had needed no change since the day it was given, "as if impressed with the seal of nature"; and it will continue in unabated force and splendor for all time to come and "remain immortal, so to speak, so long as sun and moon and heavens and the universe subsist" (*Vita Mosis* 2. 14–15). Very similar sentiments were expressed at about the same time by Flavius Josephus: "Other nations consider it an advantage not to stay on with old traditions, and whoever aspires to the farthest-reaching progress is considered the wisest of men. But we hold those men to be prudent and virtuous who stick both in deeds and in thoughts to the ancient laws—and surely there can be no better

1

proof of the excellence of our laws than the lack of any need to amend them. Being convinced that the laws a priori express God's will, it would indeed be ungodly ever to deviate from them. Who would dare to change them? Who could ever devise any law more perfect and just?" (*Contra Apionem* 2. 20–21). Jesus preached, "Till heaven and earth pass, one jot or one tittle shall in no wise pass from the law, till all be fulfilled" (Matt. 5:18); "And it is easier for heaven and earth to pass, than one tittle of the law to fail" (Luke 16:17).

The immutability of the law was finally codified in the following terms: "It is explicitly and clearly laid down in the Written Law that its norms stand forever and evermore: the Law suffers no change, no diminution and no addition; for it is written, 'Ye shall not add unto the word which I command you, neither shall ye diminish aught from it'; and it is written, 'Those things which are revealed belong unto us and our children for ever, that we may do all the words of this law' (Deut. 29:29)—hence you learn that all the words of the law are binding on us in eternity" (Maimonides, *Yessodei HaTora* 9:1 and *Moré Nevukhim* 2:39).

There is, however, no escaping the fact that with the change of generations, of social structures, of political orientations and necessities, of economic needs—the laws had to change, too, if they were to achieve any practical purpose. On the other hand, any change in the divine law would be fatal to its immutability: it would amount to a living disproof of the perfection and timelessness of God's laws. This seemingly unsoluble dilemma was solved by the creation of Oral Law. The divine law was said to consist of two components, Scripture or Written Law (*Tora SheBikhtav*), on the one hand, and Oral Law (*Tora SheBe'al Peh*), on the other hand. Like the Written Law, so was the Oral Law believed to stem from divine revelation; but while the Written Law was handed down by God Himself to Moses, who put it into writing, the Oral Law was passed on from generation to generation as a living tradition. It was the Pharisees who first claimed divine authority and divine origin also for Oral Law, thus causing a division in Judaism and the Jewish nation. In the words of Flavius Josephus, "the Pharisees have made many ordinances among the people, according to the tradition of their fathers, whereof there is nothing written in the laws of Moses; for which cause they are rejected by the sect of the Sadducees, who affirm that they ought to keep the written ordinances and not to observe those that are grounded upon the traditions of their fathers" (*Antiquitates Judaicae* 13. 10, 6). The Pharisees won a total victory: their "oral" law traditions were absorbed into divine law as part and parcel thereof; and while direct divine revelation was reserved to Written Law, it has throughout the ages remained authoritative rabbinical doctrine that the common denominator of both Written and Oral Law is their ultimate divine origin and their being clothed with divine authority.

The Oral Law did not remain "oral" for very long. It is a matter of dispute at what period new laws were first introduced into the canon and reduced to writing; but from talmudical testimonies it is evident that there must have been written statutes and law scrolls, apart from Scripture, even before the talmudic period. There was not, however, any codification of Oral Law until the completion of the Mishna. An interdict on committing the Oral Law to writing was fortunately not followed (B. *Megilla* 28a–b, B. *Sota* 22a). Though containing records of the bulk of the Oral Law, the Talmud itself is not confined to statements and descriptions of the various rules of law, nor to the processes of scriptural interpretation and of the reasoning which led to their enunciation: it contains the teachings of many schools in many different places and periods, on laws and rituals, manners and morals, history and philosophy, medicine and the natural sciences, folklore and myths. If the Talmud has, nevertheless, been described as the classic of law books and as a typically legal creation, it is because Jewish tradition sees every aspect of human and natural life as governed by "law," and does not recognize any conceptual distinction between laws governing relations of men *inter se* and laws governing relations between God and His universe or His creatures. The laws of physics and biology are divine laws no less and no different than the laws governing ethical human behavior, as the laws of property and obligations are laws of the same species as those prescribing rules of hygiene or ritual. Law is a manifestation of God, just as nature and man himself; the fact that a "law" is called by that name and is binding presupposes— and proves—the divine will and the divine authority behind it.

A substantial part of the Oral Law grew out of interpretations of Scripture. Very elaborate rules were worked out to serve as canons of construction, but it was inevitable that scriptural words and phrases would lend themselves to more interpretations than one, and there is hardly any interpretative—or other legal—problem upon which talmudical opinions were not divided. Thus it is that the most characteristic feature of the Talmud is the disputation. At times, the reader witnesses an argument between scholars who were, indeed, teaching at the same time and place and might well have been engaged in the disputation exactly as reported; but more often, a would-be argument is staged in which scholars of different ages and generations and of different places appear to participate—the dictum of a first-century scholar, for instance, being contested by a third-century scholar and then, again, defended by a fourth-century scholar, as if all three of them had met and sat together, creating an illusion of timelessness which, however objectionable it may seem to the historically minded critic, effectually reflects the timelessness of divine law.

The great difficulty presented by these divergencies of opinion is, of course, that the divinity of the law logically presupposes its certainty. God, from whom all the law is ultimately emanating, cannot be supposed to be contradicting Himself. The talmudical solution with which this difficulty was met was the blank assertion that all the divergent opinions were "the words of the One Living God" (B. *Eruvin* 13b). There is no denying the fact that the haphazards of oral transmission from generation to generation involve misunderstandings and misconceptions, and several contradictory versions of any one tradition may well each be propounded as the true and authentic one. Where the interpretations of any of God's words differ, God's truth may remain unrevealed, but no scholar may claim any greater authenticity or veracity for his particular version than his disputant may claim for his. It must in fairness be assumed that all the different versions were propounded in perfect good faith, and that each had the same potentiality of being the true and authentic one; and so, in a sense, all the scholars did, indeed, propound the word of the One Living God. Not that the scholars of those times consciously indulged in the illusion, or sought to pretend, that they acted as God's mouthpiece or spokesman; it is probable that none of the participants in the talmudical discussions ever consciously rendered himself an account of the divine mission in which he was engaged.

Indeed, where no explicit indication is given of the origin of an opinion or rule propounded in the Talmud—as, for instance, that it is transmitted in the name of an earlier authority, or based on the teachings of another school, or that it is a tradition from time immemorial—it may safely be assumed that it expresses, first and foremost, the personal views of the scholar who propounded it. In matters of procedure or ritual even such personal views may possibly reflect actual or traditional usages; but where ethical or judicial standards are laid down, what is reflected is the acumen and the value-criteria of their author. Most talmudical human-rights pronouncements are in this latter category: while clothed with divine (or quasi-divine) authority, they are but normative expressions of their authors' humanitarian creeds (as, indeed, pronouncements denying human rights may well serve as indications of their authors' neglect of, or indifference to, humanitarian concerns). The "divinity" of Jewish law is in actual practice achieved, and freely admitted to be conditioned, by human agencies operating for human ends with human methods and from human motives. Rather than being superimposed on the final human achievement, the "divinity" is inherent, so to speak, in the whole process of creation and change, determining the nature of the law as if by legal fiction.

As a matter of practical legislation, wherever opinions differed on a given legal problem, one opinion was chosen as the binding one and invested with the force of Halakha, that is, positive law. There are several recognized methods, all laid down in the Talmud, by which Halakha is created: it is the solution to the problem posed by the fact that you cannot observe two or more mutually exclusive rules on the same subject-matter at the same time, even though each of them aspires to divine backing. The sum total of norms elevated to the rank of Halakha thus became the corpus of Jewish positive law, and the great post-talmudic codifiers—Alfassi, Maimonides, *Tur*, and *Shulhan Arukh*—restated the Oral Law as if it consisted of Halakha only. Even today Jewish law is seen by Orthodox observant Jews as consisting only of halakhic law, i.e., binding positive law. In truth, however, as we have seen, one of the main characteristics of Oral Law is that it comprises, in addition to Halakha, all the divergent legal opinions and statements of law which were, by the creation of Halakha, as if relegated into the realm of legislative history or academic theory. It is the variety and diversity of legitimate and authoritative (after all, divine) dissents by which Oral Law is distinguished; and its constriction to, and petrification as, Halakha only, as postulated by the Codes, amounts to a misrepresentation of its true character.

It is a mishnaic tradition that even after Halakha is established, dissenting opinions are to be recorded and studied, whether in order "to teach the generations to come that no man should ever insist on his view, for the fathers of the world did not insist on theirs"—when the Halakha was settled contrary to their views; or whether in order to enable a later generation to prefer the view which had been discarded to that which had been adopted (M. *Eduyot* I: 4–6). This early reminder of the usefulness of reports of dissenting opinions for later generations will surprise the modern lawyer only because of its antiquity; but insofar as ancient Jewish law is concerned, it is an indication of the open-mindedness with which even the creators of Halakha contemplated future changes in the law—with the manifold divergent versions and aspects of divine law ready and available for choice and selection.

As distinguished from legal theory, however, in actual practice Jewish law became identified with the positive law as codified in the later codes. As a general rule, where the codes differ from each other, the latest would prevail as the most authoritative statement, the presumption being that the latest codifier had the earlier versions before him when he wrote, and must have had good reasons when he deviated from them. Thus, the *Shulhan Arukh* of Joseph Caro (16th cent.), the latest of the great codes, is generally regarded as the last word on binding law. With the general acceptance of the codes as binding statements of the law in force, the metamorphosis of the Oral into written law has become complete.

A second source of post-talmudic law is the responsa—legal opinions of the great jurists and scholars of their times. Contained in hundreds of volumes and not always easily accessible even to the initiated, they represent—not unlike the hundreds of volumes of law reports in a given jurisdiction—judicial lawmaking and law-expounding throughout the centuries on all aspects of life, civil and criminal, commercial and matrimonial, ritual and liturgical, private and communal. As the name "responsa" indicates, they are, more often than not, opinions of renowned scholars given to local courts or judges before whom a controversy had arisen. Rather than decide novel or complex questions of law on their own responsibility, local judges would address themselves to the leading spiritual and legal authority of their day or of their country and ask for guidance and instruction. It also happened that the local court would first decide the case at hand, so as not to delay justice, and then submit its reasoned decision to some such authority for comment, whether on its own initiative or upon request by a litigant as if by way of appeal. A good many of the responsa given before the completion of the codes were incorporated in them; still there are thousands of responsa anteceding the codes and not so incorporated; and to these must be added an enormous number written after completion of the codes, in the last four centuries, throughout the Jewish world.

A third important source of Jewish law is the commentaries. The most celebrated and authoritative commentator is Rashi (Shlomo Yitzhaki), who lived in the eleventh century in France, and whose commentaries on Bible and Talmud contain many interpretations that are regarded as authoritative statements of the law. He was followed by the school of Tossafists, so named because of their addenda (*Tossafot*) of glosses to the Babylonian Talmud; their interpretations, too, are regarded as authoritative. A great responder, Asher ben Yehiel (Asheri), also wrote a commentary on the Talmud, entitled *Halakhic Novellae;* and the great codifier Joseph Caro wrote, before embarking on his own code, commentaries on those of his two predecessors, Maimonides' *Mishne Tora* (*Kessef Mishne*) and the *Tur* (*Beit Yossef*), both regarded with no less respect and veneration than his code itself. This code, the *Shulhan Arukh*, was for its part amplified by the glosses (*hagahot*) of Rema (Moshe Isserles), which gained, at least in Western and Eastern Europe, the authority of binding law. In the course of time the codes were commented upon by a host of commentators who are, in an expressive metaphor; known as the "armor-bearers" of the codifiers; and while the authority accorded to the commentators and responders may vary according to their respective individual standing and stature, they all provide legitimate and authoritative sources of law.

The fact that some law books failed to gain recognition as authoritative statements of the law outside the immediate sphere of authority of their authors reflects another important feature of Jewish law. The Jews were scattered over many distant parts of the world, and there were many communities which had no effective communication with each other. This was true particularly of communities in North Africa, which were for many centuries virtually cut off from the Jewish life and law that developed in Europe. The responsa of North African rabbis were unknown in Europe, and those of German and Polish rabbis were unknown in North Africa—but even had they been known, or where one or the other reached some such distant community, they would not carry any authority, because their authors were unfamiliar. In consequence, the Jewish law that developed in various regions was not uniform. Until the present day, laws have differed in substantial matters in the various communities, according to their respective geographical provenance. Whereas, for instance, the prohibition of bigamy was introduced in Western Jewry by the *herem* (ban) of Rabbenu Gershom (11th cent.), a scholar of undisputed authority throughout the Western Jewish world, the prohibition did not extend to the Oriental Jewish communities, and even today does not apply to Jews of Oriental ("Sephardic") origin wherever they may now reside.

Nor is it surprising that in the various communities of the dispersion various customs and usages sprang up which, in the course of time, whether by virtue of deliberate sanction or merely by general tacit consensus or actual practice, have gained the sacrosanctity of true law. There are already in the Talmud dicta to the effect that customs may acquire the binding force of law especially when (and because) men of authority were seen to practice them. One scholar went so far as to say that a custom may even supersede the law (*Sopherim* 14:18). Customs of particular places or countries were widely resorted to in commercial and matrimonial matters, if not to supersede the law, then to complement the law (B. *Kiddushin* 49a; B. *Bava Metzia* 68b, 86a; B. *Bava Batra* 4a, 165a; et al.). The notion underlying such legalization of custom is that by conducting themselves as they did for any length of time, the people in a particular place demonstrated the existence of a tacit agreement among themselves, which the law would recognize and enforce, so long as it was not illegal. There are also instances in which mishnaic law records the existence of different customs in different places, investing those different customs with the sanction of law (e.g., M. *Pesahim* 4:1–5, M. *Ketuvot* 4:12). The older a custom, the greater its authority: the biblical injunction "Remove not the ancient landmark, which thy fathers have set" (Prov. 22:28) was held to enjoin the observance of ancient custom. But as every community had customs of its own, not necessarily identical with or even similar to those of other communities, the variety so engendered again contributed to the multifariousness, already noted, in which Jewish law excels. Communal customs having been absorbed into the law as it was known and practiced in a given community, the various communal laws became different from each other and developed differently. To some extent, therefore, "Jewish law" can be said to be a collective term for a variety of legal norms developed and conditioned by local custom; and for our purposes it may be significant that ancient laws which must be regarded as manifestly incompatible with human rights have, either universally or locally, fallen into desuetude.

A similar diversity is noticeable in the rule-making power. The Great Sanhedrin of Seventy-One, "from whom the Torah went out to all Israel" (M. *Sanhedrin* 11:2), performed the highest judicial and legislative functions. In the old tradition of the Sanhedrin, courts and scholars invested with judicial authority enjoyed at the same time the power and competence to legislate by making rules (*takkanot*). They were joined in later centuries, especially in Eastern Europe, by communal councils ("the seven best men in town") which exercised rule-making powers in matters of civic administration, taxation, health and hygiene, police offenses, and the organization of public welfare and charity. Such rules were valid only within the area of the communal authority that enacted them, or, where made by a rabbinical authority, in the places and countries where that authority was recognized. But there were *takkanot* which gained much wider recognition, at times even throughout the Western ("Ashkenazic") world, or even everywhere. Restrictions on the husband's right to be the sole heir of his wife, for instance, were almost universally adopted; and *takkanot* increasing the father's liability to maintain his children up to their sixteenth year were accepted as part and parcel of universally binding Jewish law.

While the scope of rule-making authority is virtually unlimited, there is one talmudical restriction which is worthy of note. It is that no regulation may be imposed on the community unless the majority thereof "could stand it"—that is, unless the regulation was reasonable and not too onerous. Thus, a rule prohibiting meat and wine, introduced as a sign of mourning after the destruction of the Temple, was held invalid for the reason that most people could be expected not to abide by it (T. *Sota* 15:10). In instances where a rule was held reasonable and valid at the time and place of its enactment, but after the lapse of time, or in a different place, circumstances were found to be such as to render that rule unreasonable and people could no longer be expected to acquiesce in it, the rule would be allowed (or ordered) to expire. This appears to be an exception to the general rule that while the authority which had enacted the regulation was at liberty to repeal it ("the mouth that forbade is the mouth to allow": M. *Eduyot* 3:6, M. *Ketuvot* 2:5, B. *Ketuvot* 18b, 22a, B. *Bekhorot* 36a), no other authority was competent to repeal it unless greater "in wisdom and numbers" than the enacting authority (M. *Eduyot* 1:5). Opinions differ as to how the wisdom and numbers of the later authorities are to be determined, and no clear-cut tests appear to have been finalized. In any event, the more ancient the old authorities became, the more venerable and unsurpassable they were, and their insuperable wisdom and infinite numbers have now become a matter of irrebuttable presumption. It is an open question whether it is only true modesty and humility, or rather a lack of courage, which lies at the root of the refusal of present-day authorities ever to pretend to greater wisdom and numbers such as required for legislative changes.

Before leaving the sources of the law, mention ought to be made of nonlegal sources. Generally speaking, our information and knowledge of ancient laws does not necessarily derive from legal texts only; much of our knowledge of Greek law, for instance, comes to us from the poets and philosophers, not to speak of the orators. All our biblical, apocryphal, talmudic, midrashic, medieval, and postmedieval literature abounds with nonlegal matter—an important part of which, the Aggada (being mostly nonlegal and fictional hermeneutics), was expressly held to be excluded from the legally relevant material from which conclusions as to the law may be drawn (J. *Pei'a* 2:4). Nevertheless, these sources provide important raw material for the legal historian. Subject to proper chronologization, the customs there depicted, the ideas expounded and morals preached, and the hermeneutical and exegetical theories there set forth, all contribute materially to our knowledge and understanding of legal conditions and perceptions prevailing at the time. Many of the aggadic preachers and storytellers also participated in halakhic discussions, and their aggadic pronouncements are often found to throw illuminating light on their attitudes, frames of mind, philosophies and ideas, all of which are highly relevant in analyzing their legal norms and reasonings. Into this category belong also the utterances of the prophets, from whose upbraidings the legal historian learns not only of laws which were disobeyed and individual liberties which were violated, but also of ethical standards providing the motivation both for the creation and for the implementation of the law.

While aggadic sources open the door wide to all sorts of mystical, mythical, fanciful, and speculative notions underlying legal or philosophical data, a characteristic feature of halakhic, that is, positive, law is its formalism. It is not only cogent law in the sense that it leaves little leeway to judges for anything like a "liberal" interpretation; it is even, not unlike arithmetic, a code of "measures and measurements" (*middot veshi'urin*) which are unflexible and unadaptable.

The matter is well illustrated by two discussions reported in the Talmud. Where a pigeon is found within fifty yards of a dovecote, it belongs to the owner of the dovecote; if it is found at a distance of more than fifty yards from the dovecote, it belongs to the finder. One of the disputants stood up and asked, "What if one leg of the pigeon is within the fifty-yard limit and the other leg without?" Whereupon they expelled him from the Academy for his impertinence (B. *Bava Batra* 23b). It appears that the simplest and most effective solution to a legislative problem like this was that provided by exact measurements, whether such measurements were based on general life experience or biological or physiological data, or whether they were fixed arbitrarily. The possibility that circumstances might arise in which blind adherence to preconceived measurements could lead *ad absurdum* or work injustice did not deter the talmudists: what was involved was the principle that the law could not do without exact figures; and an isolated case of potential absurdity or injustice appeared to them quite irrelevant.

When the question arose whether there should be a limitation on the period within which a widow may make a claim under her marriage contract (ketuva), it was laid down that so long as she lived in her late husband's house no period of limitation would run, but after having returned to her father's house she could make her claim only within twenty-five years. On this proposition the following discussion is reported to have taken place: "If she made her claim before sunset (on the expiration of the twenty-five years), you would say she was entitled to succeed, and if she made it after sunset you would say she failed? Should we really make matters hinge on the particle of a minute?" The answer was "Yes—all the measurements of the law are like this" (B. Ketuvot 104a).

These are not isolated instances but rather typical examples of a formalism which pervades all branches of the law. No account is taken of boundary cases: you are either within or without the rule. Thus it has been said that the application of the law is a mechanical rather than an intellectual or emotional process: once the law offers a solution to a given problem, it is automatic and inevitable. Rather than interpreting or construing the law, a judge is enforcing it as he finds it, possibly explaining to the parties what it is. The more remarkable are the discretionary powers which later jurists vested in the courts so as to attain better standards of justice (see Part III).

This sort of "mechanical jurisprudence" was bound to lead to hardships in individual cases, and not unlike other systems of law the Jewish law developed its own particular brand of equity to avoid such hardships. Such equitable jurisdiction was based on the scriptural exhortation "And thou shalt do that which is right and good in the sight of the Lord" (Deut. 6:18)—the "right and good" being, indeed, the aequum et bonum of later Roman law. Another verse reiterates the exhortation "Observe and hear all these words which I command thee, that it may go well with thee and with thy children after thee for ever, when thou doest that which is good and right in the sight of the Lord thy God" (Deut. 12:28). The observance of God's laws is not enough to make sure that it may indeed "go well with thee and thy children"; in addition to observing the laws you also have to do that which is "good and right." The talmudic interpreters wondered what the distinction was between "good" and "right" and why both the one and the other were to be done. One interpreter said that "good" is what is good in the eyes of heaven, and "right" is what is right in the eyes of man; another said that "good" is what is good in the eyes of man, and "right" is what is right in the eyes of heaven (T. *Shekalim* 2:2; *Sifrei Deut.* 79). A thirteenth-century commentator elaborated on the "good and right" as follows: "The law cannot take cognizance of all facets of man's conduct toward his fellow-men, nor of every detail of what is required for the welfare of the community or of states in general. Having stated only some of the rules of upright conduct, such as, 'Thou shalt not go up and down as a talebearer' (Lev. 19:16), 'Thou shalt not avenge or bear grudges' (ibid. 18), 'Thou shalt not stand against the blood of thy neighbor' (ibid. 16), 'Thou shalt not curse the deaf' (ibid. 14), and many more like them, he now sums up all those rules in this general exhortation to do what is good and right in every given situation and in regard to every subject-matter, including not only compromising and waiving claims, but also politeness and good manners and soft-spokenness, in short, everything that renders a man righteous" (Ramban ad Deut. 6:18).

The standard of goodness or rightness to be applied is always an objective one; either it has to be good and right in the eyes of the Lord (Deut. 6:18, 12:25 and 28; Exod. 15:26; 1 Kings 11:38; et al.), or it has to be good and right in the sight of men, that is, of all mankind. Doing what is good and right only in one's own eyes, however, is denounced as strongly reprehensible, showing as it does egotism or arbitrariness (cf. Judg. 17:6, 21:25; Jer. 26:14, 40:4; Josh. 9:25; et al.). The ways of good and right have to be taught to people before they can embark on them (cf. 1 Sam. 12:23), if not by human teachers then by God Himself (Ps. 107:7, Ezra 8:21).

Some instances of "right and good" dealings have become absorbed into positive law. Where a mortgagee had seized mortgaged property, he would be compelled to give it up again and return it to the mortgagor, even after maturity of the mortgage debt, whenever the mortgagor was in a position to repay the debt—because, however valid the mortgagee's claim to the property might be, that would be right in the sight of God (B. *Bava Metzia* 35a). Or, again because of the duty to do that which is right and good, an "equitable" right of preemption was conferred on an owner of land in respect of land immediately adjoining his own, at the same price and on the same conditions as his neighbor was willing to sell it to any buyer (ibid. 180a): "The sages said, it is right and good that the land should go to adjoining owners rather than to distant strangers" (Maimonides, *Shekheinim* 12:5).

A distinction was made between laws of men (*dinei adam*) and laws of heaven (*dinei shamayim*) in the sense that while certain acts and omissions do not, by the "laws of men" (i.e., the laws applicable to men), sound reprehensible in civil or criminal responsibility, they may still be reprehensible by the laws of heaven: therefore a God-fearing man will abstain from them, although no liability can attach to him (e.g., B. *Kiddushin* 43a, B. *Bava Kamma* 55–56, B. *Bava Metzia* 61b and 91a, et al.). Similarly, while a mere promise does not in law give rise to a cause of action, "He who took His due from the generation of the Flood will take His due from him who does not keep his promise" (M. *Bava Metzia* 4:1). Not only divine displeasure was invoked to deter people from conducting themselves unfairly or inequitably; many acts and omissions, while not prohibited by law, are said to arouse "the displeasure of the sages." Thus, a testator may validly disinherit his sons, but the sages would not like it unless the sons had grossly misconducted themselves (M. *Bava Batra* 8:6). Or, while a borrower may accept the return to him of interest unlawfully paid by him to the lender, any such acceptance would engender the displeasure of the sages, presumably because the borrower had been *in pari delictu* (B. *Bava Kamma* 94b). Conversely, the sages are said to be pleased with a man who repays his debt though it be prescribed and can no longer be claimed (M. *Shevi'it* 10:9).

Certain modes of conduct are highly recommended as the ways of the virtuous and right-minded (*middat hassidut*). For instance, while anybody was entitled to partake of the gleanings of the harvest left over by the landowner (Lev. 19:9–10), if a wayfarer who had partaken of them could afford to pay for them, the right thing for the virtuous to do would be to pay the owner (B. *Hullin* 130b). When a man has been given a defective coin, he may return it and claim to have it exchanged within a very short time after discovery of the defect (M. *Bava Metzia* 4:5), but the right thing for the virtuous to do is to exchange it even after the lapse of a year (B. *Bava Metzia* 52b). Conversely, it is sheer wickedness for a man knowingly to anticipate another in buying a chattel which that other man desired to buy (B. *Kiddushin* 59a); as it would be for a professional man, like a teacher, to enter upon unfair competition with a colleague (*Hoshen Mishpat* 2:37). Certain acts and omissions are branded as breaches of trust which, though no legal sanction attaches to them, must be avoided by the virtuous. An agent, for instance, must not delay action on behalf of his principal, because any such delay might cause him losses or inconvenience (B. *Bava Metzia* 49a); or, while no binding obligation may as yet have been incurred, it would be a breach of trust for a man to disappoint another by going back on his word (B. *Bekhorot* 13b). On the other hand, where a contract had been formally concluded and was valid and enforceable, the party who asserted that he had been induced to agree to it by a "mistake in his heart" was released from his contract, because that was the right thing to do "inside of the line of the law" (B. *Ketuvot* 97a).

While some of these instances were isolated cases decided *ad hoc* or *ad personam* and did not purport to change the law, some other equitable rules were absorbed into the law. The fact is, however, that the law recognizes an orientation of prescribed human conduct not only by the letter of the law but also by the lofty moral standards of the ancients—for which they had no yardstick other than their own ethical concepts and consciences. It is true that in a conflict with such ethics the law would always prevail, but then that was the fate of all systems of equity. It is that morals and ethics as such, at least insofar as they were spelled out in the context of the legal regulation of human relations, have become part and parcel of the system of law—whether or not any particular rule of conduct might be formally enforceable by judicial process. However well definable the boundaries between observing the laws and doing the right and the good may be, it is the sum total of all of them together that makes up Jewish law.

Once upon a time it was said of Jewish law that "it is not hidden from thee, neither is it far off. It is not in heaven, that thou shouldest say, 'Who shall go up for us to heaven, and bring it unto us, that we may hear it, and do it?' Neither is it beyond the sea, that thou shouldest say, 'Who shall go over the sea for us, that we may hear it, and do it?' " (Deut. 30:11–13). As far as legal research (as distinguished from theological study and religious worship) is concerned, Jewish law is until the present day some-

what "hidden and far off"—neither the comparative legal historian nor the general reader (however educated and erudite) has
easy access to the thousands of esoteric volumes in which this
magnificent legal creation is stored away. It is only lately—more
particularly with the publication of the *Encyclopaedia Judaica*
(Jerusalem, 1972) and *The Principles of Jewish Law* (ed. Elon,
1975) extracted therefrom, as well as with the regular appearance
of the *Jewish Law Annual* (ed. Jackson, 1978–)—that restate-
ments of and monographs on Jewish law have been published in
English in a systematic and authoritative manner.

It must be stressed that Jewish law (as here understood) belongs in the realm of legal history: it is not to be confused with
Israeli law. In fact, Jewish law presents to the State of Israel two
challenging problems—one is academic, the other political. There
is hardly any dissent in regard to the academic challenge; everybody seems to be agreed that it is one of the foremost tasks of
Israeli legal scholarship to foster research into Jewish law and
make it easily accessible to every interested lawyer and layman.
The Institute of Jewish Law at the Hebrew University of Jerusalem is doing splendid pioneering work on sifting and indexing
legal material found in medieval and postmedieval responsa, and
all other Israeli universities sponsor legal research work with a
view to unearthing and analyzing ancient Jewish law. It is indeed
a unique subject for research: its history stretches over four
millennia; it was developed in and influenced by all systems of law
throughout the Near and Middle East, Europe and America, and
had on its part a great impact on the evolution of modern law; and
it affords a classical example of a legal system which had religion—and revelation—not only for its primordial origin but also,
throughout the ages, for its fundamental guiding principle, its
Grundnorm, around which and out of which the whole normative
body of the law was allowed to grow. If it is the more immediate
concern of Israeli legal scholars to do research into Jewish law, it
is because Jewish law is part and parcel of the national cultural
heritage; but the interest and importance that attach to it for
legal historians and comparatists as such, far outreach national
or religious predilections.

The political problem posed by Jewish law in the State of Israel
has given rise to a controversy which is still far from settled. As to
the role which Jewish law can—or ought to—play in the evolution
of Israeli law, opinions are widely divided. As a matter of practical

legislative policy, Jewish law is not as yet acknowledged as a source of Israeli law except only in matters of marriage and divorce of Jews (and this exception dates back to the preceding Ottoman and British legislation, though expressly restated in an Israeli statute). Still, Jewish law is quoted very often in official communiqués submitted to Parliament to explain the "objects and reasons" of a bill, with a view to showing that proposed legislation corresponds with, or differs from, Jewish legal traditions in one way or another. A similar practice prevails in the courts, particularly in the Supreme Court. While Jewish law is not, except in matters of marriage and divorce of Jews as aforesaid, applied by the courts as positive law, it is time and again quoted by way of comparison and *obiter dictum* to show how the question before the court would fall to be determined if Jewish law had to be applied. There are a good many judges who deprecate this practice, not so much perhaps because of any objection to or prejudice against Jewish law as such, but rather because of natural judicial disapproval of *obiter dicta* not strictly necessary for deciding the issue at bar. The information on Jewish law imparted in judicial opinions by way of illustration, however, has been hailed as the most effective and the most painless way of bringing Jewish law nearer to the hearts of Israeli legal practitioners.

The core of the political controversy lies in the character of Jewish law as religious law. The secularization of Jewish law by the Israeli legislature might in the eyes of the believer in the divinity of the law amount to a profanation and desecration which in itself would constitute a gross violation of the divine law. On the other hand, it would be unthinkable to enact Jewish law in Israel qua divine law; Israel is a secular state, and its democratically elected legislature must always be free to repeal any law it has enacted or to bring such changes therein as it may from time to time think fit, regardless of any claims or dogmata of divine origins or divine prerogatives. It may therefore safely be predicted that, as in the past so in the future, the influence of Jewish law on Israeli legislation will remain indirect. Rather than adopting any particular norms of positive Jewish law, the Israeli legislature will let itself be guided by such principles of justice and equity and by such concepts of human dignity and human rights as are in the best tradition of the Jewish Sages of old.

Speaking of human rights concepts I must say at once that no

explicit concept of this kind is to be found in Jewish law. It is not
only that the formative sources of Jewish law precede by millennia the first enunciation of such slogans as civil liberties, citizens'
rights, or individual freedom; Jewish law is in no way unique or
isolated among ancient systems of law or of religion which fail to
recognize human rights specifically. It is mainly that the particular structure of Jewish law qua religious law—with God as the
central object of love and veneration, and the worship and service
of God as the overriding purpose of all law—postulates a system of
duties rather than a system of rights. It is true that the conferment of rights may be incidental to the fulfillment of duties: in
many instances, the very imposition of a duty already implies the
creation of a collateral right, and that right may even be legally
enforceable; in other instances, there may exist a duty—but
rather than incidentally conferring any enforceable right, the
performance of the duty will result only in the conferment of a
benefit. Thus, prohibitions such as "thou shalt not steal" (Exod.
20:15, Deut. 5:19) and "thou shalt not remove thy neighbor's
landmark" (Deut. 19:14), and the injunction to return lost chattels (Deut. 22:1–3), all impose negative or positive duties; but
they may be read to imply a right to property and possession—a
right which is nowhere spelled out as such. Similarly, the duty of
learning and teaching is reiterated several times (Deut. 6:7, 20–
25), but there is no right to education articulated anywhere.
There are a few isolated exceptions to this rule: in biblical law, for
instance, the right of the accidental manslayer to refuge from the
blood-avenger is laid down as a right, not only as the duty of the
blood-avenger to refrain from killing (Num. 35:11,15; Deut. 4:42).
Similarly, in talmudical law the duty to do charity is supplemented by explicit rights of the poor, if only with a view to settling
priorities among them (M. *Horayot* 3:8, B. *Bava Metzia* 71a).

In order to ascertain the existence and scope of "human rights"
in Jewish law, we shall therefore have to look at "commandments"
(*mitzvot*), including positive precepts (*mitzvot assei*) and negative injunctions (*mitzvot lo-ta'assé*), and start from the premise
that the purpose of imposing duties toward your fellowmen was
but the recognition and implementation of rights of which these
fellowmen stand possessed; or—and this comes to the same
thing—the fulfillment of their legitimate expectations and legally
recognized needs. It stands to reason that from the duty to assist

and maintain the poor a fundamental human right of every human being to his livelihood may reasonably be inferred, as the fundamental right to life may justifiably be inferred from the prohibition of homicide.

There is one other feature of the particular structure of Jewish law that must be stressed at the outset: all commands of the law are addressed to individuals. In a theocracy, all government is vested in God, and on God no duties can be imposed. Such legislative pronouncements from the mouth of God as were addressed to rulers, kings, prophets, and other such functionaries of public law relate mostly to acts of state and have no bearing on human rights. Duties toward individuals are all imposed on individuals; it is human beings who are at once the only subjects and the only objects of those duties. It is true that by performing a duty, the individual performs the will of God and hence an act of worship; but the will of God comprises, in the nature of things, not only the performance of the act but also the benefit thereby conferred on a human being. In legal terms, it is not the state which grants and implements human rights and from which their enforcement must be sought, but only the individual concerned in the particular matter. The duty imposed on that individual is often expressed in general terms, not as conferring any tangible right or even benefit on any identifiable person; and the potential beneficiary may therefore have no cause of action to have his "human right" enforced—he will have to content himself with the doubtful consolation that there must somewhere and somehow be some individual in duty bound to succor him.

Nor is the position essentially different in systems in which human rights are stated as such and not only implied from corresponding duties. The Universal Declaration of Human Rights, which enumerates rights and (except for Article 29) no duties, is as good an illustration as any. The rights listed in the Declaration are generally ("universally") recognized as existing and well-established rights of every individual—but none of them is actually and legally enforceable: none of these individuals can by national or international action claim or obtain any remedy by virtue thereof. They are *leges nudae*, or paper rights, making very lofty and sublime reading, but affording very small consolation and comfort to the oppressed and persecuted. The Declaration itself regards these rights as but "a common standard of achievement for all peoples and all nations," that is, a criterion or standard to be used by legislatures if and when enacting enforceable law; but there is nothing in the Declaration either to bind individuals to respect those rights or to obligate states to enact them.

If most of these "human rights" have, nevertheless, in the consciousness of civilized mankind become identified with fundamental liberties to be enjoyed by each individual in states governed by the rule of law, it is not because of their actual enforceability in this or that state, but because of the ethical idea they reflect—or, not so much because of their formal quality as "rights" as because of their essential quality as "human." They represent norms or patterns of behavior considered to be ingrained in the moral fiber of contemporary society; and being ultimately reducible to common morals and good conscience, it would not really matter whether they are expressed in rights or in duties. As the recognition of a right implies a duty to implement it, so does the imposition of a duty confer a right to have it duly performed.

And in the same way that the rights enumerated in the Universal Declaration reflect ethical standards postulated by the founding fathers of the United Nations as the aspirations of a new world sick of war and lawlessness, of inhuman atrocities and human sufferings, so do the duties imposed by Jewish lawgivers reflect their ethical standards, which were postulated by a legal order conditioned by, and wholly dedicated to, the service and worship of God. We have already observed that Jewish law regards obedience to the law as but another form of divine worship; not only is the service of God the paramount duty which law imposes on man, but there can be no true service of God other than by the conscientious and faithful performance of all the duties which God has chosen to impose upon man. Even the belief in God, the love of God, the fear of God, are duties imposed by law—as is, of course, the total repudiation of all other deities. But all duties, even those that are expressed in language suggesting that they are duties toward fellowmen, are in reality—and as a matter of law—duties owed to God; in this respect, again, there are no distinctions (except purely classificatory ones) between sacrificial or ritual laws on the one hand and civil or criminal laws on the other hand. The duty to God may well consist in doing, or refraining from doing, certain acts toward men; the fact that a norm regulates behavior within human society does not derogate from its character as imposing a duty to God. And this is true not only of norms contained in the Written Law and hence emanating from divine revelation, but no less of duties imposed by Oral Law which were superadded in the course of the centuries. All the later additions only widen the scope and amplify the manner in which man is to serve God. It is no accident that the whole of the law concentrates on duties and has a scanty regard for rights: it is the performance of duties by which God is served.

It is the theocratic character of Jewish law which appears to impregnate those duties, and such rights and benefits as may be incidental to them, with particular divine predilections; even unenforceable duties are clothed with divine sanctions so as to have incidental rights and benefits properly protected. The very divinity of the law implies that violations thereof will arouse divine wrath—whether or not any particular law might be enforceable also by human agencies; but any compulsory enforcement would presumably constitute at least a mitigating circumstance to allay divine anger, and at any rate it would surely serve God's purpose behind the imposition of that duty if the correlative right is implemented and the desired benefit conferred. Only where the incidental right is practically unenforceable can divine wrath become unmitigated. This is well illustrated by the prohibition of oppression of widows and orphans: though any affliction of widows and orphans is interdicted in unmistakable terms, they have no judicially cognizable right not to be afflicted. But God's law is that "if thou afflict them in any wise, and they cry at all unto Me, I will surely hear their cry. And My wrath shall wax hot, and I will kill you with the sword; and your wives shall be widows and your children fatherless" (Exod. 22:22–23). It is as if "the Creator of the World has made a covenant with them that whenever they cry out to Him, He will hear and act" (Maimonides, Dei'ot 6:10). Not only the violation of God's law or the nonfulfillment of the duty imposed by Him is the cause which stirs God to action, but rather His interest in, and patronage of, the human being aggrieved and suffering thereby. The ominous and fearful threat to make your own wives widows and your own children orphans shows just to what lengths a wrathful God may go to vindicate human rights.

Some of the duties laid down in biblical law carry the admonition "and thou shalt fear thy God"—for instance, the prohibition of cursing the deaf or putting a stumbling-block before the blind (Lev. 19:14), or the exhortation to honor the aged (ibid. 32), or the injunction not to defraud (Lev. 25:17). This admonition was interpreted as an indication that wherever anything wrong is done in private, or where the nature of the act is such that there need be no fear of human sanctions, the fear of God to be instilled in you must be potent enough to deter you from wrongdoing: an omnipotent and omniscient God will not suffer His laws to be disobeyed with impunity (B. *Kiddushin* 32b, 33b).

Not only fear of divine wrath but also promises of divine reward are used as incentives to obey God's laws. The duty, for instance, to return to the indigent debtor at night the raiment he gave you as a pledge, so that he may have something to cover himself, is in one passage accompanied by the threat of divine anger (Exod. 22:26) and in another passage by the promise of divine blessing (Deut. 24:13). God's anger threatening the exacting and merciless creditor is matched by God's blessing vouchsafed the generous and merciful one; in both cases God makes Himself the mouthpiece for the poor debtor, hearkening likewise to his anguish and his relief—as if indeed Himself partaking of them. It is significant that what is held out to the compliant creditor as his recompense is that his conduct will be regarded as "righteousness before God"; the term employed here (*tsedaka*) connotes both justice and charity, not only as courses of action but also as personal qualities of character or achievement. This divine "righteousness" has (in the felicitous phrase of Reinhold Niebuhr) been described as "a bias in favor of the poor"—of which God's bias in favor of widows and orphans is but a reflection or an illustration. Divine justice is conditioned by other divine attributes, such as compassion, generosity, and benevolence (Exod. 34:6); and no higher reward can be conceived than for man to attain the heights of divine attributes.

Another divine reward, namely a long and good life, is promised not only for honoring father and mother (Exod. 20:12, Deut. 5:16), but also for having mercy on animals: "If a bird's nest chance to be before thee in the way in any tree, or on the ground, whether they be young ones, or eggs, and the dam sitting upon the young or upon the eggs, thou shalt not take the dam with the young: but thou shalt in any wise let the dam go, and take the young to thee; that it may be well with thee, and that thou mayest prolong thy days" (Deut. 22:6–7). If a good and long life is your reward for showing compassion with and consideration for the feelings of animals, a fortiori will God so reward you for showing compassion with and consideration for human beings (cf. M. Hullin 12:5, Sifrei Deut. 228). Similarly, a long life is promised to anybody who has not in his bag "divers weights, great and small," nor in his house "divers measures, great and small," but only "perfect and just weights," "perfect and just measures"—for keeping inaccurate weights and measures in one's possession is "an abomination unto the Lord thy God" (Deut. 25:13–16). If a long life is your reward for keeping false measures out of your reach, a fortiori will God reward you for never using them to defraud others and unlawfully enrich yourself (Sifrei Deut. 295).

There is some authority to the effect that prospects of divine reward are held out not only for active compliance with the law and for actual performance of one's duties, but even for abstention from violating the law (M. Makkot 3:15)—that is, of course, where the law does not expressly prescribe any particular activity. While in secular legal systems a man who does not commit any offense and does not infringe the rights of others may trust, at best, to be left unmolested by the law-enforcement agencies, in Jewish (religious) law, even the man who just refrains from infringing the other's rights is assured of divine reward. Indeed, many human rights, such as rights to liberty or privacy, are duly and sufficiently honored by noninfringement; the duty not to violate them requires only passive abstinence. But it is the duty not to violate them, and the passive abstinence of the law-abiding, that bring the very rights into focus: they turn out to be rights whose benefit is enjoyed not only by their bearers but also by their respecters—the former enjoy the benefit of fulfillment of God's commandments, the latter enjoy the benefit of God's reward and blessing.

PART

I

RIGHTS OF LIFE, LIBERTY,
AND THE PURSUIT OF
HAPPINESS

1

THE RIGHT TO LIFE

In the midst of the Garden of Eden God planted the "tree of life" (Gen. 2:9). Unlike the "tree of knowledge of good and evil," the tree of life was not forbidden to man; God forbade only the eating from the tree of knowledge and warned man that "in the day thou eatest thereof thou shalt surely die" (ibid. 17). But when Adam and Eve ate of the forbidden tree, they did not die; instead they were expelled from paradise, "lest he put forth his hand, and take also of the tree of life, and live forever" (Gen. 3:22). So death *was* meted out to them, but it was not immediate; it was to come, in God's own time, at the end of lives of sorrow and sweat (ibid. 17, 19). Life produced by the paradisiac tree had been destined to be eternal—as is all God's creation. With the expulsion of man from (and the final disappearance of) paradise and its tree of life, man became entitled only to such span of life as would be allotted to him by divine grace—but in their hearts men continued to aspire and hope to live forever. We find the tree of life transplanted unto the nonparadisiac scene of God's laws (Prov. 3:18): the devotion to, and the constant preoccupation with, holy studies was regarded as an unfailing elixir for life in this world (B. *Berakhot* 32a, B. *Hagiga* 3b) as well as in the world-to-come (M. *Avot* 2:7)— "the world-to-come" being but the mythical formula for the eternization of life. On the one hand, "eternal life" became a concept of theology and metaphysics, an esoteric subject of religious faith and idealistic speculation; on the other hand, it became the subject-matter of detailed and manifold pronouncements in the sources of Jewish law (e.g., M. *Sanhedrin* 10, passim, T. *Sanhedrin* 12–13 passim). It is typical of Jewish law that it reacted to

27

the divine punishment of expulsion from paradise and deprivation of eternal life by creating a substitutive eternal life all of its
own.

Man's life on earth is a gift from God. The breath of life is
breathed by God into his nostrils (Gen. 2:7), and it is God who
gives life and takes it away at will: in God's hand is "the soul of
every living thing and the breath of all mankind" (Job 12:10).
Putting an end to life is God's own privilege and function; the God
who gives is the God who takes away (Job 1:21), and a human
being who spurns or "loathes" earthly life is denounced as offend-
ing God by ingratitude (e.g., *Eliahu Rabba* 14). While the greatest sin known to the law is the very denial and betrayal of God,
that is, idolatry, the next gravest is the usurpation of God's own
power and privilege to terminate human life. It is only when God
Himself has ordained the taking of life, whether by way of punishment for violating God's laws or in the course of a holy (i.e.,
obligatory) war, that man is, when putting an end to a human
life, acting as it were in lieu of God, by virtue of a quasi-delegation
of divine power. The first wanton killing of a man laid a curse
upon the earth, and the blood spilt cried out to God from the
ground (Gen. 4:10). And the first law enunciated by the Lord and
proclaimed to Noah and his sons was: "Whoso sheddeth man's
blood, by man shall his blood be shed; for in the image of God
made He man" (Gen. 9:5–6). Shedding human blood pollutes and
defiles the land, "and the land cannot be cleansed of the blood that
is shed therein, but by the blood of him that shed it. Defile not
therefore the land which ye shall inhabit" (Num. 35:33–34). This
is a typical instance of *lex talionis,* "a soul for a soul" (Deut.
19:21); the soul of man is God's property (Ezek. 18:4), and if you
take it unlawfully you forfeit your own soul to God. It is not so
much the life of the individual that is to be vindicated as God's
prerogative to bestow and to terminate human life. Where a man
is found slain, "and it be not known who has slain him," so that
there can be no retaliation and no cleansing of the land by
shedding the blood of him that shed it, a special sacrifice had to
be brought to God with this solemn prayer: "Our hands have not
shed this blood, neither have our eyes seen it. Be merciful, O Lord
. . . and lay not innocent blood unto Thy people of Israel's charge"
(Deut. 21:1–8). Every unnatural death must be accounted for to
God; until so accounted for and expiated it is a blemish on the

people as a whole, an affront to God and a diminution of His image (*Bereishit Rabba* 34), and a pollution of the land.

There is not in biblical law any explicit exception to the rule that no man's life may be taken except in the course of law or of war. But the Bible abounds with reports of kings, including even the few righteous ones, who had rebels or other adversaries put to death, ostensibly in contravention or disregard of divine law; and it was on the strength of such factual precedents that the rule evolved in talmudical law to the effect that kings enjoy the right to kill (B. *Sanhedrin* 49a). Maimonides summarized the king's prerogative to take human life as follows: "The king may execute anybody who rebels against him. Even where he commanded a man to go to a certain place and he refused, or not to leave his house and he left, he may be liable to death, and if the king so desires he may have him killed; for it is written, 'Whosoever he be that doth rebel against thy commandment, and will not hearken unto thy words in all that thou commandest him, he shall be put to death' (Josh. 1:18). Likewise, anybody who is in contempt of the king or curses him, like Shimei the son of Gera, may be executed at the king's discretion. . . . Persons accused of murder with only one witness available against them or who had not duly been warned beforehand (and who could therefore not be indicted in court or had to be acquitted), may be executed by order of the king, if he considers that times and circumstances require potential criminals to be deterred and evil hands to be broken" (*Melakhim* 3:8–10). While these wide powers truly reflect such royal justice as was in practice administered by many ruthless kings, they can hardly be said to be commensurable with the letter or spirit of scriptural law. Maimonides' quotation from Joshua is misleading, for the words there spoken are not a command from God, nor even from Joshua, but an undertaking given by the people themselves and binding (if at all) on them only and in respect of Joshua only and not in respect of any other ruler. As to the precedent of Shimei the son of Gera, it is reported not only that he cursed the king but also that he cast stones at him and his servants, but King David rejected the advice he was tendered to have Shimei executed then and there, (2 Sam. 16:5–10); it was only on his deathbed that David recalled the imprecations uttered against him by Shimei and recommended him to his son's vengeance (1 Kings 2:8–9); eventually he found his death at King

Solomon's behest, not without having first committed another offense against the king (ibid. 36–46). When the people clamored for a king to rule over them, they were warned by the prophet Samuel in unmistakable and rather gruesome terms of the far-reaching and unsavory powers that a king would be entitled to wield over them (1 Sam. 8:11–18); but there is no mention there at all of any royal power over life and death. Scriptural law is explicit in making the king subject to all God's laws, "that he may learn to fear the Lord his God, to keep all the words of this law and these statutes, and to do them" (Deut. 17:19), and there is no valid reason to assume that the king would not also be subject to, and bound by, the fundamental prohibition of shedding blood.

But once the royal prerogative to mete out capital punishment had been established, it was soon extended to authorize the regular courts to impose extralegal capital punishment, "where time and circumstances require potential criminals to be deterred and evil hands to be broken." Extralegal measures such as these were stated to be justified or even mandatory whenever the court considered them necessary for upholding the law's authority and enforcing its observance (B. *Yevamot* 90b, J. *Hagiga* 2:2). With the lapse of capital jurisdiction in the year 70 (with the destruction of the Temple), this emergency power was called in aid to enable the courts to administer criminal law and uphold law and order generally; the lapsing of jurisdiction created the "emergency" which justified the assumption of such powers. Thus, courts were exhorted to inflict punishment—including capital punishment—on offenders who were not liable to be so punished under the law (Maimonides, *Sanhedrin* 24:4). It was stressed, however, that no change of the law was to be involved in any exercise of any such power. Courts had to act on an *ad hoc* basis and to satisfy themselves first that in the particular case before them justice required them to act as they did (ibid.); and they were in duty bound not only to consider "the necessities of the day" but always to respect the sanctity of human life and human dignity (ibid. 10). This is a remarkable instance of the adaptability of Jewish law to changing conditions and to the requirements of particular unforeseeable situations: not even God's own prerogative to take human life, or to lay down in what cases and under what circumstances human life may be taken, could stand in the way of providing for the taking of life in cases of necessity for upholding the law.

It appears that such extralegal emergency measures were in fact taken only in the most extreme cases. Indeed, post-talmudical jurists could (and would) look to their talmudical predecessors for a fundamentally negative attitude to all capital punishment. It is reported of four of the foremost second-century talmudists that they engaged in the following discussion: "A court (Sanhedrin) that passes capital sentence once every seven years is to be called lethal. R. Elazar ben Azarya said, once every seventy years. R. Tarfon and R. Akiva said, had we ever sat in the Sanhedrin, no man would ever have been executed. R. Shimon ben Gamliel said, they (i.e., R. Tarfon and R. Akiva) would have caused murderers to multiply in Israel" (M. *Makkot* 1:10). In a later discussion of this mishnaic exchange of opinions, the question was raised as to how such great scholars could have performed their judicial duties according to law and still have abstained from passing sentences of death. The answer was proferred that the most complicated (and often rather absurd) forms of cross-examination would be devised to confuse the witnesses, make them contradict each other and themselves, and thus render their evidence untrustworthy—which would unavoidably result in the acquittal of the accused (B. *Makkot* 7a). It comes to this: that these scholars would have gone to any lengths within the procedural possibilities to circumvent the law which compelled them to impose capital punishment—the divine will and command reflected in this law notwithstanding; and it is rather significant that their opponent does not use against them the argument of disregarding the divine will, but only invokes the criminal-policy requirement of deterring potential murderers. Maimonides was not at all satisfied with such humanitarianism; he writes that courts must at all times be careful in weighing the evidence, but once they are satisfied that there is sufficient and reliable evidence to support a conviction, it is their duty to pass sentence of death and "to have even a thousand convicts executed on one day if that is what the law of the Torah requires them to do" (Commentary ad M. *Makkot* 1:10). There is nothing surprising in such a legalistic-positivistic approach; what is surprising is the spirit of liberty and independence with which the great talmudists overcame explicit commandments of God's own laws for the sake of saving human lives.

Theoretically and theologically there can be no doubt not only that the laws prescribing punishments and allocating them to the

various offenses are emanations of God's own will, but that their
primary purpose is expiation and the pacification of God's blazing
anger (Deut. 13:18, Num. 25:4): criminals and their crimes are
an abomination in the eyes of God (Deut. 18:12, 22:5, 25:16,
27:15) and for this reason alone ought to be eliminated. While
this purpose is, in the case of most offenses, served by the duty
imposed on human judicial agencies to impose capital punishment, the most eminently and inherently divine among all the
punishments ordained by God is that meted out by God Himself.
Divine punishment is not only the residuary sanction for all
evildoing (Lev. 26:14–45 and Deut. 28:15–68), whether or not
punishable or punished by human courts, but there are many
specific offenses for which biblical law provides divine punishment (kareth). The usual formula is that the soul who committed
the particular crime "shall be cut off from among the people" (e.g.,
Lev. 18:29, 20:3, 5, 18, et al.). The threat of being "cut off" from
the living by the hand of the Lord, in His own time and manner,
hovers over the offender constantly and inescapably; he is not
unlike the patient who is told by his doctor that he might die any
day or any hour from his incurable disease. However merciful,
because of its vagueness and lack of immediacy, this threat of
punishment may appear to modern criminals, in ancient times
its psychological effect must have been devastating. The wrath of
an omnipotent and omniscient God being directed particularly at
you of all people, and being certain to strike at you with unforeseeable force and intensity any day of the year and any minute of
the hour, was a load too heavy for the believer to bear. Discerning
the inhumanity inherent in the divinity of this kind of punishment, the talmudists set about abolishing it, divine and God-
willed or not. The law was laid down that all offenders liable to
kareth shall be flogged, and having undergone the punishment of
flogging shall no longer be liable to forfeit their lives at the hand of
God (M. Makkot 3:15).

   The problem of how to be sure that God would not after all mete
out His punishment as threatened, regardless of any judicial
flogging, did indeed agitate the minds of the reformers. However
deeply convinced they were of the divine inspiration which guided
their own legislative pronouncements, and however firm their
belief in a merciful God who would surely approve of their abhorrence of cruel and inhuman punishments, there was no escaping

the risk that the Lord might not honor their promise that the offender would be free from *kareth*. They had (as usual) no great difficulty in finding in God's own words the required sanction for their bold innovations. In the context of the punishment of flogging, God said: do not exceed the number of lashes, lest "thy brother should seem vile unto thee" (or, in the translation of the Jewish Publication Society, lest your brother "be degraded before your eyes") (Deut. 25:3). After having been flogged he is called "your brother"; being your brother he must be deemed as innocent and pure of sin as you can be yourself, that is, as having fully and duly expiated any sin of which he may have been guilty (M. *Makkot* 3:15; Maimonides, *Sanhedrin* 17:7). The expiation of sin, even such sin as may carry divine punishment, causes it to cease altogether, and no punishment can any longer attach to it.

Some later scholars chose not to rely on such hermeneutics but preferred to resort instead to fundamental principles of law which—or so they took for granted—even God Almighty would not disregard: the principle, for instance, that no man may be punished twice for the same offense. In the language of Maimonides, "Nobody is liable to two punishments (for one offense); once flogged he can no longer be liable to divine punishment" (Commentary ad M. *Makkot* 3:1). For the application of this rule it does not matter what the punishment was that, according to law, ought to have been imposed for the particular offense. The rule is that two sanctions—even if the one be civil damages and the other penal—may never be imposed for a single act or omission (B. *Ketuvot* 32b, B. *Bava Kamma* 83b, B. *Makkot* 4b, 13b), and the rule that nobody may be punished twice for the same offense would follow *a minori ad maius*. What remains baffling and unexplained is the usurpation of power by the human court to forestall the divine punishment prescribed for the particular offense and to confront the Lord with a *fait accompli*.

These reforms did not, however, command the unanimous support and approval of the talmudists. The substitution of flogging for the divine *kareth* met with the dissent of R. Yitzhak, an outstanding jurist, who appears to have subscribed to the view that divine punishment, depending as it does on divine mercy and being always open to divine reconsideration, was a lighter punishment than flogging, which caused immediate pain and suffering, and therefore should not be replaced at all (B. *Megilla*

7b, B. *Makkot* 22b). Another scholar was prepared to accept the substitution of flogging for *kareth*, but in order to make sure that the substitution would indeed be acceptable also to God, he made it subject to the condition precedent that the offender first duly repent—the premise being that he who has done penance will no longer be punished by God (B. *Yoma* 86a). The difference between divine and human justice is, *inter alia*, that the repentant sinner ceases to be liable to divine but remains liable to judicial punishment; and we find authoritative warnings to the effect that to have undergone judicial punishment might avail the offender nothing if he comes unrepenting before the seat of divine judgment (*Mekhilta Yitro* 7, J. *Yoma* 8:7, J. *Shevuot* 1:7). But if the offender has duly repented and hence is no longer liable to divine punishment, the question arises, why should he be flogged? If the divine punishment attaching to his offense is served by repentance, any subsequent flogging might amount to double punishment. However that may be, absolution from divine punishment ought in any case, in reason and fairness, to absolve also from any punishment substituted therefor. Perhaps the answer is that the reform will not appear as daring as all that, or as not daring at all, if it can be based on the assumption that God has forgiven the offender anyway, or that the substitution of the relatively light penalty of flogging for the very severe divine threat of being cut off from the living, required for its psychological reasonableness at least the mitigating fact of repentance. The desire to add and attach some educational and religious objective to the flogging substitute may also have been involved. This could best be achieved by the postulate of repentance. By taking the reform out of the purely legal and penological sphere and clothing it with theological meaning, one made it eminently and ostensibly God-sent.

The humanization of punishment, in the sense that human organs take over from God to save human lives which God would destroy, was justified by interpreting the verse "for the Lord will not hold him guiltless that taketh His name in vain" (Exod. 20:7, Deut. 5:11) as meaning that the Lord will not hold him guiltless but the courts down on earth will (B. *Shevu'ot* 21a, B. *Temura* 3a–b). If it is God's privilege to punish and not to take mercy on human lives, the earthly judges claim the privilege to save human lives and not to punish. In a later discussion the question was raised whether this was not a misinterpretation of God's word and whether the Lord's intransigence did not, on the contrary, require even more intransigence on the part of His servants, who ought to be eager to imitate Him (ibid.): acquittal by a human court where God would convict, or corporal punishment by a human court where God would take away life, surely amounts to a wanton frustration of God's purpose and to a usurpation of powers contrary to divine will. Nevertheless the law substituting flogging for death at the hand of God was left intact—and God Almighty was held no longer to be seized of the matter of capital punishment.

While there is no explicit recognition in biblical or talmudical law of a right to life, it may well be said that life and its fulfillment is the ultimate purpose of the whole divine law: "I call heaven and earth to record this day against you, that I have set before you life and death, blessing and cursing: therefore choose life, that both thou and thy seed may live" (Deut. 30:19). You "choose life" by "loving God, obeying His voice, and cleaving unto Him; for He is thy life and the length of thy days" (Deut. 30:20). Betraying God and worshipping other gods is choosing death—not so much because you are liable to be executed or "cut off," but rather because a life of barbarian lawlessness is not worthy of the name. "Man doth not live by bread only, but by every word that proceedeth out of the mouth of the Lord doth man live" (Deut. 8:3).

These generalities were concretized in talmudical law. The verse "Ye shall therefore keep my statutes and my judgments, which if a man do, he shall live in them" (Lev. 18:5) was supplemented to the effect that he shall live in them and not that he shall die in them (B. *Yoma* 85b, B. *Sanhedrin* 74a, B. *Avoda Zara* 27b, 54a). None of God's laws need—or may—be obeyed or performed in a way or in circumstances involving any danger to life. The "danger" to life was very liberally determined: any doubt in a matter of life would be dissolved in favor of transgressing the law rather than allowing any risk to life to be incurred in obeying it (B. *Shabbat* 129a, B. *Yoma* 83a–84b, B. *Ketuvot* 15a, B. *Bava Kamma* 44b, B. *Sanhedrin* 79a). Wasting time in investigating whether indeed the situation is such that a "danger" to life exists may amount to shedding blood (*Orah Hayim* 328:2, 13, 329:1), and an expert who lets himself be consulted on a question like this is blameworthy (Tur, *Orah Hayim* 328). For a man to endanger his life in order to perform God's commandments is considered not praiseworthy but wicked; his piety and devotion are rejected as stupid (Nahmanides, *Torat HaAdam, Sha'ar Hassakana;* Radbaz, *Responsa* 3:885).

Rather than a right to life, these norms reflect at first sight a paramount duty to live—a duty which seems to supersede all (or almost all) other duties to God imposed by law. Positive commandments such as "take heed to thyself, and keep thy soul diligently" (Deut. 4:9) and "take ye therefore good heed unto yourselves" (ibid. 15) were interpreted as imposing an explicit duty to preserve one's life (cf. *Rotzei'ah* 11:4), just as such commandments as "neither shalt thou stand against the blood of thy neighbor" (Lev. 19:16) and thou shalt not "bring blood upon thine house" (Deut. 22:8) were interpreted as imposing an explicit duty to preserve the lives of others (*Rotzei'ah* 1:14, 11:1–3). It was asserted that whoever causes the soul of any man to be lost is deemed to have caused the loss of a whole world; and whoever preserves the life of a single human being is deemed to have sustained the whole world (M. *Sanhedrin* 4:5).

But the right to life is necessarily implied both in the duty of others and in the duty of oneself to preserve it; the fact that the law does not provide any sanctions to enforce that right is irrelevant for its existence. Moreover, the fact that the divine lawgiver relegated all (or almost all) other duties owed to Him to the preservation of life implies a recognition of a right of priority and preeminence which God conceded to human life. Nor can it derogate from the character of a right that it is clothed in terms of a duty; this is the common characteristic of human rights in divine law which we have already noted.

The only exceptions to the general rule that the right to life or the duty to live take precedence over all other commandments of the law are the cases of idolatry, homicide, and incest: rather than commit any of these cardinal crimes you must even give up your life (B. *Sanhedrin* 74a). But even this exception was further restricted to apply only where the transgression takes place in public ("in the presence of at least ten men from Israel"), the reason being that by subjecting yourself to being killed rather than commit the crime, you sanctify the Holy Name, and such sanctification is prescribed in public ("I will be hallowed among the children of Israel," Lev. 22:32). If the crime takes place in private, no desecration of the Holy Name is involved, and you must commit it rather than let yourself be killed (*Yessodei Ha-Tora* 5:1–2). Again, no man ought to assume exaggerated piety and volunteer to die rather than commit the crime. Maimonides goes so far as to say that by submitting to being killed he commits not only a grave offense against his own life but also the crime of desecration of the Holy Name—just as he would have sanctified the Holy Name if he had submitted to being killed where he was in duty bound to do so (ibid. 4).

The injunction "thou shalt not stand against the blood of thy neighbor" (Lev. 19:16) was also invoked to establish the rule that whenever a human being is in danger of death you must do all you can to rescue him, even to the extent of killing his pursuer (M. *Sanhedrin* 8:7, B. *Sanhedrin* 73a). You must be careful not to kill the pursuer if you can prevent him by other means from carrying his homicidal intent into effect, as for instance by wounding him (*Rotzei'ah* 1:7); but if you kill a man with the intention only of preventing him from killing another, you are not liable to capital punishment, even though the homicide could perhaps have been prevented by other means (ibid. 13). Nor is mere inaction in failing to try and save another's life ever punishable as a crime at the hand of human courts; only acts, and never mere omissions, can provide cause for criminal sanctions in Jewish law (B. *Makkot* 16a; Maimonides, *Sanhedrin* 18:2). But whoever is in a position to save a human life and fails to do so is highly reprehensible—so much so that his omission is deemed tantamount to actively shedding blood (*Rotzei'ah* 1:16).

The conflict between the right to live and the duty to die is most strikingly reflected in the dilemma which arises when both your own life and the life of another person are in jeopardy and you can save only one, either yours or the other's. "Where two men traveling together had only one bottle of water: if they both drank, both would die; if only one drank all, he could reach a place of human habitation and be saved. Ben Pattura held, better they should both drink and die than that one should see the other die; R. Akiva held, it is written, 'that thy brother may live with thee' (Lev. 25:36)—hence your own life takes precedence over the life of your brother" (B. *Bava Metzia* 62a). In terms of the right to life, Akiva's ruling amounts to a vindication of the natural instinct for self-preservation; your own right to stay alive is paramount, and the duty to preserve another man's life is subordinate to it. Ben Pattura, on the other hand, postulates a human solidarity and the equality of value of human lives. How can you know, as another talmudical dictum has it, that your blood is redder than his—maybe your brother's blood is redder than yours (B. *Sanhedrin* 74a, B. *Pessahim* 25b); and even from a purely egotistical point of view it may well be easier and better for you to die yourself than behold, and be the cause of, the death of your brother. It was later held that when several men are threatened by heathen oppressors that they will all be killed unless they deliver one of them up for killing, they must all suffer death rather than surrender a single soul (T. *Terumot* 7:20, J. *Terumot* 8:10). Again, it is your duty to die rather than be the cause—however involuntary—of the death of another human being. The prohibition of surrendering a fellowman to be killed is deduced, *a minori ad maius,* from the biblical prohibition of stealing a man for the purpose of selling him into slavery (Deut. 24:7) and of "deliver[ing] unto his master the servant which is escaped from his master" (Deut. 23:16): if you may not surrender anybody to a person suspected of treating him harshly, *a fortiori* you may not surrender him to a potential killer. (For the crime of surrendering Jesus ascribed to him, Judas Iscariot is said in one source to have committed suicide [Matt. 27:5] and in another to have suffered a violent death, ostensibly by way of divine punishment [Acts 1:18–20].)

In this context a problem was debated which agitated the minds of the talmudists of many generations. What if the man to be surrendered for killing had already been singled out by the oppressors? Is he not doomed to death anyway? Should he not be surrendered in order to save the lives of the others? R. Shimon ben Lakish said, even he may be surrendered only if he had already forfeited his life to God by committing a capital offense against God's laws for which he had not yet been punished; R. Yohanan said, he may be surrendered even if he had committed no such offense (J. *Terumot* 8:10; the example here given is that of Sheba son of Bichri, who committed treason and thus forfeited his life to the king [2 Sam. 20:21]; but *quaere* that an offense against the king could for this purpose be tantamount to an offense against God; and *quaere* whether the criminal had not first to be duly convicted by judicial process). Maimonides adopts the ruling of Shimon ben Lakish, adding a proviso that the fact that he had already forfeited his life may not be brought to the attention of the oppressors (*Yessodei HaTora* 5:5). It is submitted that the condition here postulated of the man having already forfeited his life to God was of little or no practical importance, the coincidence being highly improbable that it would be a criminal guilty of but not yet punished for a capital offense whose surrender would be demanded. This wholly speculative case was devised to demonstrate once again that the only legitimate exception to the prohibition of taking human lives was the execution of criminals where God's law prescribed the death penalty for their offense.

Even where a man has been sentenced to death by due judicial process, the law is that before any other person may lay hands on him, the witnesses who testified against him must first lay hands on him to execute the sentence (Deut. 17:7), a provision probably intended to impress potential witnesses with the gravity of the responsibility they are taking upon themselves. It is only if and when the action of the witnesses does not result in death that it becomes the duty of anyone present to take part in the execution (ibid.; M. *Sanhedrin* 6:4). This duty was practically abolished by talmudical law reformers who substituted for the biblical stoning the execution by pushing the convict from a high "stoning-house" down into the depth, with death resulting immediately (M. *Sanhedrin* 6:1–4) and any participation by the general public thus becoming superfluous (B. *Sanhedrin* 42b, 45a). As though distilled by some chemical process, the execution by stoning, whose main attribute was that it absorbed public vengeance and, even when judicially organized and supervised, provided an outlet for public fury and aggressiveness, reappears in an entirely new shape, without public and without fury. How deep-seated was the apprehension of the sages that even this reformed mode of execution might still smack of aggressive or malicious action is shown by the dictum that the stoning-house was to be erected on a hill at some distance from the courthouse, "so as not to let the court appear to be murderous" (B. *Sanhedrin* 42b).

A man who awaits execution pursuant to a final sentence of death duly passed on him is deemed in law to be a dead man already (B. *Sanhedrin* 71b, *Mamrim* 5:12), another good reason why putting him to death cannot amount to unlawful homicide. For the same reason no civil liability would arise for inflicting any personal injury on such a "dead man" (T. *Bava Kamma* 9:15). It seems that the only offense which still can be committed against him is to be cursed or beaten by his own children or grand-children (B. *Sanhedrin* 85a, *Mamrim* 5:12). A puzzling problem arose in the purely theoretical case of a man who committed another capital offense after having been sentenced to death. It was suggested that he could be put on trial and sentenced a second time, and that the sentence which provided for the more severe mode of execution should be carried out; but if it was the second sentence which was the more severe, how can you execute an already dead man? It was held that the fiction of death ought not to stand in the way of severity (B. *Sanhedrin* 81a).

It comes to this: that the duty imposed by divine law to live, implicit in the divine gift of life, may be suspended only by divine command; but whenever man finds himself in a situation in which he himself must decide between life and death, the situation may well be such as to require in law the preference of death over life, however cardinal and paramount the duty and virtue of choosing and preserving life may in general be.

Not only life but a long life, "the length of days and years" (Deut. 30:20; Pss. 21:5, 91:16; Prov. 3:2, 16), is a gift from God. Talmud-ical tradition has it that the Lord allots to every person at birth a potential span of life, or number of days, in advance. It is consid-ered a blessing from God if a man is allowed to live out the whole of the term originally allotted to him (Exod. 23:26; God is said to sit "filling up the years of the righteous day by day": B. *Rosh HaShana* 11a, B. *Sota* 13b). Opinions are divided as to whether this fulfillment of the days will always be limited to the maximum determined in advance, or whether divine generosity and omnip-otence would not rather allow for the prolongation of lives even beyond their original span. God's promise to add fifteen years to the days of King Hezekiah (2 Kings 20:6, Isa. 38:5) was taken by one school as an addition out of Hezekiah's preallotted term and by another school as an additional divine donation over and above that term (T. *Eduyot* 1:15, B. *Yevamot* 50a). But all are agreed that the fulfillment of one's days and, *a fortiori,* the extension of one's predetermined life-span are left to free divine discretion—a consensus which is the premise for holding out prospects of being rewarded for good deeds by long life, and for threatening with being punished for misdeeds by early death.

In Scripture we find prolongation of life promised as the reward for walking in the ways of the Lord and obeying His statutes and commands (Deut. 4:40, 5:33, 6:2, 11:8–9, 32:47); and, in particular, for honoring father and mother (Exod. 20:12, Deut. 5:16), keeping weights and measures "perfect and just" (Deut. 25:15), and showing compassion for animals (Deut. 22: 6–7). A special prolongation of their days was reserved for kings whose hearts were not lifted up above their brethren and who abode by the laws (Deut. 17:20, 1 Kings 3:14). King Solomon attributes long life to hatred of covetousness, love of wisdom, fear of God, charity and honesty (Prov. 10:2, 11:4, 13:14, 14:12, 16:25, 28:16). The talmudists provided additional long lists of recipes for prolonging one's life—for instance, devotion to prayers (B. *Berakhot* 13b et al.), reticence and abstinence from excessive sexual intercourse (B. *Berakhot* 22a), regular wearing of phylacteries (B. *Menahot* 44a)—and quite a number of famous scholars who had been blessed with long lives volunteered to their disciples their own surmises for what good deeds they might have been rewarded— among which cleanliness, tolerance, humility, and spurning gifts and riches rank high (B. *Ta'anit* 20b, B. *Megilla* 27b–28a). The ever-recurring experience that divine promises in this respect are so often and so flagrantly broken was easily explained away by transferring the lengthening of the days to the world-to-come (B. *Kiddushin* 39b, B. *Hullin* 142a)—but, then, existence there is probably of unlimited duration anyway.

King David's prayer, "Lord, make me to know mine end, and the measure of my days, what it is" (Ps. 39:5), was not answered. God will not disclose to man the secret of his end or the measure of his days (B. *Shabbat* 30a), though He has occasionally given some forewarning of the impending end (e.g., to Moses; Deut. 31:14). Man's span of life is God's well-kept secret; were it not, there would be no incentive for man to try and prolong his life by good deeds. However much he tries, man can never be sure of God's response: "not every righteous man has his days prolonged, and not every wicked man has his days shortened, but all according to the choice of the Creator" (*Emmunot veDei'ot* 6:8). Rabbis are reported to have wept on reading the prophetic utterances to the effect that righteousness, self-humiliation, justice, and good deeds would only "perhaps" give hope for divine grace (Lam. 3:29, Amos 5:15, Zeph. 2:3)—"all this and only 'perhaps'?" (B. *Hagiga*

4b). The Talmud comments on two great scholars and righteous men who both experienced God's grace in having their prayers for rain granted: one of them lived ninety-two years, and the other only forty years (B. *Mo'ed Kattan* 28a). The conclusion was inevitable that long life may in reality not be a matter of merit but rather a matter of luck; but we are given to understand that good luck may certainly be fortified by good deeds (Tossafot ad B. *Yevamot* 49b).

If it is by God's decree that man dies, whether at the end of his days or before his time, it would stand to reason that the instrument chosen by God to put him to death, even if it be a murderer, ought not to bear responsibility for having brought about the result which had anyway been divinely predetermined. The murderer would, indeed, legally and logically be in a position similar to that of an executioner: both are performing God's will—the one consciously, the other unwittingly—and both are intentionally killing their victim at the very moment and in the very manner God willed him to die. They differ from each other not only in their motivations but also in the knowledge the executioner probably has, and the murderer probably has not, of any particular offense for which God decreed the death; but then both motivation and knowledge may for legal purposes be wholly irrelevant. The sages sought to solve the problem by distinguishing between the act of killing and the event of death. The act of killing may entail personal responsibility like every other human act, the character and quantum of such responsibility being determined by law. The event of death, however, is and remains in the hands of God, as indeed all "natural" consequences of our acts are in the hands of God. Had the killer—be he murderer or executioner—abstained from killing, the victim would nevertheless have died at the same divinely predestined moment, unless God in His mercy fell in with the repentant killer and willed it otherwise (*Emmunot veDei'ot* 4:5).

While this kind of speculation left both divine predetermination and human responsibility ostensibly intact, it failed to provide an incentive for the individual to do something about prolonging his life, since the moment and manner of his death would anyway not depend on him. Even if he committed suicide he would only terminate his life at the moment and in the manner God had willed him to die, and insofar as his responsibility for his wrongful act was concerned, he might well have to undergo divine punishment in another world, but such delayed sanction might be regarded by him as rather irrelevant to his present earthly death. Not only was this conception unsatisfactory from the point of view of legal policy, but it seemed unconsonant with those scriptural and talmudical texts which (as we have seen) conceded to man a much more decisive role in the shaping of his own destiny.

It was Maimonides who initiated a new line of thought. Combining the devotion of the faithful with the rationalism of the physician and the utilitarianism of the jurist, he wrote that it was one of the main objects and purposes of divine law to cause man to abstain from intemperance and such activities and indulgences as were likely to "injure the body and destroy life before his natural time arrives" (*Moré Nevukhim* 3:33). Not only ethics and morals but also laws, particularly including the dietary laws but also the personal-injury laws and even the ritual laws, were destined to lead to the prolongation of human life. Indeed, man differs from animal in that he is able, by exercising his reason, to submit to deliberate restraints with a view to maintaining good health and thus prolonging life (ibid. 1:72).

The opportunity to enlarge on the subject came to Maimonides when the following formal question was addressed to him: "Is the life of man in this world predestined to a fixed date which he necessarily reaches and no affliction can shorten or destroy it, or are there perhaps shortening afflictions which may ruin life if man does not beware of them? Is it that unless he takes care and actively avoids or eliminates those afflictions he does not stay alive, but if he prepares and equips himself to meet and endure them he will live longer than he would have lived, had he not so prepared and equipped himself?" The Maimonidean responsum starts with the proposition that there is no predetermined period of life. "A living organism lives as long as the osseous lymphs which melted away are being replaced. As Galen taught, the cause of death is the destruction of the balance of natural heat, either for internal or for external causes" (*Responsum*, p. 27). He then proceeds to give a most detailed and elaborate description of the physiology of each of three internal and six external causes, and asserts that a man who bewares of all these causes will not have his life cut short but will reach his "natural age" (ibid., p. 30).

The physiological argument is then fortified by four "proofs" from divine law, "all mathematical, biological, or metaphysical studies, nay even the science of logic, being but preparatory to the study of the Torah, which alone leads to real perfection" (ibid.). The first proof he adduces is from the law requiring parapets to be built on house-roofs (Deut. 22:8): this is but an illustration of the general rule that precautions must be taken to avoid danger to life. The rule implies that taking such precautions will remove the danger, for unless they were apt to remove it the law would make no sense: "if it had already been decreed that the man would fall off the roof, there would be no purpose to the parapet, and erecting it would be useless. Seeing that God exhorts us to erect parapets, they must be useful, and the precaution effected by them efficacious; and those who hold that life has a predetermined end which cannot be guarded against must be wrong" (ibid.).

Another proof is deduced by Maimonides from the laws relating to cities of refuge where a manslayer is entitled to seek asylum from the blood-avenger (Num. 35:11–32, Deut. 4:41–43, 19: 2–10). Had it been predestined for the manslayer to die at the hands of the blood-avenger at a certain date, there would have been no use and no purpose in setting up cities of refuge; and they would have been equally unnecessary had it been predestined that he would not die at the hands of the blood-avenger (Responsum, pp. 31, 78). In essence, cities of refuge are also just another of the precautions calculated to avoid dangers to life.

A third proof is seen by Maimonides in the law dispensing the newly-married from war service, "lest he die in the battle, and another may take her" (Deut. 20: 5–8). Again, dispensation from war service is in the nature of a precaution to avoid death in battle. The conclusion is inescapable that the death which would have occurred at the front would not occur at home (Responsum, p. 31).

A "conclusive" proof is seen by Maimonides in the fact that the people of Nineveh, who were doomed to die within forty days, were pardoned and did not die: "God repented of the evil, that he had said he would do unto them, and he did it not" (Jonah 3:4, 10). Had the end of the forty days been predetermined as their date of death, no repentance on their part could have saved them; and had the end of their days been predetermined for the date on which they eventually did die, their sinfulness could not have brought about their death at any earlier date even though they did not repent. "This shows that life in this our world is not preallotted in such a way that afflictions could not shorten it (*Responsum*, p. 31).

Corroboration for these proofs is provided, according to Maimonides, by Scripture itself. King Solomon asserted that "the fear of the Lord prolongeth days, but the years of the wicked shall be shortened" (Prov. 10:27). Jeremiah's prophecy that he who abides in the city shall die by the sword, by famine and pestilence, but he that leaves the city shall live, "and his life shall be unto him for a prey" (Jer. 21:9), was authoritatively interpreted as meaning that "his life shall be as if he had rescued it or snatched it away from death" (Rashi ad loc.). And then there are the divine promises of reward by the prolongation of life for obedience to the laws, and the actual prolongation of King Hezekiah's life, which we have already mentioned.

It is therefore up to man to lengthen or shorten his life, by living either healthily and in conformity with divine law or intemperately and sinfully; and the length of his life depends entirely on man alone. The role assigned to God, however, is not just that of a passive observer and onlooker, but rather that of a benign dispenser of life who responds favorably to the efforts and precautions taken for the prolongation of life, but who reacts adversely to intemperance and misconduct calculated to bring about premature death. As to God's foreknowledge of when and how a man will die, Maimonides absolves himself from entering into any discussion of the subject by stating that we know nothing, and cannot know anything, of the nature of divine knowledge, nor can we draw any conclusions from what we know about human knowledge to that of God (*Teshuva* 5:5, *Moré Nevukhim* 3:20–21): "no human mouth can express it, no human ear can hear it, no human heart can understand it" (*Yessodei HaTora* 2:10). What we do know is that man is free to do and act as he chooses: "never let it enter your mind, as the fools of other nations and many of the Jewish robots have it, that God decrees man from his birth to be good or bad. . . . there is nobody who compels him or commands him or draws him unto one of the two ways, but he of himself and of his own understanding inclines to whatever way he chooses. This is what Jeremiah said, 'Out of the mouth of the

Most High proceedeth not evil and good' (Lam. 3:38), that is to say, not the Creator destines men to be good and not to be bad: it follows that it is the sinner who is destroying himself" (*Teshuva* 5:2). What is written, "See I have set before you this day life" (Deut. 30:15), is a "fundamental principle of the Torah: I have set before you life so that the liberty is yours" and the life is in your hands (*Teshuva* 5:3).

This total exclusion of divine omniscience from the consideration of the nature of human freedom to act may have been a stroke of genius, but it left the theological problem unsolved. While later philosophers tried to solve it by limiting God's omniscience to everything that is "ordered," as distinguished from what is "contingent"—or, in other words, to matters which God chose to reserve for His own determination, as distinguished from matters which He chose to allot to human determination (Ralbag, *Milkhamot HaShem* 3:1–6)—Maimonides dismissed the possibility of any such diminution of Divinity *in limine* and preferred the shortcomings of human understanding to any doubt as to the absoluteness of divine omniscience. He must have been well aware of the likelihood that divine omniscience—of the exact nature of which he had professed his total ignorance—conflicted with the human freedom which he so unequivocally postulated; still, as a matter of law or ethics, he would probably dismiss any such conflict as irrelevant and insist on the absoluteness of human liberty for his pragmatic purpose at hand.

The ancient notion of divine predetermination of the length of our days and of the inescapability of divinely predestined death was thus superseded by a theory of human self-determination, extending even to the individual's well-nigh absolute power over his own life. Instead of being the unfathomable source of inescapable decrees, God becomes but the instrument in the hands of man for the preservation or loss of his life. God appears to have divested Himself of any "right" to the life of man when He breathed the breath of life into his nostrils (Gen. 2:7) and to have vested the right to life in the living human being. Coming from God it is a divine trust which man is expected and commanded to keep and cherish.

2

THE RIGHT TO LIBERTY AND SECURITY OF PERSON

Although we know from biblical sources that both administrative detention and punitive imprisonment were widespread in ancient Egypt (Gen. 39:20, 42:16–19; Exod. 12:29), among the Philistines (Judg. 16:21, 25) and Assyrians (2 Kings 17:4), as well as in Persia (Ezra 7:26), there is no biblical law explicitly authorizing imprisonment. It is true that we find persons accused of blasphemy (Lev. 24:12) and of violation of the Sabbath (Num. 15:34) "put in ward" pending trial, even on divine instructions; but the special reason given for the arrest in both cases is that the law had not yet been revealed and it was not known what exactly should be done to those persons (ibid.). Whether or not the conclusion is justified that where the substantive law was known the offender had to be tried forthwith and could not be detained pending conviction, it can at any rate be asserted for sure that a person could lawfully be deprived of his liberty pending trial only in order to prevent his escape, and that he could not lawfully be deprived of his liberty by way of punishment or for purposes or reasons of security.

An apparent exception to this rule is, again, to be found in the powers of the king. From biblical reports it would appear that the kings of both Judah and Israel maintained prisons (described by various names: 1 Kings 22:27; Isa. 24:22; Jer. 37: 4, 15, 16, 18, 21; 38:6, 7, 9–13, 28), and some of the prophets who raged against the kings found themselves incarcerated. This royal usage may have been an imitation or adoption of laws and customs prevailing in neighboring countries, or it may have been an autocratic usurpation of powers and means of repression: there is no authorization in law to support its legality. But here again the actual practice of the kings gave rise to legislation, formulated at a time when kingship had long ceased, to the effect that kings were entitled "to inflict imprisonment and corporal punishment" (*Melakhim* 3:8). More surprisingly the Persian law which Ezra was authorized to introduce in Judea, and which recognized imprisonment as a legal mode of punishment, was later called in aid as authority to empower the courts applying Jewish law to also impose imprisonment (B. *Mo'ed Kattan* 16a). The heathen origin of this law was allowed to fall into oblivion, and its rather wide application made it appear as if it were indigenous.

Talmudical law appears to have taken the two biblical instances of detention pending trial as authority for the proposition that all persons accused of capital offenses are to be detained pending trial (*Sifrei, Shelah* 114), but we have no record that this was indeed the actual practice, and the rule dates from a period when capital jurisdiction had long ceased. In the particular case of the rebellious elder—that is, a person who has committed the offense (stated in Deut. 17:12) of presuming to lay down and practice the law contrary to the majority rule—his detention was provided for pending inquiries into the nature of his teachings by three different courts, each of which had to give him an opportunity to recant before he could be found guilty (M. *Sanhedrin* 11:2–4), but then, again, there is no record that any person was ever accused or convicted of any such offense. Another particular instance of pretrial detention is to be found in the case of a man who has inflicted a serious wound on another person; he is to be detained until it can be determined whether or not the wound was mortal (i.e., whether or not the victim survives) and thus whether the charge against him should be homicide or assault (B. *Ketuvot* 33b; *Mekhilta, Nezikin* 6; B. *Sanhedrin* 78b; Rashi ad *Pessahim* 91a).

The point was raised, however, as to how the detention of a person not yet convicted and hence presumed to be innocent, with the embarrassment and public affront involved in his arrest, could possibly be justified (J. *Sanhedrin* 7:10)—an eminent human rights issue, formulated by R. Yossei (4th cent.), which apparently agitated the minds of the members of the academy. It was eventually agreed that any such detention could be held permissible only where the names of the two witnesses testifying that they had seen the accused committing the offense were already known, and the detention appeared necessary only until the witnesses could be brought before the court (ibid., and Ran ad *Sanhedrin* 56a). In a similar vein we find an admonition never to let a man be degraded in public even though he may be suspected of having sinned (M. *Avot* 3:11, B. *Menahot* 99b, B. *Bava Metzia* 58b).

A person convicted of a capital offense was deprived of his liberty—not necessarily imprisoned, but held under guard—until his execution (M. *Sanhedrin* 6:1–3). One of the sages opined that executions should take place immediately following the verdict so as to avoid unnecessarily tormenting the convict by imprisoning him pending execution (T. *Sanhedrin* 11:3). But that same scholar (R. Yehuda) also held that where different persons were arrested for different murders and then got mixed up in such a way that it could no longer be established clearly which person was to be accused of which murder, they should all be indefinitely detained but not executed (M. *Sanhedrin* 9:3), dissenting from the majority opinion that they should all have the benefit of the doubt and be discharged (ibid.). The sages later sought to apply R. Yehuda's dissent to a situation in which the mix-up was of persons already convicted of murder and persons still standing trial: those convicted should certainly not be released, even if the doubt as to their identity precluded their execution (B. *Sanhedrin* 79b). Needless to say, these were all purely theoretical exercises in dialectics.

Distinctly punitive imprisonment was introduced by talmudical law for recidivists. A person who committed a noncapital offense after having previously undergone the punishment of flogging for the same kind of offense was to be incarcerated (M. *Sanhedrin* 9:5), but this rule was later restricted to offenses carrying the divine punishment of *kareth*, for which flogging had been substituted (B. *Sanhedrin* 81b; for *kareth* see above p. 32). The restricted rule would then apply only to grave offenses, and its *ratio* would be that a man who had repeatedly committed such grave offenses had thereby demonstrated that his detention was required to secure the public peace. It is, however, remarkable that although *kareth* was in essence capital punishment, even rec¹divists were not allowed to be executed. Detention being regarded as necessary for the protection of the public, its duration was unlimited, and the potential danger posed by the convict must be presumed to subsist so long as he was at liberty; and it was laid down that while in prison he should be kept on a barley diet (M. Sanhedrin 9:5, T. Sanhedrin 12:8), believed to shorten his natural life and hence the agony of his imprisonment. A man not previously convicted and punished who admitted, on or before being convicted of an offense, that he had already committed at least three such offenses, was also liable to imprisonment (B. Sanhedrin 81b), though he could not, on the strength of his confession, be flogged for his previous offenses (Maimonides, Sanhedrin 18:5): but the diet prescribed for him was (semble) not barley but bread and water (T. Sanhedrin 12:7). For similar reasons of protecting the public, imprisonment was also prescribed for murderers of whose guilt the court was persuaded, but who could not be convicted and executed for lack of sufficient evidence—as where, instead of the requisite minimum of two eyewitnesses (Deut. 17:6), only one eyewitness, however creditable, was available (M. Sanhedrin 9:5, B. Sanhedrin 81b); or where the murderer, though seen in flagranti by two eyewitnesses, had not been duly warned beforehand by two competent witnesses that it was unlawful for him to kill and that if he murdered that man he would be executed by decapitation (Rotzei'ah 4:8; for warning see below Chap. 24); or where the evidence of the witnesses or any of them had formally to be rejected because of some discrepancy, contradiction, or other defect, though being regarded as trustworthy (ibid.). While the law is that only perpetrators of the act, not procurers or instigators, are criminally liable (B. Kiddushin 42b–43a), it was held that where a man hired or procured another to kill, even though he could not be convicted of murder, the court was "under obligation," for the protection of the public as well as for the deterrence of potential murderers, to inflict on them both corporal punishment and imprisonment "for many years" (Rotzei'ah 2:5). It appears that there was no scriptural authority enabling imprisonment to be introduced as a mode of judicial punishment (the reference in B. Sanhedrin 81b to the verse in Ps. 34:21, "evil shall slay the wicked," would indicate capital or corporal punishment rather than imprisonment). The deprivation of a man's liberty was held

RIGHTS OF LIFE, LIBERTY, AND THE PURSUIT OF HAPPINESS   51

to be legally justifiable only where the peace of the community was threatened by his going free—a justification which sprang from political or penological necessity rather than from any conceptual or ideational relation back to the principles of Jewish law.

In later periods imprisonment became the standard sanction for contempt of court, including the collection of judgment debts from recalcitrant debtors and the enforcement of divorce orders (Rashi ad *Pessahim* 91a). But even this use of imprisonment was always regarded as contrary to the true spirit of Jewish law: "It is the law of the Torah that when a creditor has sued for the debt due to him, he may satisfy himself out of the debtor's property except such as is exempt from attachment; and if it is found that the debtor has no property or that all his property is exempt, then let him go his way; he may not be imprisoned, nor may he be called upon to prove that he is destitute, nor may an oath of insolvency be administered to him—such as is the rule in the laws of the gentiles" (Maimonides, *Malvé veLové* 2:1). Not unlike the political and penological purposes behind the justification of imprisonment for offenders are the economic purposes behind the justification of the imprisonment of debtors. Not only were severe sanctions thought necessary in order to regulate the money market and encourage lenders to grant loans, but intractable debtors were regarded as cheats and swindlers and transgressors of divine law (*Rivash* 484). While (as from about the sixteenth century) imprisonment for debt was taken over from contemporary alien legal systems and actually practiced, Jewish legal literature abounds with statements to the effect that any such imprisonment is incompatible with the spirit and letter of the law (e.g., *Semag* 1:93; Asheri, *Responsa* 18:5, 68:10; *Hoshen Mishpat* 97:15; et al.).

In the Middle Ages and later we also find punitive imprisonment imposed for sexual offenses (*Rivash* 351), property offenses (*Ritba* 159), religious offenses (ibid. 179), nonpayment of community taxes (Asheri, *Responsa* 7:11), and sundry other transgressions (Assaf, *Onshin* 25–31).

Talmudical law contains several provisions conferring benefits on or making allowances for persons in prison (M. *Pessahim* 8:6, M. *Sota* 4:5, M. *Yevamot* 12:5) or released from prison (M. *Mo'ed Kattan* 3:1). These benefits may differ in extent depending on whether the man was confined in a Jewish or a non-Jewish prison (B. *Pessahim* 91a, J. *Pessahim* 8:6), the only extant indication of the existence of Jewish prisons alongside the Roman prisons. (The prisons from which, according to the custom reported in the New Testament, prisoners were released on the occasion of a feast [Matt. 27:15, Mark 15:6, Luke 23:17, John 18:39] were probably Roman.)

The law favors not only the man released from prison but also the man fleeing from prison; he may not be overcharged for transport facilities (B. *Yevamot* 106a; *Gezeila* 12:7), and there is no differentiation here between Jewish and non-Jewish prisons. Or, a slave released or escaped from prison thereby gains his liberty not only from imprisonment but also from slavery, and his master is compelled to release him and set him free (B. *Gittin* 38a).

There is a special prayer prescribed for a man who had been imprisoned and regained his liberty: "Blessed be the Lord who did mercy unto me" (B. *Berakhot* 54b).

It appears that a man deprived of his liberty, or a prisoner of war, could regain it by being ransomed (at least where non-Jewish authorities were concerned). The maxim that "no prisoner can release himself from prison" (B. *Berakhot* 8b, B. *Nedarim* 7b, B. *Sanhedrin* 95a) was applied to all sorts of situations where one needed the help of others in order to achieve a certain object; but the act of helping a prisoner to regain his liberty was elevated to the rank of a "high commandment" (B. *Bava Batra* 8a–b). In the language of Maimonides: "The release of prisoners takes precedence over the maintenance of the poor. There is no greater commandment than the release of prisoners, the prisoner being included in the hungry and thirsty and naked in danger of their lives; and whoever abstains from ransoming them, transgresses the prohibitions of 'thou shalt not harden thine heart nor shut thine hand' (Deut. 15:7), 'thou shalt not stand against the blood of thy neighbor' (Lev. 19:16), and 'the other shall not rule with rigor over him in thy sight' (Lev. 25:53), as well as violates the injunctions of 'thou shalt open thine hand wide unto him' (Deut. 15:8) and 'thou shalt love thy neighbor as thyself' (Lev. 19:18), and many other similar exhortations—and there is no greater commandment for you than this" (*Matnot Aniyim* 8:10). Even where money has been raised for other charitable or public purposes, it must, whenever a case of ransom arises, first be applied to ransoming a prisoner (ibid. 11). Any delay in ransoming a prisoner may result in danger to his life; regaining his liberty is, therefore, tantamount to saving his life (*Yorei Dei'a* 252:3).

Two restrictions have been placed on the duty to ransom prisoners: one is that one ought not to pay excessive ransoms, and the other that one ought not to aid a prisoner in unlawfully escaping (M. *Gittin* 4:5). The reason for both these restrictions is given as the maintenance of the order of the world (*tikkun ha-olam*, ibid.): excessive ransoms may lead to a multiplication of arrests so as to make more money, and aiding to escape may result in torture and other acts of revenge when the fugitive is rearrested (Bartenura ad M. *Gittin* 4:5, B. *Gittin* 45a). One scholar was apprehensive of retaliatory measures against the prisoners who had not been rescued and had to stay in prison rather than of anything that might happen to the fugitive (ibid.). But "the order of the world" readily suffers any bribe to be paid to secure the release of a prisoner, as well as any aid to be given to him to escape; it is the adverse consequences of such acts which are likely to disturb that order, not any efforts to bring about the release of a person to liberty.

The "security" of the person was in biblical times threatened— apart from the threat of crime and criminals—mainly by the blood-avengers who enjoyed a legitimate right to kill the slayer of their next of kin (Num. 35:19, 27). The law intervened so as to interpose judicial process (ibid. 24): if the slayer was found guilty of murder, he would be sentenced and executed (ibid. 16–21); if the killing was found to have been unpremeditated or accidental, the slayer would find "refuge" from the blood-avenger in one of the six cities of refuge assigned for this purpose (ibid. 13–15, Deut. 4:41–43, 19:2–10). These cities were populated towns in which the manslayer would not only be immune and secure from persecution by the blood-avenger (and, *a fortiori*, by the authorities), but could lead a normal life and earn his livelihood—the words "and that he might live" (Deut. 4:42, 19:5) being interpreted to mean that he was entitled to all normal amenities of life. If he was a scholar he was allowed to take his school with him, if a pupil he would have his teacher brought to him (B. *Makkot* 10a). In order to discourage avengers from frequenting these cities, certain trades, such as the manufacture of textiles, ropes, and glassware,

were banned from them, because they would cause increased
commercial intercourse (T. *Makkot* 3:9); and the sale of arms and
hunting tools was prohibited there so as not to provide avengers
or their agents with weapons or other dangerous instruments (B.
Makkot 10a). According to a later tradition it was not only the six
cities of refuge proper, but also the forty-two cities allotted to the
levites (Josh. 21:39), which provided refuge to manslayers (B.
Makkot 13a, Rotzei'ah 8:9); but while in the original six cities
immunity from persecution was automatic, in the other cities
there had to be an express request for asylum (*Rotzei'ah* 8:10).
Moreover, in the former housing could be claimed as of right (T.
Makkot 3:6), whereas in the latter rent had to be paid (B. *Makkot*
13a). In order to secure the manslayer's safe escape to the city of
refuge, road signs had to be put up at all crossings clearly
showing the nearest way leading to them (B. *Makkot* 10b, T.
Makkot 3:5), and all roads leading there had to be straight and
level and always kept in good repair (*Rotzei'ah* 8:5). On arrival the
man had to present himself at the city gate before the elders, who
would give him accommodation (Josh. 20:4); afterwards he would
be taken to court, escorted by two men learned in the law (M.
Makkot 2:5) who would not only advise him as to his rights but
also dissuade the blood-avenger, should they encounter him on
the way, from exercising his avenging rights (Bartenura ad loc.,
Rashi ad B. *Makkot* 9b). The manslayer was re-escorted into the
city of refuge if found guilty of manslaughter and not guilty of
murder, and there he had to remain until the death of the high
priest; when the high priest died, he was to return to his former
home (Num. 35:25). If he prematurely left the city of refuge and
the blood-avenger found and killed him, the avenger would not be
guilty of any offense (ibid. 26–27); but if he killed him after the
demise of the high priest, he would be guilty of murder (ibid. 28,
Rotzei'ah 7:13). Opinions were divided as to whether the home-
coming manslayer should automatically be restored to his former
position or office. The law was settled to the effect that he should
be (M. *Makkot* 2:8 and Bartenura ad loc.), but Maimonides held
that he had lost his standing forever, "because of this great
misfortune that had come by his hands" (*Rotzei'ah* 7:14). Within
the city of refuge, however, the manslayer could occupy all posi-
tions of trust and honor, provided that he first disclosed to the
people there that he had come to seek refuge (M. *Makkot* 2:8, T.

Makkot 3:8). And in order to prevent refugees from praying for the early death of the incumbent high priest, it is reported that mothers of priests would have food and clothing and other presents sent to them so as to persuade them to pray for a long life for all the priests, including the high priest, notwithstanding their opposite interest (M. *Makkot* 2:6).

Perhaps in order to give an outlet to the "hot anger" of the blood-avenger (Deut. 19:6), some later jurists allotted him the function of prosecutor and initiator of court proceedings (Ran ad *Sanhedrin* 45b, Me'iri, ibid.); others relegated the avenger to the role of executioner, it being both his right and his duty (Num. 35:19) to execute the death sentence of the court (*Rotzei'ah* 1:2; *Ritba* ad *Makkot* 10b). That the avenger had indeed some *locus standi* in court appears probable from the injunction that the court "shall decide between the slayer and the blood-avenger" (Num. 35:24). It was even laid down that where no next of kin was available or came forward, a blood-avenger was to be appointed by the court (B. *Sanhedrin* 45b).

There is little doubt that legally all the rights and duties of blood-avengers have become obsolete (*Havot Ya'ir* 146). But the opinion was proffered that the killing of a manslayer or, *a fortiori*, a murderer by a next of kin qualified as a blood-avenger ought to be regarded as no more than unpremeditated manslaughter (*Ketzot haHoshen* ad *Hoshen Mishpat* 2).

3

SLAVES AND SLAVERY

A "slave" in the legal sense is a person who may not dispose of his time and labor and has no capacity to hold property of his own: he is the property of his master, who may freely dispose of him as well as of his time and labor. There was no civilization in antiquity in which slavery was not legally recognized and widely practiced; nor was there any religion (including the Christian) or any ethical or political philosophy (including the Greek and the Indian) which raised its voice in protest. If biblical law differs from all other contemporaneous systems, it is because of the far-reaching reforms it introduced, mainly—but not solely—with regard to the treatment of slaves and their "human rights."

The following classes of slaves are to be distinguished:

1. *Hebrew slaves.* A "Hebrew"—that is, a citizen—could become a slave either by order of the court on conviction of theft, if he was unable to make restitution (Exod. 22:2), or by giving himself into bondage because of his inability to pay his debts (Lev. 25:89; and cf. Prov. 22:7, Isa. 50:1, Amos 2:6 and 8:6; for actual instances, see 2 Kings 4:1, Neh. 5:5). It was against the law to acquire a Hebrew slave in any other way (Lev. 25:42).

2. *Alien ("Canaanite") slaves.* "Both thy bondmen and thy bondmaids, which thou shalt have, shall be of the heathen that are round about you; of them shall ye buy bondmen and bondmaids. Moreover, of the children of the strangers that do sojourn among you, of them shall ye buy, and of their families that are with you, which they beget in your land; and they shall be your possession" (Lev. 25:44–45).

3. *Prisoners of war.* The booty of war, including "man and

56

beast," was to be divided into two parts: one part for the men "that took the war upon them, who went out to battle," and the other part to the state (Num. 31:26–27). The more ferocious Deuteronomist provided bondage for prisoners of war only where the enemy surrendered without battle (Deut. 20:11)—otherwise "thou shalt smite every male thereof with the edge of the sword" (ibid. 13), and may take into bondage only the women and children (ibid. 14); but it has been rightly observed that this law was "unreal" and never put into practice (de Vaux I 81). When, as the result of a war between the Kingdoms of Judah and Israel, "Hebrew" prisoners were taken and the attempt was made to take them into bondage, the prophet Oded intervened and caused them to be set free and clothed, shod, and fed (2 Chron. 28:8–15).

4. *Female slaves.* A father may sell his daughter into slavery (Exod. 21:7), usually for household duties and eventual marriage (ibid. 7–11).

5. *Slave descendants.* The status of slaves devolved upon their offspring (Exod. 23:12: "the son of thy handmaid"; Gen. 17:13: "he that is born in thy house, and he that is bought with thy money"; Lev. 22:11: any soul bought with his money "and he that is born in his house"; and cf. Jer. 2:14).

The main difference between Hebrew and non-Hebrew slaves is that the former serve six years only and must be freed in the seventh (Exod. 21:2, Deut. 15:12), while the latter serve in perpetuity (Lev. 25:46). The short period of service of the Hebrew slave appears to have been regarded as sufficient to make up for the loss which his master had suffered owing to the cause of the bondage—the theft or the nonpayment of debts; and the master is admonished, lest "it shall seem hard unto thee, when thou sendest him away free from thee; for he hath been worth a double hired servant to thee, in serving thee six years" (Deut. 15:18). If the slave refuses to go free and wishes to retain his status as his master's slave, then the master is to pierce his ear with an awl, and in this way the slave is bonded to him forever (Exod. 21:5–6, Deut. 15:16–17); but even then is he able to be freed and to "return unto his own family and unto the possession of his father" in the year of jubilee (Lev. 25:40–41), in which liberty is proclaimed "throughout all the land unto all inhabitants thereof" (ibid. 10).

Female slaves sold into bondage by their fathers go free if their master's sons—whose concubines they were to become—deny them their matrimonial rights (Exod. 21:11). And every slave had to be released for grievous bodily harm done to him: the master had to let his slave go free "for his eye's sake" or "for his tooth's sake," if either be gouged out or knocked out by him (Exod. 21:26–27). A master who caused his slave's death committed a criminal offense (Exod. 21:20); but where the slave survived the homicidal attack and died only later, the master was not to be punished (ibid. 21). (In other ancient codes, only cruelty to another man's slave, but not cruelty to one's own slave, provides a cause of action for damages; cf. *Codex Hammurabi* 199. In later Roman law, only the murder of a slave with malice aforethought was punishable, not causing his death as a result of chastisement: *Codex Theodosianus* IX 12.)

Slaves were members of the master's household, and as such entitled to rest on the Sabbath day and, indeed, in duty bound to keep the Sabbath (Exod. 20:10, Deut. 5:14, 15) and the holidays (Deut. 16:11, 14). They were to participate in the rejoicing over Temple worship and sacrifices (Deut. 12:12, 18) and receive their share in the offerings to their priestly masters (Lev. 22:11). They had to be circumcised even if they were non-Jews (Gen. 17:12–13) and, when circumcised, partook of Passover celebrations and sacrifices (Exod. 12:44). They inherited their master's estate where there was no direct issue (Gen. 15:3), and perhaps even where there was (Prov. 17:2); and such inheritance must have constituted an exception to the rule that they could not hold property of their own. (We find that Ziba, Saul's slave, had slaves of his own [2 Sam. 9:10] and was given further properties by King David [ibid. 16:4]; but this may be explained either by Ziba's possible earlier manumission, or by the use of the title "slave" in a figurative sense, as indicating a devoted follower. Cf. "the slave of God": Deut. 34:5.) An alien slave is disqualified from testifying as a witness in court (Maimonides, *Eidut* 9:4).

As for the treatment of slaves, no distinction may be made between them and hired laborers (Lev. 25:40, 53); no master may rule over them "with rigor" (ibid. 43, 46, 53) nor ill-treat them or oppress them (Deut. 23:16). There is implied in the prohibition of oppression a warning that the maltreated slave may legitimately run away (Deut. 23:15–16); and "if thou treat him ill and he runs away, what way shalt thou find him?" (Ben Sira 33:31). A master was (semble) allowed to chastise his slave to a reasonable extent (Ben Sira 33:26), but wounding him was strictly prohibited (Exod. 21:26–27). The workload of a slave should be commensurate with his physical strength and never exceed it (Ben Sira 33:28–29).

A slave who ran away from his master, presumably because he had been maltreated, was not to be returned to his master but to be given refuge: "He shall dwell with thee, even among you, in that place which he shall choose in one of thy gates, where it liketh him best" (Deut. 23:15–16). The rule was later interpreted to relate only to a slave who had fled from abroad—the repetitive exhortations that he shall dwell "with thee," in thy "place," in thy "gates," being taken as an indication that he has not come to you personally to seek refuge, but to your country—and it is from the country that he may not be extradited (cf. Maimonides, *Avadim* 8:10). This is an entirely unwarranted misreading of the text; the language of the verse is clear and unambiguous to the effect that the compulsory return to his master of any fugitive slave is prohibited, and that everybody is under a personal obligation to receive him into his house and let him live wherever he likes (literally: wherever he feels good). But the fact that the rule was narrowed down by later interpretation is significant enough: the tendency is unmistakable to reduce the interference with the aggrieved master's legal rights to such a minimum as would appear unavoidable if God's explicit will is not to be thwarted. Withholding fugitive slaves from their rightful masters, and giving them refuge and shelter, must not only have been regarded as a highly unfriendly act against the masters, being instrumental in depriving them of their property, but in earlier systems of law had been branded as a severe criminal offense, punishable even with death (*Code of Hammurabi* 15, 16, 19), and would in the minds of the peoples of antiquity be associated with moral turpitude of the worst kind—and it remained, indeed, a criminal offense, albeit not capital, even in later Roman law (*Codex Theodosianus* V 17.2). The priority divinely ordained for the wellbeing and protection of the unlawfully escaped slave over the lawful rights of his wronged master demanded some rather revolutionary thinking, not easily palatable to legally trained minds. The fugitive slave may be taken, in this context, for the prototype of any oppressed outcast whose human dignity can possibly be saved only by escape into freedom: whatever the legal rights and wrongs may be, it is the rescue of the human being that matters; and by granting him refuge and shelter, you do justice and excel in righteousness (cf. Isa. 16:3–5).

Talmudic law, while limiting the duty to give asylum to fugitive slaves from abroad, also deemed it necessary to ensure that the master, as legal owner, be reimbursed for his loss. It was ruled that the man in whose house the fugitive had found refuge had to bring him into court forthwith, and the court would order the fugitive slave to make a promissory note in favor of his owner in the amount of his value as assessed by the court; upon execution of that note and its deposit with the court, the court would then, in exercise of its expropriating powers, declare the slave to be liberated—unless the owner could be summoned and was present and willing to effect the manumission himself (B. *Gittin* 45a, Maimonides, *Avadim* 8:10–11). By this contrivance the slave made good his escape into freedom, and God's will was duly fulfilled; but he who had sought refuge was required to make good the loss to his legal owner out of his future earnings—and thus the law was vindicated.

In biblical times, the laws providing for the release of slaves after six years' service appear to have been widely disobeyed. We hear that King Zedekiah had to make a "covenant" with the people that every man should let his slaves go free "at the end of seven years"—but hardly had the people released their slaves than they turned round and brought them back into subjection. In retribution for the failure to grant liberty to the slaves, the prophet warned that God would proclaim liberty "unto the sword, unto the pestilence, and unto the famine" (Jer. 34:8–17). Nehemiah succeeded in having the (legislative) assembly of the people proclaim an unlimited moratorium, by virtue of which men and women who had been enslaved for nonpayment of their debts were freed and their properties returned to them (Neh. 5:9–13).

The law was that upon the release of a slave, the master had to give him a subsistence allowance, and he was exhorted to be generous: "Thou shalt not let him go away empty; thou shalt furnish him liberally out of thy flock, and out of thy floor, and out of thy winepress; of that wherewith the Lord thy God hath blessed thee thou shalt give unto him" (Deut. 15:13–14). So long as slavery was rampant, it would appear that this law had no better chance of compliance than the law for the obligatory release of slaves; but no sooner was slavery virtually abolished than this law was applied to provide gratuities and severance pay to laborers and servants upon their dismissal or the determination of their work (B. *Kiddushin* 16b; *Sifrei, Re'ei* 119). The opinion was expressed that the grant should be made out of the contributions which the servant had made to the enrichment of his master (R. Elazar ben Azarya, B. *Kiddushin* 17b).

In talmudical times slavery was gradually seen to abate. At the beginning of the period, we still hear of Tebi, the slave of Rabban Gamliel (M. *Berakhot* 2:7, M. *Pessahim* 7:2, M. *Sukka* 2:1), and of a freed slave formerly belonging to Tobiah the physician (M. *Rosh HaShana* 1:7). And in a later period we hear of men selling themselves into slavery as gladiators (B. *Gittin* 46b–47a), apparently from dire necessity (J. *Gittin* 4:9), and into Roman service. But there is a strong talmudic tradition to the effect that all bondage of Hebrew slaves had ceased with the cessation of jubilee years, the theory being that where liberation in the year of jubilee is no longer feasible, the whole institution of slavery must be deemed to have come to an end (B. *Gittin* 65a, B. *Kiddushin* 69a, B. *Arakhin* 29a, Maimonides, *Avadim* 2:10).

The question of exactly when the jubilee years ceased to be observed is in dispute among scholars. There is an early talmudic source to the effect that they had already ceased to be observed with the Assyrian capture of the cities of the Reubenites, Gadites, and the half-tribe of Manasseh (1 Chron. 5:18–26), i.e., in about 730 B.C.E. (B. *Arakhin* 32b; *Sifra, Behar* 2; J. *Shevi'it* 10:3).

According to another talmudic source, the prophet Jeremiah restored the jubilee institution, albeit only for a short period, namely, until the destruction of the First Temple (B. *Megilla* 14b and Rashi ad loc.). On the other hand, second-century talmudists relate that slaves were formally freed not on the first day of the jubilee year but on the tenth, the Day of Atonement, and during those ten days they would be feted and entertained (B. *Rosh HaShana* 8b), from which it would appear that jubilee was still practiced in their times. For our purposes, it is sufficient to state that the law was laid down to the effect that without automatic release with the advent of a generally observed jubilee year, the institution of slavery itself could not be allowed to subsist (Maimonides, *Shemitta veYovel* 10:9). If there was any slavery in talmudic times at all, it was confined to non-Hebrew slaves.

The more momentous are the talmudical elaborations upon

biblical law. In order that your bondman may be "well with thee" (Deut. 15:16), he must share your own food and drink—not that you eat fine bread and give him coarse, you drink old wine and give him new, you sleep in a bed and let him lie on hay (Sifra, Behar 7; B. Kiddushin 20a); hence the saying that whoever acquires a slave sets a master over himself (B. Kiddushin 20a, 22a). When you have only one bed, for instance, you may not use it for yourself, for then you would not let your slave be "well with thee," that is, no less well than you yourself are. Not to use the bed at all would be a wrongful waste and would smack of parsimony (a "Sodomite" attribute), so there is nothing left for you to do but to let the slave have your bed (Tossafot ad Kiddushin 20a, s.v. kol ha-koneh). There are, moreover, quite a number of services which you may not demand from your slave so as not to hurt his feelings: carrying your things after you, dressing or undressing you, and the like personal services which you may ask a freeman, like your own son, to perform, but never your slave (Sifra, Behar 7). Nor may you require your slave to perform any services for others, e.g., as hairdresser or laundryman, unless that was his former trade and he wishes to continue it (Maimonides, Avadim 1:7). The worst and most strictly prohibited sort of forced labor is to make a man work just in order to keep him busy: to rule over slaves "with rigor" (Lev. 25:43, 46, 53) means to employ them for no good purpose—you may employ your slaves only in useful and productive work (Maimonides, op. cit. 6).

The verse "he hath been worth a double hired servant to thee" (Deut. 15:18) was interpreted by some scholars as allowing slaves to be given double the amount of work usually allotted to hired laborers: while the latter work only during daytime, slaves may be required to work also at night (Sifrei, Re'ei 123). Others ruled that the "duplicity" involved refers to the master's right to give a bondwoman in marriage to the slave so as to enjoy the benefit of both of them and their children (B. Kiddushin 15a).

In talmudical law, slaves were known and allowed to hold property of their own (T. Arakhin 1:2, M. Shekalim 1:5, B. Pessahim 88b, J. Yevamot 7:1, T. Bava Kamma 11:1, B. Bava Batra 51b–52a, B. Sanhedrin 91a and 105a, B. Ketuvot 28a, et al.), but could not dispose of it by will (Rashi and Tossafot ad Nazir 61b). A slave who had no property of his own could not be made answerable for his torts; only if he came into property after his release could he be made liable in damages for torts committed during bondage (M. *Bava Kamma* 8:4). A slave to whom his master bequeaths all his property becomes *ipso facto* emancipated (M. *Pei'a* 3:8, B. *Gittin* 8b–9a), as he becomes emancipated by marriage to his master's daughter (B. *Pessahim* 113a) or to any other freewoman (B. *Gittin* 39b–40a).

A slave has the right to be domiciled and stay in the land of Israel, and may not be sold for export (M. *Gittin* 4:6); if he is with his master abroad, he may compel his master to take him back home (B. *Ketuvot* 110b), and on being refused he may flee home with impunity (B. *Gittin* 45a).

Maimonides sums up the position of the slave in talmudic law as follows: "It is permissible to work the slave hard; but while this is the law, the ways of equity and prudence are that every master should be just and merciful, not make the yoke heavy on his slave, and not press him hard; and that he should let him partake of all food and drink. And this is what the early sages used to do: they gave their slaves of everything they ate and drank themselves, and had food served to their slaves even before partaking of it themselves. . . . Slaves may not be maltreated or offended: the law destined them for service, not for humiliation. Do not shout at them or be angry with them, but hear them out . . ." (*Avadim* 9:8). An in another context Maimonides wrote that the laws relating to slavery were all dictated by "mercy, compassion, and forbearance: you are in duty bound to see that your slave makes progress; you must benefit and enlighten him and not hurt or offend him. He ought to rise and advance with you, be with you in the place you chose for yourself, and when fortune is good to you, do not grudge him his portion" (*Moré Nevukhim* 3:39).

4

THE RIGHT TO PRIVACY

The most effective and frequent threat to the privacy of oneself and one's home emanates from unsatisfied creditors: they are apt to invade your privacy as if rightfully, whether in order only to confront you and make their demands or in order also to seize what they can as security for the debt.

Though in modern systems of law a creditor may not take the law into his own hands, still the entrance by lawfully authorized execution officers into private homes, and the search for and seizure of chattels and valuables to be attached in satisfaction of the judgment, has remained the most frequent and most dreaded invasion of privacy. Of all systems of law, ancient and modern, biblical law was the only one to prohibit any such interference with the privacy and the home of a defaulting debtor: "When thou doest lend thy brother any thing, thou shalt not go into his house to fetch his pledge. Thou shalt stand abroad, and the man to whom thou doest lend shall bring out the pledge abroad unto thee" (Deut. 24:10–11). The injunction to "stand abroad" (literally: to remain standing outside) has been held to apply both to the creditor himself and to any "messenger of the court," i.e., any execution officer (*Sifrei, Teitzei* 276; B. *Bava Metzia* 113a; T. *Bava Metzia* 10:8; Maimonides, *Malvé veLové* 2:2). Even when proceeding on judicial business of law enforcement, you must "remain standing outside"; in a conflict between the creditor's lawful right to be repaid and the debtor's right to privacy and the inviolability of his home, the latter prevails—and the home of the debtor remains inviolable even in face of the exigencies of the judicial process.

64

It is evident that the observance of lofty human rights such as this could lead to serious obstructions of the money market; and it was for the sake of pacifying creditors that the debtor's right of privacy was gradually more and more restricted. First, it was held to apply, according to the scriptural text, to debts arising from loans only, and not to debts arising from any other contract or obligation (B. *Bava Metzia* 115a); then it was held to apply to the home of the debtor only, but not, for instance, to the home of his surety (ibid.; Maimonides, op. cit. 3:7); later it was held not to apply to debtors who fraudulently used their private homes to conceal therein goods or chattels liable to attachment for their debts, or to such debtors as failed to disclose goods or chattels outside their homes which could be so attached (*Tur, Hoshen Mishpat* 97:26 and *Beit Yossef* ad loc.); and finally it was held to apply only before maturity of the debt but not after judgment had issued thereon (*Hoshen Mishpat* 97:15). All these later incursions into the debtor's right to privacy cannot, however, and were certainly not intended to, derogate from the fundamental principle that the private home of a person is inviolable, even though he may be your debtor. The fact that the principle was stated apropos of the special relationship between creditor and debtor allows a conclusion *de maiore ad minorem*—if even the creditor may not enter your house on his (lawful or at least) legitimate business, a person without such legitimate business may certainly not do so.

Although talmudical law allows a man to take the law into his own hands and possess himself of his property which he finds in the hands of another (B. *Bava Kamma* 27b–28a, Maimonides, *Sanhedrin* 2:12), it has been said that he ought not to enter that other's house in order to take his own property without the landlord's permission, "lest he may look like a thief" (B. *Bava Kamma* 27b, T. *Bava Kamma* 10:38). Where a man was seen entering another's house and leaving it with some chattels in his hand, he is not to be believed when he says that the chattels were his or that he had taken them with the owner's permission, but he is presumed to have stolen them until he can prove his title (Maimonides, *Gezeila vaAveida* 4:12; *Hoshen Mishpat* 364:2).

One may not enter the house of another without permission, and if one does so, the landlord is entitled to eject him even by force; but if the landlord in the course of ejecting the trespasser hurts him, he will be liable in damages, "for he has the right to eject him, but he has no right to injure him" (Maimonides, *Hoveil uMazik* 1:15). The landlord will, however, be exempt from any liability if he had no knowledge of a trespasser being on his premises and had injured him unintentionally (*Bava Kamma* 48b, *Hoshen Mishpat* 421:7), though, in general, a man is responsible even for his unintentional wrongs (M. *Bava Kamma* 2:6; Maimonides, op. cit. 11).

Among the four things which, according to R. Shimon ben Yohai, are detested by God and not liked by men, is entering into a house suddenly—not only into another's but even into one's own house (B. *Nidda* 16b); and R. Akiva is said to have left his son seven pieces of advice, among them, "do not enter your house unannounced, and certainly not the house of your friend" (B. *Pessahim* 112a). This advice is elsewhere based on divine precedent: before God revealed Himself to Adam, he first called out unto him, "and said unto him, Where art thou?" (Gen. 3:9)—and these good manners every man can learn from God (*Derekh Eretz Rabba* 5:2). The reason given for the rule is that by entering a house unannounced, you may surprise somebody inside the house and embarrass him or her (Rashi ad *Nidda* 16b and ad *Pessahim* 112a). Thus it is related of R. Yohanan that before entering a house, he would always make himself heard from the outside first, if only by coughing loudly (*Vayikra Rabba* 21), just as the high priest was to make "his sound heard" even when entering the Holy Temple (Exod. 28:35).

Further rules to protect the privacy of the individual are to be found in the law relating to neighbors and joint owners of land. A particular kind of damage, known as "damage of sight," is caused by a person peering into the window of another's house; and if he is the owner of an adjacent house, he may not construe any window in his own house so as to enable him, or anybody else, to peep into his neighbor's (M. *Bava Batra* 3:7, Maimonides, *Shekheinim* 5:6, *Hoshen Mishpat* 154:3). Nor may any landlord change his premises in such a way that the quiet formerly enjoyed by his neighbors is likely to be disturbed (B. *Bava Batra* 59b–60a; Maimonides, op. cit. 7; *Hoshen Mishpat* 154:1–2). The fact that the neighbor knowingly suffered, for any length of time, other people to disturb his privacy, whether by peering into his premises or otherwise, does not prevent him from claiming the damage to be abated in future (B. *Bava Batra* 59b, *Tur, Hoshen*

Mishpat 154:16); for it is not so much his own interest—which he may have waived—that is at stake, as rather a general interest in morality, decency, and public peace (Nahmanides and Alfassi, as quoted in *Tur,* loc. cit.).

5

THE RIGHT TO REPUTATION

The right of every human being to his good name and reputation is one of the best-documented human rights in biblical and talmudical law. Many divine utterances could be, and duly were, taken as clues and sources for prohibitions of slander and defamation. "Thou shalt not raise a false report" (Exod. 23:1) was interpreted as prohibiting not only the uttering of, but also the listening to, any slanderous statement (*Mekhilta, Kaspa* 20); and as the preceding verse speaks of casting something to the dogs, it has been said that whoever makes or accepts any vilification of another is worthy of being cast to the dogs (B. *Pessahim* 118a). "Keep far from a false matter" (Exod. 23:7), on the face of it a prohibition of lying, was taken also as a "warning to slanderers" (*Yalkut Shimoni* 352). "Thou shalt not go up and down as talebearer among thy people" (Lev. 19:16) served as authority for the proposition that slander was unlawful whether it was true or false (*Dei'ot* 7:2), and for the deprecation of all gossip which might eventually lead to calumnies (*Hafetz Hayim,* passim). The general admonition "keep thee from every wicked thing" (Deut. 23:9) was particularized as another prohibition of insult (B. *Ketuvot* 46a). "Thou shalt not curse the deaf" (Lev. 19:14) and "Thou shalt not put a curse upon the ruler of thy people" (Exod. 22:27) were interpreted as particular instances of a general prohibition against cursing and reviling (*Sifra, Kedoshim* 2; *Mekhilta, Kaspa* 19; B. *Shevu'ot* 36a). The injunction to "rebuke thy neighbor and not suffer sin upon him" (Lev. 19:17) was to be obeyed by reproving and admonishing your fellowman to his face without in any way insulting him or putting him to shame; you may never "rebuke" him behind his back; and if by "rebuking" him you make

68

him angry or furious, you incur grave guilt (*Sifra, Kedoshim* 4; *Dei'ot* 6:7–8). Even the fundamental "Love thy neighbor as thyself" (Lev. 19:18), as well as the complementing "Thou shalt not hate thy brother in thy heart" (ibid. 17), was invoked to invest the prohibition of maligning your fellowman with divine authority (*Hafetz Hayim*, passim).

The law distinguishes between an innocent talebearer and a malicious slanderer. It is summed up by Maimonides as follows: "A talebearer is one who collects gossip and goes from one to the other, saying, 'This is what that man has said, this is what I have heard about him'; even if he speaks the truth, he destroys the world. But there is a far graver sin than that, namely defamation—and that is where he vilifies another, even if he speaks the truth. And if what he speaks is untrue, he is called a calumniator. The ordinary slanderer is one who sits around and says, 'This or that some other man has done, such and such were his ancestors like, this and the other thing have I heard about him'—or made any derogatory remarks about him; of such a man Scripture says, 'The Lord shall cut off all flattering lips and the tongue that speaketh proud things' (Ps. 12:4). . . . Our sages have said that slandering people is tantamount to denying God, for it is written, 'Who have said, "With our tongue will we prevail, our lips are our own: who is lord over us?" ' (ibid. 5). And our sages further said that three victims suffer from slander: the one who utters it, the one who receives it, and the one who is slandered—and the one who willingly receives it is worst of all" (*Dei'ot* 7:2–3).

But though regarded as a violation of express biblical negative injunctions, slander is not punishable even by flogging—the lightest punishment known to biblical law. The reason—which stems, of course, from talmudical jurisprudence only—is that punishment may only be inflicted for criminal *acts*, and the mere utterance of words is never considered an "act" (B. *Sanhedrin* 63a; Maimonides, *Sanhedrin* 18:1). The only instance of defamation for which biblical law prescribes a penalty is that of the bride whose virginity was falsely impugned by her husband (Deut. 22:13–19), but that defamation may be said to be in the nature of a matrimonial stratagem rather than of a specifically libelous offense. It has also been suggested that the sanction in Deut. 22:19 is within the realm of civil damages rather than that of criminal punishment.

The fact that no punitive sanctions were attached to defamation, and that the many exhortations against speaking evil of a fellowman were binding only religiously and morally but not judicially enforceable, appeared to talmudical jurists highly unsatisfactory. They proceeded to provide for certain sanctions, but they did so in their own casuistic way, if and when the necessity arose to have them imposed. Thus, a person who called another a slave was ordered to be ostracized; a person calling another a bastard (*mamzer*) was held liable to forty stripes; and where a person called another wicked, the offended party was held entitled to compensation out of the slanderer's earnings (B. *Kiddushin* 28a). Legal scholars sought to explain these particular sanctions as talionic in nature (Tossafot and *Me'iri* ad loc.), but these efforts seem to be rather far-fetched afterthoughts. The ban to which the person is liable who has called another a slave has been codified (*Maimonides, Talmud Tora* 6:14, *Yorei Dei'a* 334:43). As for the administration of disciplinary, as distinguished from penal, floggings (*makkat mardut*), the rule was eventually held to be subject to local custom; where customary local regulations provided for different sanctions for slander, those were to prevail (Asheri, *Responsa* 101:1; Rema ad *Hoshen Mishpat* 420:41). In fact, disciplinary floggings appear to have remained the most common sanction in most places, at least for graver cases (Maharshal 11:28, 59, and *Yam shel Shelomo* ad *Bava Kamma* 8:34, 48, 49). In lighter cases fines were imposed, and we find fines often substituted for bans or floggings at the option of the injured person who had first to be appeased (*Tur, Hoshen Mishpat* 420:33 and *Beit Yossef* ad loc.).

A particular aggravation of slander is insulting a scholar. A person found to have insulted a scholar is liable not only to be ostracized but also to pay one litra of gold to the aggrieved scholar (B. *Mo'ed Kattan* 16a, *Talmud Tora* 6:12). This amount appears to have later been increased to thirty-five gold dinars (J. *Bava Kamma* 8:6, *Hoveil uMazik* 3:5), though normally a person is not liable in damages for mischief done by word of mouth only (B. *Bava Kamma* 91a, *Hoshen Mishpat* 420:39). The insulted scholar, however, may always forgo such payment (*Hoveil uMazik* 3:6). Soon enough the benefit originally reserved for scholars was extended to all pious people (Asheri, *Responsa* 15:10; *Tur, Hoshen Mishpat* 420:32), and eventually it became obsolete when sanctions for defamation were no longer confined to any privileged class.

Another particular instance of slander is that of widows and orphans. "Ye shall not afflict a widow or a fatherless child" (Exod. 22:22) means not only that you may not cause them distress by physical or other tangible means, but that if you cause them any distress just by insulting them or speaking evil of them, and they cry unto God, He will hear their cry: "And my wrath shall wax hot, and I will kill you with the sword; and your wives shall be widows, and your children fatherless" (ibid. 23–24). This is a typical instance of purely divine punishment: the court will not impose any punishment for offenses committed solely by word of mouth; therefore "a covenant was concluded between widows and orphans and the Creator of the World, that whenever they cry out, He hears and acts" (Dei'ot 6:10).

A grave sin is slandering the dead, to be expiated by fasting and prayer; but the court may also impose a fine on the slanderer (Mordekhai ad Bava Kamma 81–82; Rema ad Hoshen Mishpat 420:38).

God is said not to suffer slanderers living with Him in the same world (B. Arakhin 15b), for it is written, "Whoso privily slandereth his neighbor, him will I cut off; him that hath a high look and a proud heart will I not suffer" (Ps. 101:5). The men "that did bring up the evil report upon the land, died by the plague" (Num. 14:37); if death by plague is the fate of those who slander "trees and stones," how much more dreadful must be the fate of those who slander human beings (B. Arakhin 15a). The Solomonic proverb "Death and life are in the power of the tongue" (Prov. 18:21) was quoted as authority for the proposition that destroying the good name and reputation of a person is tantamount to taking his life (B. Arakhin 15b). Divine revulsion against slanderers being what it is, the sages were convinced that no slanderer would ever escape divine punishment; if he did not die from the plague (Avot deRabbi Natan 19), he would surely be visited by a stroke (B. Arakhin 16a) or by leprosy (ibid.), and at any rate will never enter paradise but end up in hell (M. Avot 3:11, B. Berakhot 19a, B. Arakhin 16a).

The classical biblical case of slander is that reported of Miriam and Aaron, who "spake against Moses because of the Ethiopian woman whom he had married: for he had married an Ethiopian woman" (Num. 12:1). And in the manner of evil tongues they proceeded from the insults on account of his wife to insults on account of his standing (ibid. 2); "And the anger of the Lord was kindled against them" (ibid. 9). In this particular instance divine punishment was swift and drastic: "Miriam became leprous, white as snow" (ibid. 10), and it was only the prayer of Moses, the slandered man himself (ibid. 13), that moved a merciful God to heal her again (and see below, Chap. 16).

Joseph, who brought his father an "evil report" of his brothers (Gen. 37:2), is said to have been divinely punished by being sold into bondage (J. Pei'a 1:1). Even the prophet Isaiah suffered an untimely and violent death only for the reason that he "slandered" his people as being of "unclean lips" (Isa. 6:5), and did so—in contradistinction to the many other highly critical reflections on the character of the people contained in his prophecies—without claiming divine authority for this derision (B. Yevamot 49b and Rashi ad loc.).

The psalmist's query, "What man is he that desireth life, and loveth many days, that he may see good?" (Ps. 34:13), was answered on the spot: "Keep thy tongue from evil, and thy lips from speaking guile" (ibid. 14). This verse became the first sentence of a prayer attributed to a fourth-century scholar and since then included in the daily liturgy: "My God, keep my tongue from evil and my lips from speaking guile; let my soul be silent to those who curse me, as if my soul were dust for all [to tread upon]" (B. Berakhot 17a). Indeed, readiness to suffer insults with patience and good grace was elevated to the same ethical standard as total abstinence from using offensive language: "The insulted who do not insult, those who hear abuse and do not retort, who act from love and gladly accept affliction—of those it is said, 'let them as love him be as the sun when he goeth forth in his might' (Judg. 5:31)" (B. Shabbat 88b, B. Yoma 23a, B. Gittin 36b). And the rule that every man should aspire to be of the persecuted and not of the persecutors, of the slandered and not of the slanderers, found its place of honor in the Maimonidean code (Dei'ot 5:13).

6

FREEDOM OF MOVEMENT AND RESIDENCE

The patriarch Abraham is reported to have moved, with his parents, from Ur of the Chaldees to Haran (Gen. 11:31), where God's command was addressed to him, "Get thee out of thy country . . . unto a land that I will show you" (Gen. 12:1), and from that primordial upheaval originated the never-ceasing urge of the Jews to move, and more particularly to go to the land that God had shown Abraham, that is, the land of Israel. God's promise that, having gone to the new land, Abraham would be made into a great nation (ibid. 2) gave rise to a discussion among talmudic scholars as to whether it was *any* change of domicile that would bring good fortune or whether it was only going to the land of Israel that would bestow the blessings (B. *Rosh HaShana* 16b). At any rate it was said that he who has not made good in one place and fails to move and try his luck in some other place has only himself to complain about (B. *Bava Metzia* 75b). To secure facility of movement, it was laid down that public roads must have a certain minimum width to allow convenient passage to everybody, that interurban roads must be still wider, that roads leading to cities of refuge must be wider still, and that the king may expropriate private property to build roads of any width (M. *Bava Batra* 6:7, B. *Bava Batra* 100a–b). The biblical "Is not the whole land before thee?" (Gen. 13:9) may have served as a kind of motto to seekers after fertile land and prospectors for distant treasures; and the freedom to choose one's own place of residence found its most marked expression in the permission given to the

73

tribes of Reuben and Gad to settle outside the land which had
been destined by God for the whole nation (Num. 32, passim).

Freedom of movement in the biblical period is also well illustrated by the telling story in the Book of Judges: "And there was a
young man out of Bethlehem-Judah . . . and he sojourned there.
And the man departed out of the city from Bethlehem-Judah to
sojourn where he could find a place; and he came to Mount
Ephraim to the house of Micah, as he journeyed. And Micah said
unto him, 'Whence comest thou?' And he said unto him, 'I am a
Levite of Bethlehem-Judah, and I go to sojourn where I may find a
place.' " (17:7–9).

The preference to be given to moving to the land of Israel, over
all other changes of domicile, found halakhic application in the
laws relating to husband and wife (and master and servant). The
general rule is that the wife goes after the husband. A man living
in country A, who married a wife from country B, is entitled—
unless some other agreement was reached beforehand—to set up
the matrimonial domicile in country A, and if the wife refuses to
follow him, he may divorce her (T. *Ketuvot* 13:2; Maimonides,
Ishut 13:17; *Even Ha'ezer* 75:1). If after marriage the husband
wishes to change the matrimonial domicile, the wife may be
compelled to go after him only if he improves the domicile, that is,
moves from a village into a city, or from an ugly to a beautiful
place, or from any country to the land of Israel, or from any place
in the land of Israel to Jerusalem; and if the wife insists on
moving from any country to the land of Israel, or from any place in
the land of Israel to Jerusalem, the husband will be compelled to
go after her (M. *Ketuvot* 13:10–11; Maimonides, *Ishut* 13:18–20;
Even Ha'ezer 75:3–4); if he refuses, the wife will be granted a
divorce (B. *Ketuvot* 110b). This rule was restricted during the
Middle Ages to the effect that a spouse could be compelled to
follow the other into the land of Israel only where the voyage
entailed no danger to life (*Even Ha'ezer* 75:5). In the same way
that a wife can compel her husband to go after her to the land of
Israel, a servant or slave can compel his master (B. *Ketuvot* 110b;
and see above, p. 63); and if the master refuses, the servant is free
to go on his own (B. *Gittin* 45a).

A husband who wishes to go abroad and leave his wife behind
may be prevented from leaving without first making provision for
her or, at her option, divorcing her (*Even Ha'ezer* 154:8); but they

are, of course, free to travel together beyond the seas so long as there is "peace between him and her" (M. *Yevamot* 15:1).

Though, as a matter of law, everyone has the right to go and reside wherever he likes, we find dicta to the effect that nobody ought to leave the land of Israel (B. *Ketuvot* 111a, Maimonides, *Melakhim* 5:12), but everybody should establish his residence there, for he who resides in the land of Israel is deemed to be near to God (B. *Ketuvot* 110b), and he who leaves the land of Israel is deemed to deny God (by being far and estranged from Him) (Maimonides, loc. cit.). It is significant that this rule, pronounced as it was in Babylonian academies, was countered by a further rule that if you resided in Babylon, you should not leave Babylon either (B. *Ketuvot* 111a), if only for the sake of the many great institutions of learning available there (Rashi ad loc.); and as scriptural authority the prophecy was invoked, that the people banished to Babylon would remain there until the day of divine redemption (Jer. 27:22). Small wonder that this prophecy was promptly extended and applied to all countries of dispersion where God had banished the Jews (Tossafot ad *Ketuvot* 111a), providing the needed legitimation of residing in the Diaspora, even where the possibility of going to reside in the land of Israel had offered itself. There is, on the other hand, a dictum to the effect that if there is a famine in the land of Israel, you may go abroad (B. *Bava Batra* 91a, T. *Avoda Zara* 4:4); but that was what Elimelech and Naomi and their sons did (Ruth 1:1–2), and they had to die for having done so (ibid. 3 and 5; B. *Bava Batra*, loc. cit.; T. *Avoda Zara*, loc. cit.; Maimonides, *Melakhim* 5:9). The rule was eventually settled that residents of the land of Israel may not leave it to take up residence elsewhere, but they may freely move about and proceed abroad for trade and commerce, or to assist and succor any other person in any predicament (Maimonides, loc. cit.). Apart from the preferential provisions applying to the land of Israel, the rule as finally codified is that any person may reside anywhere in the world (Maimonides, op. cit. 7).

7

THE RIGHT TO ASYLUM

We have already seen that for the unintentional killer cities of refuge were provided where he was secure from blood-avengers (pp. 53–55). We have also seen that fugitive slaves were entitled to asylum and may not be returned to their masters (pp. 59–60). These are but particular instances of the right of refuge, expressly accorded to those who, in view of the vested rights of blood-avengers and slave-owners, stood in particular need of it. It was, however, early observed that if divine law provided "paths and ways for homicides to save themselves, how much more must the right of refuge by accorded to the righteous" (*Bamidbar Rabba* 23:13).

Any persecution or oppression compelling a man to go into exile, whether at the hand of an individual or a national enemy, is considered the worst fate—next to death—that can befall him. In the wrath of God, and in the day of His fiercest anger, people will have to flee "as the chased roe, and as a sheep that no man taketh up. . . . Every one that is found shall be thrust through, and every one that is joined unto them shall fall by the sword" (Isa. 13:13–15). The extreme threat of divine punishment is to be scattered among alien peoples: "the sound of a shaken leaf shall chase them; and they shall flee, as fleeing from a sword, and they shall fall when none pursueth. . . . And ye shall perish among the heathen, and the land of your enemies shall eat you up" (Lev. 26:33–38). And when "the Lord shall scatter thee among all peoples, from the one end of the earth even unto the other . . . among these nations thou shalt find no ease, neither shall the sole of thy foot have rest; but the Lord shall give thee there a

76

trembling heart, and failing of eyes, and sorrow of mind. And thy life shall hang in doubt before assurance of thy life . . ." (Deut. 28:64–66).

It is not only that the vicissitudes of exile were thus brought home to the people by scriptural warnings; nor is it only that the divine threats were actually carried into effect, and the people went into exile time and again and bitterly experienced the affliction of dwelling among the heathen and finding no rest (Lam. 1:3), being pursued in the mountains and laid wait for in the wilderness and hunted in the streets (ibid. 4:18–19)—but that even before attaining nationhood they had suffered affliction as strangers in the land of Egypt (Exod. 1:11–14). It is mainly this prenational experience which biblical law postulated as the underlying reason for the requirement to receive the stranger with love and affection and compassion: "Love ye therefore the stranger, for ye were strangers in the land of Egypt" (Deut. 10:19), and you "know the heart of a stranger" (Exod. 23:9) and what it means to be stranded in a foreign land. It is now generally assumed that most of the "strangers," that is migrants, who, in antiquity, left their own lands and went into foreign parts were refugees in the modern sense—if not from individual persecution and oppression, at any rate from famine (cf. Gen. 12:10, Ruth 1:1, 2 Kings 8:1) or some other disaster; and from the biblical prescriptions relating to them it is abundantly clear that they were among the poor and needy who had to be given shelter, food, and raiment (Lev. 19:10, 23:22; Deut. 10:18; et al.). That they were, indeed, given "asylum" in the proper sense of the term, would appear from the repeated references to them as belonging to a particular household: "the stranger sojourning with thee" (Exod. 12:48); "the stranger or sojourner living with thee" (Lev. 25:35); "thy stranger" in the same context with thy son, thy daughter, thy manservant, and thy maidservant (Exod. 20:10, Deut. 5:14); or "the stranger with him" (lit. "his stranger") in the same context with his brother (Deut. 1:16)—all indicating that the "stranger" was received into the family and became a member of the household (de Vaux I 20). The many exhortations to love the stranger and treat him as your equal in every respect (see below, p. 166) give this duty to shelter and protect him a distinctly humane import.

Later prophets stressed this duty of protecting and sheltering the persecuted in no mistakable terms. Although the Moabites had always been hostile to the Hebrews (Num. 22:3), had declared war on them (Judg. 3:12–13), and had held them in derision (Jer. 48:26–27) and reviled them (Zeph. 2:8), and although the Moabites were condemned by the prophets for their wickedness and insolence (Isa. 16:6, Jer. 48:29), yet when Moab fell and her people were put to flight, this was the occasion for the prophet to say that his heart cried out for Moab (Isa. 15:5) and to expostulate: "Let every one wail for Moab. Give counsel, grant justice . . . Hide the outcasts, betray not the fugitive; let the outcasts of Moab sojourn among you: be a refuge to them from the destroyer" (Isa. 16:3–4; translation of Heschel, p. 87). This is immediately followed by the assurance that "then a throne shall be established in mercy, and there shall sit on it in truth . . . a judge who seeks justice and excels in righteousness" (Isa. 16:5)—mercy, truth, justice, and righteousness being invoked to extend even to former enemies the protection that is due to the outcast and persecuted. In the same vein, a prophetic appeal is made on behalf of Arab desert tribes: "To the thirsty bring water, meet the fugitive with bread. . . . For they have fled from the swords, from the drawn sword, from the bent bow, and from the press of battle" (Isa. 21:14–15; translation of Heschel, loc. cit.).

Instances of practical asylum actually given are rare. We find that when King Ahab persecuted the prophets and Queen Jezebel had them "cut off," Obadiah, "which was the governor of his house," "took a hundred prophets, and hid them by fifty in a cave, and fed them with bread and water" (1 Kings 18:3–4), an act of humane mercy so highly appreciated by the talmudists that they (wrongly) asserted that as a reward from God Obadiah was himself invested with prophetic vision (B. Sanhedrin 39b). It was the prophet Obadiah, however, who preached, long after his predecessor Obadiah's act of compassion, not to stand "in the crossway to cut off those that did escape," nor to "deliver up those that did remain in the day of distress" (Obad. 1:14).

The rule that the right to asylum from persecution is not available to people prosecuted for nonpolitical crimes (Art. 14.2 of the Universal Declaration) has in our sources been deduced from a verse in Proverbs to the effect that a man who committed a crime of violence "to the blood of any person" shall not be saved, even when fleeing "to the pit"; only "whoso walketh uprightly shall be saved" (Prov. 28:17–18). It is related of Rabbi Tarphon that he ruled that fugitives from justice, accused of murder, should not be hidden or given shelter (B. *Nidda* 61a). We find that rule later extended to robbers, thieves, and other common criminals (*Sefer Hassidim* 181), the reason adduced for the duty of turning them back being that criminality is an infectious disease, and by receiving criminals into your midst, you may eventually see your children turn into criminals. On the other hand, turning back righteous people who want to settle in your town will eventually be visited upon you by yourself or your children being expelled from that town and compelled to live elsewhere (ibid.).

In this context, mention should be made of the very ancient belief that God's altar provided a sanctuary where no fugitive could be apprehended. The first we hear in biblical law of this ancient institution is that the altar could not serve as sanctuary to the murderer: "if a man come presumptuously (i.e., with premeditation) upon his neighbor to slay him with guile, thou shalt take him from my altar that he may die" (Exod. 21:14). Indeed, we find that King Solomon ordered the sanctuary of the altar to be disregarded in the case of Joab, who had "fled unto the tabernacle of the Lord and caught hold on the horns of the altar" (1 Kings 2:28), because he had killed "two men more righteous and better than he" and was to be punished for the murders (ibid. 32–33). On the other hand, when Adonijah, who had been a pretender to King Solomon's throne, was afraid of the king's displeasure and vindictiveness, he "arose and went and caught hold on the horns of the altar. . . . And Solomon said, 'If he will show himself a worthy man, there shall not a hair of him fall to the earth; but if wickedness shall be found in him, he shall die.' So King Solomon sent, and they brought him down from the altar. And he came and bowed himself to King Solomon; and Solomon said unto him, 'Go to thine house' " (1 Kings 1:50–53). The episode appears to disprove a later talmudical theory to the effect that it was only the roof of the altar and not the horns that could provide a sanctuary (B. *Makkot* 12a). In the event, the rule was codified that the altar in God's Temple provided an inviolable sanctuary for any fugitive from the king's wrath or from other executive action, as distinguished from the due process of a competent court (Maimonides, *Rotzei'ah* 5:14).

8

THE RIGHT TO MARRY AND FOUND A FAMILY

"Before the law was given, a man would meet a woman in the street, and when both he and she so desired, he would take her into his house and cohabit with her, and she would become his wife. The law now having been given, the people of Israel are commanded to take their wives by way of acquisition (see p. 170) before witnesses and thus marry them" (Maimonides, *Ishut* 1:1). The prelegal requirement, however, that both he and she should desire to marry each other has been preserved in the law. While a wife could be divorced against her will under the ancient law (see p. 171), she could never be married against her will (B. *Kiddushin* 2b; Maimonides, *Ishut* 4:1). It is true that the father's right to give his infant daughter in marriage to whomever he pleased was deduced from the verse "I gave my daughter unto this man for wife" (Deut. 22:16; M. *Kiddushin* 2:1; Maimonides, op. cit. 3:11); but it was laid down in talmudical times that "no man ought to give his infant daughter in marriage, but he should wait until she comes of age and says, this man I want" (B. *Kiddushin* 41a; *Even Ha'ezer* 37:8). The question as to whether a marriage was valid if the husband had been coerced gave rise to a dispute among later authorities: some held it to be valid, because the husband, if he did not desire it, could at once unilaterally dissolve it (Maimonides, ibid. 4:1); others held it to be invalid, because it lacked the husband's consent (*Tur, Even Ha'ezer* 42:1 and *Beit Yossef* ad loc.). The view holding the marriage to be valid is, of course, the more favorable one for the wife; it is only under a valid marriage that she may have acquired rights of maintenance and compensation. The law would now appear to be settled to the effect that lack of consent on the part of the husband invalidates the marriage no less than lack of consent on the part of the wife— if only for the reason that the husband is no longer allowed to dissolve the marriage unilaterally (see p. 172).

The marriage is invalid where the husband is a minor (M. *Kiddushin* 2:6; B. *Kiddushin* 50b; Maimonides, op. cit. 4:7; *Even Ha'ezer* 43:1); but where the wife is a minor, the marriage is valid until she has made a formal declaration of refusal (M. *Yevamot* 13:1–2; Maimonides, op. cit. 7–8 and *Geirushin* 11:1) to the effect that she does not wish to be married to her husband (Maimonides, *Geirushin* 11:8–11). Such a declaration of refusal is not, however, open to her where she was given into marriage by her father; nor is it any longer open to her when she has come of age or when she has already cohabited with her husband (B. *Nidda* 52a; Maimonides, op. cit. 4). Rabbis performing marriages were expressly warned not to perform the marriage of an infant girl when "their eyes could see" beforehand that the girl would in all probability eventually make a declaration of refusal (Rema ad *Even Ha'ezer* 115:1).

Limitations on the right to marry "due to race, nationality or religion" were imposed by biblical law only in respect of the "seven nations" enumerated in Deut. 7:1, namely, the Hittites, the Girgashites, the Amorites, the Canaanites, the Perizzites, the Hivites, and the Jebusites (in Exod. 34:11 only six nations are listed, the Girgashites being omitted). With these nations no covenant may be made, "Neither shalt thou make marriages with them; thy daughter thou shalt not give unto his son, nor his daughter shalt thou take unto thy son. For they will turn away thy son from following Me, that they may serve other gods" (Deut. 7:3–4; to the same effect, Exod. 34:16). Additional prohibitions of intermarriage were imposed in respect of the Ammonites and the Moabites (Deut. 23:4) and, limited to three generations only, in respect of the Edomites and the Egyptians (Deut. 23:10). But early talmudical authorities already established the fact that all these particular peoples could no longer be identified as such and had, after the Assyrian conquests, been confounded and become irrecognizable (M. *Yadayim* 4:4, T. *Yadayim* 2:17–18, B. *Berakhot* 28a), so that the biblical prohibitions of intermarriage became in fact unenforceable.

The only absolute limitation on the right to marry a woman of any nationality or race is imposed on the high priest: "he shall take a virgin *of his own people* to wife" (Lev. 21:14). While regular priests may not marry "a wife that is a whore or profane" or divorced from a previous husband (Lev. 21:7), no limitation is imposed on their right to marry a woman of another people or religion. And while kings are exhorted not "to multiply" wives to themselves (Deut. 17:17), there is no restriction imposed even on them in respect of the national or religious provenance of their wives, though the kings themselves must be chosen "from among thy brethren" (Deut. 17:15) and may not be of foreign origin (Maimonides, *Melakhim* 1:4).

Apart from the prohibited nations, then, the right to marry any person, regardless of race, nationality, or religion, was unrestricted to all except only the high priest. The Bible provides many examples of intermarriages between Jews and non-Jews; and apart from the fact that from the earliest (even prelegal) times people preferred and sought marriage ties within their own immediate circles and with their own kindred (Gen. 24:3–4, 27:46), and were apt to look askance at foreign and strange intruders into their families (cf. Num. 12:1), no legal or moral blemish whatever attached to any "mixed" marriage. Moses, the great lawgiver and God's own faithful servant (Num. 12:7), himself married first a Midianite (Exod. 2:16, 21) and later an Ethiopian woman (Num. 12:1), and was in both instances vindicated by miraculous divine intervention (Exod. 4:24–26, Num. 12:9–10). Samson took a Philistine wife, and as against his parents' objection, "Is there never a woman among the daughters of thy brethren, or among all my people, that thou goest to take a wife of the uncircumcised Philistines?", his answer that "she pleaseth me well" was conclusive even in the eyes of his parents (Judg. 14:1–3). One of the wives of King David was Maacah, the daughter of the king of Geshur (2 Sam. 3:3); and King Solomon "loved many strange women, together with the daughter of Pharaoh, women of the Moabites, Ammonites, Edomites, Zidonians, and Hittites; of the nations concerning which the Lord said unto the children of Israel, 'Ye shall not go into them, neither shall they come in unto you; for surely they will turn away your heart after their gods'; Solomon clave unto these in love. And he had seven hundred wives, princesses, and three hundred concubines; and his wives turned away his heart" (1 Kings 11:1–3). The reproach lay, firstly, in the proliferation of King Solomon's marriages, and, secondly, in his breach of the prohibition in respect of the particular "seven nations"—and it was the wives from these prohibited nations who did actually turn away his heart from God; but no reproach whatever attached to his marriage to the daughter of the Pharaoh of Egypt (1 Kings 3:1), nor to his marriage to Naamah the Ammonitess, who became the ancestress of the kings of Judah (1 Kings 14:21). On the contrary, we find the psalmist full of praise for the queen from Ophir and the daughter of Tyre, who forget their own people and their father's house and are brought to the king, who greatly desires their beauty (Ps. 45:9–12); and in the Talmud the Moabitess Ruth and the Ammonitess Naamah are said to have been the blessing which God had promised to Abraham (Gen. 12:3, B. *Yevamot* 63a).

We find not only non-Jewish women married to Jews but also Jewish women married to non-Jews. Jael, a Jewess, was married to Heber the Kenite (Judg. 4:17), who was of Midianite ancestry (ibid. 11), and her being the wife of a non-Jew in no way diminished her standing and her popularity (cf. Judg. 5:24). Bath-sheba, the daughter of Eliam, of a good Jewish family, was the wife of a Hittite, Uriah (2 Sam. 11:3), a marriage which, while violated by King David's sin, was upheld by God's own prophet (ibid. 12:10). Jether the Ishmaelite took a Jewish wife, Abigail (1 Chron. 2:17), and their own son Amasa was called by King David, "of my bone, and of my flesh" (2 Sam. 19:14). Hiram of Tyre, whom King Solomon sent for to build the Temple, was the son of a Jewish mother of the tribe of Naphtali and of a Tyrian father (1 Kings 7:14). Esther was given in marriage to the king of Persia (Esther 2:16–17), and her success in being chosen by the king from among her many competitors is unabashedly applauded.

Special mention must be made of the Book of Ruth. Elimelech took his wife, Naomi, and his sons to the country of Moab, and there both his sons "took them wives of the women of Moab" (1:4). When Elimelech and his sons had died, Naomi "arose with her daughters-in-law that she might return from the country of Moab" (1:6), and "her two daughters-in-law went with her on the way to return unto the land of Judah" (1:7). When Naomi suggested to them that they had better return to their mothers' houses, instead of going with her to a strange and unknown land, one went back, but the other, Ruth, "was steadfastly minded to go with her" (1:18); and the words she is reported to have said to her mother-in-law, "thy people shall be my people, and thy God my God" (1:16), were in later law called in aid as authority for the proposition that a non-Jewish woman may not be married to a Jew unless and until she converts to the Jewish religion (B. *Yevamot* 47b). When they arrived in Bethlehem, Ruth's first and natural thought was to find a man "in whose sight I shall find grace" (2:2); and when Boaz noticed her among the reapers of his fields, she was introduced to him as "the Moabitish damsel that came back with Naomi out of the country of Moab" (2:6). What made such an impression on Boaz was that she had left the land of her father and mother "and come unto a people which thou knewest not heretofore," in order not to leave and abandon her mother-in-law; and he prayed for her that "a full reward be given thee of the Lord God of Israel, under whose wings thou art come to trust" (2:11–12). Throughout the story, the heroine is called "Ruth the Moabitess" (2:21, 4:5, 4:10), and no formal change of her status took place until Boaz acquired her in marriage, together with "all that was Elimelech's" and all that belonged to his sons, in order "to raise up the name of the dead upon his inheritance, that the name of the dead be not cut off from among his brethren, and from the gate of his place" (4:9–10), as ancient custom prescribed. And so Ruth the Moabitess was married to Boaz the Jew and became the ancestress of King David (4:17).

The first biblical prohibition of mixed marriages occurred in the days of Nehemiah (5th cent. B.C.E.), when all the people made a solemn covenant "that we would not give our daughters unto the people of the land, nor take their daughters for our sons" (Neh. 10:31). A similar covenant had been made shortly before, in the days of Ezra (Ezra 10:3), and had also received popular assent (ibid. 10–12), but in practice had resulted only in a relatively small number of husbands divorcing their non-Jewish wives (ibid. 18–43). The practical result of the second covenant may have been better, for we hear that "they separated from Israel all the mixed multitude" (Neh. 13:3). In summing up this operation, Nehemiah said: "In those days also saw I Jews that had married wives of Ashdod, of Ammon and of Moab; and their children spake half in the speech of Ashdod, and could not speak in the Jews' language, but according to the language of each people. And I contended with them, and cursed them, and smote certain of them, and plucked off their hair, and made them swear by God, saying, 'Ye shall not give your daughters unto their sons, nor take their daughters unto your sons, or for yourselves. Did not Solomon king of Israel sin by these things? yet among many nations was there no king like him, who was beloved of his God, and God made him king over all Israel; nevertheless even him did outlandish women cause to sin' " (ibid. 23–26). The renewal of Jewish religious and national autonomy in the land of Israel after the first Babylonian exile necessitated, in the eyes of the leaders, the elimination of non-Jewish wives and the prohibition of intermarriage with non-Jews; it was a political decision, conditioned by the circumstances prevailing at that time, that brought about a change in the law.

The talmudic prohibition of all intermarriage with non-Jews is by Maimonides expressly referred back to the decree of Ezra and Nehemiah (Issurei Bee'a 12:1). In the talmudical sources themselves, the biblical prohibition in respect of the "seven nations" is extended to all foreign nations, for the reason that the ratio legis of the biblical prohibition applied with equal force to all non-Jewish religions, and the danger of being turned away from God and led to serve other (i.e., the wife's) gods was acute in the case of any marriage with any non-Jew (B. Avoda Zara 36b, B. Kiddushin 68b). So the law was eventually settled to the effect that a marriage between a Jew and a non-Jew was invalid (M. Kiddushin 3:12), the non-Jew being regarded by later jurists as having no capacity to marry under Jewish law (Tur, Even Ha'ezer 44:8), and the ceremony of marriage according to Jewish rites can have no legal effect on the status of a non-Jew (Maimonides, Ishut 4:15). Only if and when the non-Jewish partner has been converted to Judaism is he or she fully capacitated to marry, even though he or she may have originated from one of the prohibited nations (Maimonides, Issurei Bee'a 12:25).

That the family is, indeed, "the natural and fundamental group unit of society" was, in Jewish tradition, the subject of the very first exhortation which God gave Adam: "And the Lord God said, It is not good that the man should be alone" (Gen. 2:18); hence it was said that a man living alone without a family has (or is) no "good" (B. Yevamot 62b). Nor has he any joy, because it is written, "and thou shalt rejoice, thou and thine household" (Deut. 14:26);

nor any blessing, because the blessing rests "in thine house" (Ezek. 44:30). The "house" or "household" is, in biblical parlance, the term for a man's family, whereas the Hebrew term "family" (mishpaha) denotes the wider family or clan (cf. Josh. 7:14).

God created the earth "not in vain, He formed it to be inhabited" (Isa. 45:18); and in order that the earth may be inhabited, God wants man to "be fruitful and multiply" (Gen. 1:28). Thus, founding a family is regarded as a religious duty; and the duty has been held to be fulfilled when a man has procreated at least one son and one daughter (M. Yevamot 6:6; T. Yevamot 8:4; Maimonides, Ishut 15:4)—God Himself, in whose image man was created, having created male and female (Gen. 1:27). A man who practices ascetic abstinence or otherwise willfully refrains from procreation is said to be unworthy of the description "man" and to be diminishing the image of the Creator (B. Yevamot 63a–b). "Therefore shall a man leave his father and his mother, and shall cleave unto his wife" (Gen. 2:24); and "thy wife shall be as fruitful vine by the sides of thine house; thy children like olive plants round about thy table. Behold, that thus shall the man be blessed that feareth the Lord" (Ps. 128:3–4). Children are said to be the heritage of the Lord (Ps. 127:3) and the crown of men (Prov. 17:6); and the wise and virtuous wife builds her house (ibid. 14:1), blessed by her children and praised by her husband (ibid. 31:28).

There is a talmudic tradition that two days in the year were set apart for the daughters of Jerusalem to go out and dance in the surrounding vineyards, all dressed in white; and they sang to the boys to come and choose a wife from among them (M. Ta'anit 4:8). A groom who has betrothed a bride but not yet married her is exempt from military service (Deut. 20:7); and "When a man hath taken a new wife, he shall not go out to war, neither shall he be charged with any business; but he shall be free at home one year" (Deut. 24:5). This unique and very liberal provision to foster family life even at the cost of a national war effort had later to be restricted, apparently under the force of circumstances, to wars of expansion ("voluntary wars"); in wars of "duty" ("involuntary wars"), bride and bridegroom also had to be recruited even from under their canopy (M. Sota 8:7; T. Sota 7:24; Maimonides, Melakhim 7:4).

9

THE RIGHT TO PROPERTY

It is one of the tenets of the Jewish faith that God is the "possessor of heaven and earth" (Gen. 14:20), and that everything on
earth is God's riches (Ps. 104:24). It is God who "giveth thee land
to possess it" (Deut. 19:14), in the land "which the Lord thy God
giveth thee for an inheritance" to possess it and to dwell therein
(Deut. 26:1). It depends only on God's will whether man will have
property and enjoy it and see it yielding fruits (Lev. 26:3–4), as
well as whether he will be "plenteous in goods" (Deut. 28:11) or
one of the poor that "shall never cease out of the land" (Deut.
15:11): "The Lord maketh poor and maketh rich. . . . He raiseth
up the poor out of the dust, and lifteth up the beggar from the
dunghill, to set them among princes, to make them inherit the
throne of glory" (1 Sam. 2:7–8).

Rights of ownership and possession that human beings can
acquire are therefore always subject to the overriding title of God.
This overriding divine claim finds nowhere more beautiful expression than in the law relating to "the sabbath of the land": six years
may you sow your fields and prune your vineyards and gather in
the fruit thereof; "but in the seventh year shall be a sabbath of
rest unto the land, a sabbath for the Lord: thou shalt neither sow
thy field, nor prune thy vineyard" (Lev. 25:2–4). The land was left
"to rest and lie still," and what grew thereon during the sabbath
year had to be left to the poor (Exod. 23:11), and was not to be
reaped or gathered by the owner (Lev. 25:5). The resting of the
land involved a resting for the workers on the land, slaves and
hired laborers and maids and everybody sojourning with the
owner (ibid. 6).

Nor were the land and the workers on the land the only beneficiaries of the sabbatical cycle: with the advent of the seventh year,
slaves had to be freed (Exod. 21:2, Deut. 15:12, and see above, pp.
57, 60); and at the end of every seven years debts had to be released
and could no longer be exacted (Deut. 15:1–2). The sabbatical
cycle stems, of course, from God's own rest on the seventh day
from all the work of the creation (Gen. 2:2, Exod. 31:17). Not only
must everybody rest from his work on the seventh day, including
your slaves and servants, and even your animals (Exod. 20:10,
Deut. 5:14), in imitation of God, but the seventh year was to
entail a particularly far-reaching restriction on the enjoyment of
your property, bestowing at the same time a correspondingly far-
reaching benefit on your slaves and debtors—the victims, so to
speak, of your property rights. The law relating to the release of
slaves differed from that relating to the release of debts, in that
slaves were released after six years of individual service, whereas
debts were released at the end of the sabbatical year, which
recurred at fixed intervals of seven years, irrespective of the date
at which the debt had been incurred; and creditors had to be
admonished not to withhold loans because "the seventh year, the
year of release, was at hand" (Deut. 15:9).

Later law proved the admonition to have failed. "People abstained from lending money to each other," because they lost it in
the sabbatical year when the debtors were automatically released,
so it was laid down, "for the betterment of the world" (M. *Gittin*
4:3), that every loan should be deemed to have been sued upon
and merged in a judgment debt (M. *Shevi'it* 10:3; B. *Gittin* 36a).
This legal fiction, by the simple expedient of replacing the creditor, who was the one enjoined to release the debt and "not to exact
it of his neighbors" (Deut. 15:2), with the court, which was not
(expressly) so enjoined, had the effect of practically abolishing the
release of debts. To the creditor it could be said, "that which is
thine with thy brother, thine hand shall release" (ibid. 3), but not
to the impersonal court and the disinterested judge. The abolition of the biblical release of debts gave rise to vehement discussions. One of the scholars called it an impertinence and an insult,
and added that if he had the power, he would revoke it—but the
power he had not (B. *Gittin* 36b). It was also debated whether this
new rule was to be valid only for the particular generation of
people who "abstained from lending money to each other," or

whether it was to remain binding for all generations; it was eventually made binding in perpetuity, not only because there would never be any authority great enough to revoke it, but presumably also because it was based on human nature: people would not readily lend money if they had to fear losing it. The biblical restriction on the property rights of the creditor was thus removed, by talmudical law, in order to increase the debtors' prospects of obtaining finance; but authority is still found to the effect that if and when the idyllic times of biblical life should recur, the biblical restriction would have to be reintroduced (Maimonides, *Shemitta ve-Yoveil* 9:16).

In the fiftieth year, after seven times seven years (Lev. 25:8), liberty is proclaimed "throughout all the land to all inhabitants thereof: it shall be a jubilee unto you; and ye shall return every man unto his possession" (ibid. 10). All land acquired at any time during the fifty years otherwise than by inheritance had to be restored to its original owner—it being assumed that nobody would sell his land unless under the pressure of debts or other untoward circumstances. The temporariness of all dispositions of land is expressly attributed to the ultimate divine ownership of land: "The land shall not be sold forever: for the land is Mine: for ye are strangers and sojourners with Me. And in all the land of your possession ye shall grant a redemption for the land" (ibid. 23–24).

In later law, the temporariness of dispositions of land was divested of its theological implications; it was made lawful to dispose of land, and of any chattel, by way of sale or gift, for a predetermined and limited period, for which the purchaser or donee acquired full ownership rights, and after the expiration of which the ownership would revert to the vendor or donor (B. *Kiddushin* 6b, B. *Bava Batra* 137b). The difference between a sale of the fruits of the land (or a gift of the fruits of the land) for a given period and an outright sale (or an outright gift) of the land itself for such a period is that if you acquire the land itself, you may not only enjoy its use and reap its fruits during that period but may also build houses thereon and demolish them and change the character or form of the land—in short, do everything that a perpetual owner could do (Maimonides, *Mekhira* 23:5–6). Having thus introduced the institution of temporary sales in which the land anyway reverts to its original owner, the talmudists proceeded, logically enough, to exempt such temporary sales from the applicability of the law of restoration in the year of Jubilee (B. *Bava Metzia* 79a; Maimonides, *Shemitta ve-Yoveil* 11:2). The price of the land had to be fixed taking due account of the number of years for which it was sold or which would expire until the year of Jubilee (Lev. 25:15); to exact any higher price than justified by the length of that period would be an act of oppression (ibid. 14).

With the cessation of Jubilee years (above, p. 61), lands (or chattels) sold would no longer revert to their original owner unless the sale had been for a limited period; but sales and gifts for such limited periods survived the institution of Jubilee and became a well-established legal institution in their own right.

But it appears that even before the cessation of the Jubilee years, sales in perpetuity were actually concluded (e.g., cf. 1 Kings 21: the vineyard would have been sold to the king were it not for Naboth's insistence that he would not sell "the inheritance of his fathers"). Even lands taken in execution or foreclosure for debts appear not to have always been restored in Jubilee years. The bitter complaints made to Nehemiah by the people who had mortgaged their lands and been dispossessed (Neh. 5:1–5) prompted him to appeal to the "nobles" and have them take the oath that they would restore the property they had taken away (ibid. 8–12); it seemingly required a voluntary renunciation on their part, and the Jubilee was either ineffective or no longer in force. We find a prophetic foreboding of the seller's mourning because he will no more "return to that which is sold" (Ezek. 7:13)—from the mouth of the same prophet who reiterated the law that gifts to one's sons are given in perpetuity, but gifts to others are theirs only until "the year of liberty" (Ezek. 46:16–17).

On the strength of ultimate divine ownership in all property, divine claims are made and restrictions placed on earthly property rights. The poor had a right of redemption at any time, and at the original price, of land sold by them in distress (Lev. 25:25–27; but in respect of urban property the right had to be exercised within one year: ibid. 30); and if they themselves could not afford to redeem, their relatives had the right and the duty to do it for them (Lev. 25:25, Jer. 32:7, Ruth 3:13, 4:3–6); if the relatives could not afford it either, the property would revert to its original owner gratis in the Jubilee year (Lev. 25:28). Land was not allowed to be harvested fully; part of its fruits had always to be left for the poor, the stranger, and orphans and widows (Lev. 19:9–10, 23:22; Deut. 24:19–21). Property in your hand was not to be used only for your own enjoyment, but to aid the needy; if you open your hands wide (Deut. 15:8), God will bless you and increase your property (ibid. 10; Ps. 112:3, 5, 9; et al.). Later law made charity obligatory; every citizen had to be assessed as to what his contribution should be, and such contributions were then levied by compulsory process (Maimonides, *Matnot Aniyim* 7:10; *Yorei Dei'a* 248).

While the right to acquire and hold property was always fully recognized and legally enforced, the law looking upon the property of men with benevolence and solicitude (J. *Terumot* 8:9), amassing property was always looked upon askance. It is part of "human vanity" that "he that loveth silver shall not be satisfied with silver, nor he that loveth abundance, with increase" (Eccl. 5:10). The more wealth a man accumulates, the less sleep will he enjoy at night (ibid. 12), and the more troubled will be his days (M. *Avot* 2:7); "there is a sore evil which I have seen under the sun, namely, riches kept for the owners thereof to their hurt" (Eccl. 5:13). The wise king prayed to be given neither poverty nor riches (Prov. 30:8); he knew that a man may be rich and have nothing, and that another man may be poor but have great riches (ibid. 13:7). We find prophetic censures on the rich who buy up lands, "add house to house and join field to field, till there be no place, that they may be placed alone in the midst of the earth!" (Isa. 5:8); on luxury buildings of summer houses and winter houses and "the houses of ivory" (Amos 3:15); on feasting on wines and the harp and the viol, the tabret and the pipe (Isa. 5:11–12); on "tinkling ornaments" and extravagant dresses (Isa. 3:18–23); and generally, on indulging in a life of "ease" and lavishness (Amos 6:1–6). Small wonder that the rich are often suspected of having come by their wealth by unlawful means: if "they covet fields, they take them by violence; if they covet houses, they take them away by oppression" (Mic. 2:2); and a man who makes haste to be rich will never establish his innocence (Prov. 28:20). Not that his riches will avail him much: "As the partridge sitteth on eggs, and hatcheth them not, so he that getteth riches and not by right, shall leave them in the midst of his days, and at his end shall be a fool" (Jer. 17:11).

A mishnaic tradition lists four different classes of property owners: he who says, "mine is mine and thine is thine," is the average man; he who says "mine is thine and thine is mine," is uneducated and silly; he who says, "mine is mine and thine is mine," is wicked; and he who says "mine is thine and thine is thine," is righteous (M. *Avot* 5:10). The rights of any other man to his property must be as important to you and as near to your heart as your own property rights (M. *Avot* 2:12); and it has been said that while your neighbor's property may look to you as desirable and radiant as the stars of heaven, when you lay hands on it, it will bury you deep in the earth (*Tanna debei Eliahu Zuta* 13).

The prohibition not to "covet thy neighbor's house . . . nor any thing that is thy neighbor's" is, of course, the tenth commandment (Exod. 20:17, Deut. 5:21); and early commentators already asked themselves how a commandment like that could possibly be enforced. As far as human agencies are concerned, it was laid down that no cognizance could be taken of any such coveting unless it was accompanied by some overt act (*Mekhilta, Yithro* 8; Maimonides, *Gezeila vaAveida* 1:9). Later commentators stressed the psychological rather than the legal aspect of the prohibition: "Many people will wonder what this commandment is about. How can a man abstain from desiring in his heart a beautiful thing which he sees? But like a poor villager who sees a beautiful princess, and does not desire her because he would not desire the impossible, or like a man who would not desire his beautiful mother because the inviolability of his mother was imbued to him from earliest childhood—so ought every educated person to discipline himself not to desire the inappropriate and incongruous: anyway property is acquired not by wisdom or skill but by luck and God's will" (Ibn Ezra ad Exod. 20:14). And covetousness has been said to be the mother of all deceit and theft, nay even of murder and rape (Ibn Ezra, loc. cit.). However that may be, the fact that coveting your neighbor's property is raised to the status of one of the ten most grievous sins speaks eloquently indeed for the respect in which property rights are held—as well as for a divine predilection for such rights.

It is not only that the law prohibits interfering with the property of another, whether by larceny (Exod. 5:15, 21:37; Lev. 19:11; Deut. 5:19), or robbery (Lev. 5:21, 19:13), or embezzlement (Exod. 22:6–12), or trespass (Deut. 19:14), but that, rather than making such interferences criminal offenses, the law insists that restitution be made to the owner, often with the addition of double or three or four or five times the value by way of punitive damages (Exod. 21:37, 22:3, 6, 8, 11, 13; Lev. 5:23–24). The notion that interference with property rights gives rise to civil rather than criminal remedies survived into later law (Maimonides, *Gezeila vaAveida* 1:1, *Geneiva* 1:1), and the owner had a cause of action in the regular civil courts (M. *Sanhedrin* 1:1). It was always regarded as more important that the property should be restored to the owner than that the offender should suffer punishment.

When kings ruled over Israel, it appears that they usurped the power to confiscate private property (see King Solomon's self-laudatory account in Eccl. 2:4–9). Indeed, when the elders came to Samuel and asked him to give them a king, "like all the nations" (1 Sam. 8:5), he warned them that "the manner of the king that shall reign over you" will be to "take your fields and your vineyards and your oliveyards, even the best of them, and give them to his servants. . . . And he will take your menservants and your maidservants and your goodliest young men, and your asses, and put them to his work . . ." (ibid. 11, 14, 16). While Samuel intended, of course, to deter the people from monarchic rule and therefore threatened them with royal confiscations without mentioning any compensation, the law was eventually settled to the effect that the king was, for purposes of warfare, entitled to confiscate private property and recruit manpower, but was under obligation to pay a fair price therefor (Maimonides, *Melakhim* 4:3, 6). Only for purposes of road-building and similar public works was the king allowed to confiscate property without paying compensation (M. *Sanhedrin* 2:4; Maimonides, op. cit. 5:3). If he confiscated property for any other purpose, especially for his private use, it was branded as sheer plunder (Maimonides, op. cit. 3:8).

By later talmudical law, wide powers of expropriation were vested in the courts of justice (B. *Gittin* 36b, B. *Yevamot* 89b), on the strength of a precedent reported in the Book of Ezra, in which it was threatened that disobedience to lawful orders of the court would be visited with confiscation of property (Ezra 10:8). Courts used this power of expropriation in order to impose fines and damages even where no such fines or damages were provided for by law (B. *Mo'ed Kattan* 16a), or where the fines or damages provided for by law were regarded as insufficient (B. *Bava Kamma* 96b). In post-talmudic times ample use appears to have been made of this expropriatory power in the judicial battle against lawlessness and violence (Maimonides, *Sanhedrin* 24:6; *Hoshen Mishpat* 2, and Rema ad loc.). A talmudic source seems to indicate that semi-confiscatory powers for punitive purposes could also be vested in nonjudicial authorities: a Temple inspector who found a guard asleep on duty was authorized to take his clothing away and burn it (M. *Middot* 1:2).

Judicial expropriations were not confined to criminal or quasi-criminal sanctions. They were also used for public-utility purposes, on the authority of Joshua and the elders, who distributed the land among tribes and families (Josh. 19:51), divesting an owner of some of his property and vesting that property in someone else. While punitive confiscation presupposes some guilt and blameworthiness on the part of the owner (Tossafot ad *Yevamot* 90a), public-utility expropriations could also lawfully deprive innocent persons of some of their property (*Responsa Akiva Eger* 105).

The most important use made of judicial expropriations, however, was quasi-legislative in nature. This use is best illustrated by some examples. A man who had acquired a chattel in the *bona fide* belief that it was abandoned had it expropriated by order of the court, which vested the property in the original owner who had lost it (B. *Bava Metzia* 27b, and Rashi ad loc.). Where a son had disposed of his father's property before the latter's death, in payment of his father's debts, the court would expropriate the property from the father and vest it in the creditor who had *bona fide* received it (B. *Bava Metzia* 16a). Dispositions by infants of property in their hands could be validated by judicial expropriation in favor of the grantees (B. *Gittin* 59a). The above-mentioned great law reform by which debts remained recoverable notwithstanding their remission in the sabbatical year was later sought to be justified by the expropriatory powers of the court (B. *Gittin* 36–37). In these and similar cases the expropriatory powers were invoked in theory only, by way of legal fiction, and mostly *ex post facto:* what had already been done or ordered for the sake of justice was retrospectively explained as an exercise by the court of its power of expropriation.

It is believed that this judicial power of expropriation is unique. Rather than endangering the inviolability of vested property rights, it enables the court to leave, transfer, or distribute property where in justice and equity it should be. (In this respect it is but the counterpart of the equitable powers assumed by the praetorial court of Rome and the chancery courts of England.) There are almost unlimited possibilities for its application. Where the court desired to dissolve a marriage (by abduction), which could not otherwise be dissolved without the husband's concurrence, it retroactively expropriated from the husband the property (the ring) with which he had acquired the wife in marriage (B. *Yevamot* 110a). A husband's overriding right to inherit his wife was judicially expropriated from him in order to validate the wife's bequests to third parties (*Responsa Asheri* 55:10). Or, as a wife does not inherit her husband (see p. 173), the husband's estate was expropriated by the court in order to leave it in her undisturbed possession after she had in good faith taken possession thereof (J. *Ketuvot* 9:3, J. *Kiddushin* 1:3).

It may well be that the courts, whose function it is to administer God's laws, do but recognize, in the exercise of these expropriatory powers, that ultimate and overriding right of divine ownership to which all property rights must always be subject, and which can—at least in the hands of human judges—have no purpose other than justice and equity.

10

THE RIGHT TO WORK AND REMUNERATION

It is often mistakenly assumed that labor—"the sweat of thy face"—was imposed upon man as divine punishment for his primordial sin (Gen. 3:19). In fact, however, God planted the Garden of Eden and put Adam there "to dress and keep it" (Gen. 2:15), thus entrusting him, long before he committed his sin, with the duty of work by way of a blessing. Indeed, so long as "there was no man to till the ground" (Gen. 2:5), God's creation was incomplete and unworkable.

As God did the work of creating the world in six days (Gen. 2:2), so man was exhorted to labor and do his work six days of the week (Exod. 20:9, Deut. 5:13); the duty to work six days and the duty to rest on the seventh day are interdependent and collateral (*Avot deRabbi Natan*, Version I, 11, Version II, 21).

Both biblical and talmudical sources abound in extolling work and industry. When the sun rises, "man goes forth unto his work and to his labor until the evening" (Ps. 104:22–23), and happy is the man who eats the fruit of his own labors (Ps. 128:2, Ben Sira 40:7). Sweet is the sleep of the laborer (Eccl. 5:12); and he who tills his land will have plenty of food (Prov. 12:11). The ways of the ant, which, "having no guide, overseer or ruler, provideth her meat in the summer and gathereth her food in the harvest," are set as an example to the sluggard who likes to sleep (Prov. 7:6–9). And the great prophetic vision of the ideal world sees the instruments of warfare transformed into tools of work and labor, such as plowshares and pruning hooks (Isa. 2:4), it being self-evident

96

that the ideal and idyllic state of life can be attained only when man is able to pursue his work in peace.

In talmudical literature we find manual labor raised to the standard of (at least) a moral duty. Even the study of Holy Writ and the preoccupation with law and religion are of no use, and may lead to sin, unless they are accompanied by some work (M. *Avot* 2:2). (On the other hand, one scholar said of himself that he would leave all the crafts in the world and rather spend all his time studying the Torah [Nehorai, M. *Kiddushin* 4:14].) Work should be loved and sinecure hated (M. *Avot* 1:10), and nobody ought to be heard to say that he is too high-born or too highly stationed to do manual work (B. *Bava Batra* 110a). While engaged in his work, a laborer is excused from standing up and paying the (otherwise prescribed) respect to scholars (B. *Kiddushin* 33a). Labor honors the person engaged in it (B. *Nedarim* 49b), so much so that the laborer is held in higher esteem than the god-fearing (B. *Berakhot* 8a).

In order to comply with the divine exhortation to choose life (Deut. 30:19), man is in duty bound to choose one of the crafts for his livelihood (J. *Pei'a* 1:1), as he is also in duty bound to teach his son one of the crafts (B. *Kiddushin* 29a). Not educating one's children to a life of work and labor is tantamount to educating them to a life of crime (ibid., and 30a). Fathers are advised to choose for their children clean and easy trades (M. *Kiddushin* 4:14, B. *Kiddushin* 82a), and while it is true that all the trades have to be manned, happy is he whose trade is clean and easy (ibid. 82b). But the word of the Preacher that God "hath made everything beautiful in his time" (Eccl. 3:11) has aptly been interpreted to mean that God makes everybody see his own trade as the most beautiful of all (B. *Berakhot* 43b).

Everybody should exercise his right to work, because idleness and indolence endanger life and accelerate death (*Avot deRabbi Natan*, Version II, 21). They are also a cause of slander, people being likely to ask whence that sluggard provides for his livelihood (ibid.). A man at work is like a vineyard well protected against the outside so that no trespasser and no animal can enter and do damage, or like a wife well protected by her husband so that no stranger will inconvenience her (T. *Kiddushin* 1:11), whereas the idle and indolent person is like an unprotected woman of whom people talk loosely and in derision (*Avot deRabbi*

Natan, loc. cit). Great scholars used to engage in heavy manual trades so as to keep their bodies fit and warm (B. *Gittin* 67b), the surest way to remain in good health (Maimonides, *Dei'ot* 4:2). Others performed even menial services, so as never to be in need of charity or the benevolence of others (B. *Bava Batra* 110a). Some authorities hold that a man must hire himself out as a menial servant if he cannot otherwise maintain his wife (*Tur, Even Ha'ezer* 70; Rema ad *Even Ha'ezer* 70:3).

As distinguished from the duty to work, however, the right to work (or to abstain from work) finds expression in the legal rule that the laborer is at liberty to quit work and withdraw his labor at any time, irrespective of the nature of work or the length of time for which he had been engaged (B. *Bava Metzia* 10a, B. *Bava Kamma* 116b)—the reason given for this *prima facie* surprising inequality between employer and employee being that man is the servant of God only (Lev. 25:55), and not the servant of God's servants. Where the laborer has been paid in advance, he has to return to the employer the proportionate unearned part of his wages (*Hoshen Mishpat* 333:3); and where the advance wages are irrecoverable because the laborer is without means, he may not withdraw from work, because the law is that he has the right to abstain from work, but not that he has the right to defraud his employer (*Knesset Hagedola* and *Arukh Hashulhan* ad *Hoshen Mishpat*, loc. cit). If he has not been paid in advance, he is entitled to a *quantum meruit* for the work actually done by him before he withdrew (B. *Bava Metzia* 76b; Maimonides, *Sekhirut* 9:4). It is worthy of note that the right to stop work is accorded only to the laborer who wishes to withdraw from work entirely, either in order to exercise his right not to work or because of illness of himself or a member of his family or other such circumstances beyond his control; it is not accorded to a laborer who stops work in order to compel his employer to increase his pay (Bah ad *Tur, Hoshen Mishpat* 333; Rema ad *Hoshen Mishpat* 333:3), nor, it seems, to a laborer who leaves his employer because he has found a better one, that is, who does not abstain from work but only changes his place of work. Where an employer promised to increase the laborer's pay beyond the customary or agreed wages, under duress of the laborer's threat to exercise his right and stop working altogether, he would not be bound by his promise (*Responsa Asheri* 104:2; *Tur, Hoshen Mishpat* 333:4).

Remuneration for work is to be paid either according to custom (M. *Bava Metzia* 7:1) or according to a specific agreement between employer and employee. Where customary rates vary in a given community, the average rate is applicable (B. *Bava Metzia* 87a; Maimonides, *Sekhirut* 9:2), unless the employee agreed to accept the lower rate (B. *Bava Metzia* 76a; Maimonides, op.cit. 9:3). Custom also determines whether wages do or do not include subsistence pay, board or lodging, and the like (M. *Bava Metzia* 7:1); but the biblical rule that "when thou comest into thy neighbor's vineyard, then thou mayest eat grapes thy fill at thine own pleasure; but thou shalt not put any in thy vessel" (Deut. 23:24) has been held to apply particularly to workmen, who may in no way be restricted in their right to eat and drink from the produce of their work in the fields to their hearts' content, provided they do not take anything off the employer's premises (M. *Bava Metzia* 7:2–5; Maimonides, *Sekhirut* 12:1). The workman cannot, however, be compelled to take the produce of his work, or some share therein, in lieu of wages (M. *Bava Metzia* 10:5; Maimonides, op.cit. 9:10; *Hoshen Mishpat* 332:2); he is entitled to be paid his wages in cash (Shah ad *Hoshen Mishpat* 332:18).

There is another injunction laid down twice already in biblical law and hence regarded as establishing one of the fundamental rights of the worker: "the wages of him that is hired shall not abide with thee all night until the morning" (Lev. 19:13)—or, in the language of the Deuteronomist: "Thou shalt not oppress a hired servant that is poor and needy, whether he be of thy brethren, or of thy strangers that are in thy land and within thy gates. At his day thou shalt give him his hire, neither shall the sun go down upon it; for he is poor, and setteth his heart upon it: lest he cry against thee unto the Lord, and it be sin unto thee" (Deut. 24:14–15). Talmudical scholars were divided as to what amounts to "oppression" of the hired servant. According to one opinion, oppression consisted in putting the worker off from one day to the other with promises of payment, saying to him, "go, and come again, and tomorrow I will give" (Prov. 3:28); others held oppression to be the denial that any wages were due at all; still others held oppression to be the denial that any work had ever been ordered by the employer—while the nonpayment of wages due was considered to be not oppression but outright robbery (B. *Bava Metzia* 111a). To avoid any delay in the payment of wages, elaborate rules were laid down fixing the time when wages were payable to hourly, daily, nightly, weekly, and monthly workers (M. *Bava Metzia* 9:11; Maimonides, *Sekhirut* 11:2; *Hoshen Mishpat* 339:3–5); and any dilatoriness in paying wages on maturity is decried as if it meant taking from the worker his heart which he has "set upon it" (B. *Bava Metzia* 111a; Maimonides, loc.cit.). The fact that the worker has set his heart upon his wages gave rise to yet another rule, namely, that where the employer denies having employed the worker, or where he claims to have already paid him, the worker is entitled to recover on his oath that the wages are due to him—he having "set his heart" on his wages, whereas the employer has all sorts of other matters bothering him (M. *Shevu'ot* 7:1, B. *Shevu'ot* 45a–b, Maimonides, op.cit. 6). And all possible facilities are to be accorded to the workman who resorts to the court for his remedies against his employer; the court even has to comfort him so that he does not take the matter to heart (Maimonides, op.cit. 9).

But as the employer is under obligation to pay the worker's wages punctually, so is the worker under obligation not to defraud the employer by working negligently and unconscientiously and wasting the employer's time and implements (Maimonides, *Sekhirut* 13:7). As a matter of law, the worker is responsible for the employer's property in his hands as if he were a bailee (M. *Bava Metzia* 6:6; Maimonides, op.cit 10:3–5); thus, he is liable in damages for any such property lost or damaged by him, and the employer is entitled to set-off the damages due to him against the wages due to the worker (Maimonides, op.cit. 10:5–7). It is obvious that the law depriving a worker of all or part of his wages for any negligent act or omission must cause great hardship; and it is therefore hardly surprising that we find relief provided by an outspokenly equitable jurisdiction. The story goes that laborers were employed to repair wine barrels. Instead of repairing them, they broke them. Whereupon the employer took their gowns from them. They went to the judge, and the judge told the employer to give them their gowns back. The employer asked, "Is that the law?" and the judge replied: "It is: That thou mayest walk in the ways of good men" (Prov. 2:20). So he returned them their gowns. Then the laborers said, "We are poor, and we worked all day, and we are hungry, and we have nothing." Said the judge: "Give them their wages." He asked, "Is that the law?" and the judge replied: "It is: And keep the paths of the righteous" (ibid.). So he paid them their wages (B. *Bava Metzia* 83a, J. *Bava Metzia* 6:8). The proverbial advice to walk in the ways of good men and keep the paths of the righteous is not, of course, formal law; but it was Scripture enough to be invoked in justification of the equitable remedy. In later periods, courts would entertain the employer's claim for damages and make a formal adjudication of the worker's liability but insist at the same time on a declaration of the employer that the judgment would serve him only as a declaration of the duty of care incumbent upon his workers and would not be put in execution against them (*Responsa Havat Ya'ir* 169).

The right of workers to form and join trade unions for the protection of their interests is also recognized in talmudical law. The rule that townspeople may regulate prices, weights, measures, and wages (B. *Bava Batra* 8b) was extended to authorize the members of a given trade to fix hours and places of work and minimum or maximum wages for their trade (Asheri ad *Bava Batra* 1:33; Maimonides, *Mekhira* 14:10; *Tur, Hoshen Mishpat* 231:30 and *Beit Yossef* ad loc.; *Hoshen Mishpat* 231:28). In particular, woolspinners and dyers may combine to put the income of each of them into a common fund, bakers may combine to distribute work among each other, donkey- and camel-drivers may combine to replace, from a mutual insurance fund, animals lost to any of them (T. *Bava Metzia* 11:24–26); and these are presumably but instances to illustrate the general rule. As distinguished from townspeople, however, who appear to enjoy full autonomy in these matters (*Responsa Rivash* 399), wage regulations by trade unions are said to require the consent or approval of the leading scholar of the city (Maimonides, *Tur,* and *Hoshen Mishpat,* loc. cit.), and are valid and binding without such consent only where wages are not increased by such regulations and "no damage is done to others" (Ran, quoted by Rema ad *Hoshen Mishpat* 231:28), or where no such leading scholar is available (*Responsa Rashba* 4:185). It seems that some outside control was thought necessary to curb the natural enrichment tendencies of organized labor. We also find various trades having common offices or labor exchanges where customers would be directed to a craftsman willing and available to serve (T. *Sukka* 4:6, B. *Sukka* 51b).

Some indication of minimum wages providing for "a standard

of living adequate for the health and well-being of himself and his family" (Art. 25.1 of the Universal Declaration of Human Rights) is to be found in the rule that if the legally fixed salaries paid to public employees, such as scribes and judges, appear to be insufficient, they are, even without any application on the part of the employees and even against their will, to be increased so as to meet "the needs of themselves, their wives and sons and members of their households" (Maimonides, *Shekalim* 4:7, elaborating on B. *Ketuvot* 106a).

11

THE RIGHT TO LEISURE

Jewish law limits working hours according to the custom prevailing in any particular place; and no employer may compel his workman to work at earlier or later hours than local custom permits (M. *Bava Metzia* 7:1). Where the workman resides in a place with shorter working hours and is hired to work in a place with longer working hours, he may stipulate that the custom of his place of residence be followed; otherwise the determining custom is that of the place where the work is to be performed (J. *Bava Metzia* 7:1), or, according to some later jurists, of the place where the contract of employment was made (Rema ad *Hoshen Mishpat* 331:1). But any such choice of custom applies only where there is no express agreement between employer and workman as to what the working hours shall be (Tossafot ad *Bava Metzia* 83a, s.v. *hassokher; Responsa Gershom Me'or Hagola* 72; *Hoshen Mishpat* 331:1).

The time needed for going to work is charged to the employer, it being his interest that the workman come to his working place; but the time lost in going home from work is charged to the workman, it being his interest to get home (B. *Bava Metzia* 83b and Tossafot ad loc.). Working hours start, therefore, with the workman leaving his home to go to his place of work, but they cease with the stoppage of work, and his going back home is not reckoned as working time.

Where there is no local custom, and failing agreement between employer and workman, the psalmist's verse, "the sun ariseth. . . . Man goes forth unto his work and to his labor until the evening" (Ps. 104:22–23), was resorted to as fixing or indica-

103

ting the normal working day from sunrise till sunset (B. *Bava Metzia* 83b).

Particular provisions were made for Fridays, the eve of the Sabbath, on which the workman must be released from work in time to make his preparations and purchases for the Sabbath— and the time required therefor is reckoned as if within working hours and charged to the employer (J. *Bava Metzia* 7:1; *Tur, Hoshen Mishpat* 331:5). Opinions differed as to how much time is needed and may be charged; some said, two hours and a half (Rashi ad Pessahim 50b q.v. *min*), others five hours and a half (*Mordekhai* ad *Pessahim* 603); eventually a modern authority accepted the former opinion for workmen who worked within their own city walls and the latter for workmen who worked in the fields (*Mishna Berura* ad *Orah Hayim* 251:1). The rules applying to eves of Sabbaths apply also to eves of holidays (cf. M. *Pessahim* 4:1).

From the biblical comparison between a slave and a hired servant, the former being "worth a double hired servant" (Deut. 15:18), it was deduced that while a slave could be made to work day and night, a hired workman could be required to work during the day only and never at night (B. *Kiddushin* 15a, J. *Kiddushin* 1:2). The better law, however, appears to be that slaves could not be required to work at night either, if only because slaves were, by biblical command, to be treated in every respect as if they were hired servants (Lev. 25:40; *Mekhilta, Mishpatim* 1). Night work was, however, permissible for workmen who did not work during the daytime and whose work was, by its nature, required to be done at night (cf. M. *Bava Metzia* 9:11).

A man may not do any work during the seven days of mourning for his near relatives—parents, children, spouse, brothers, sisters—but is entitled to his contractual wages, his failure to perform his work being ascribed to circumstances beyond his control (B. *Bava Metzia* 77a).

Later authorities also recognized a right of permanent employees, such as teachers or rabbis, to annual vacations with full pay (e.g., *Responsa Tashbatz* 3:109).

During working hours, reasonable time must be allowed to workmen at the expense of the employer for meals and refreshment (B. *Bava Metzia* 86a and Tossafot ad loc.) as well as for prayer (B. *Berakhot* 16a, T. *Berakhot* 5:24). Prayers may be recited at the place of work and need not be recited at places of prayer (cf. M. *Berakhot* 2:4).

The most incisive and lasting reform which biblical law accomplished in this area is, of course, the establishment of the compulsory weekly day of rest, the Sabbath. We have already seen that the scrupulous observance of the Sabbath was incumbent on all and sundry, householders and their families as well as strangers, servants, and slaves, nay even domestic animals (Exod. 20:11, Deut. 5:14). Theologically, the sabbatical rest is an imitation of God's own rest on the seventh day after six days of effort in creating the world (Gen. 2:1–3), and, as such, "a perpetual covenant" between God and the children of Israel (Exod. 31:16–17); but theological considerations were soon matched by social and humanitarian rationalizations. In the context of provisions for the benefit of the poor and the stranger, you are exhorted to do your work six days of the week, "and on the seventh day thou shalt rest: that thine ox and thine ass may rest, and the son of thine handmaid, and the stranger, may be refreshed" (Exod. 23:12). The Bible already spelled out some particular instances of resting, such as abstaining from work in general (Lev. 23:3), and from plowing and harvesting in particular (Exod. 34:21); carrying no burdens (Jer. 17:21–22); pursuing no trade (Amos 8:5, Neh. 13:19); kindling no fire (Exod. 35:3)and gathering no sticks for firewood (Num. 15:32–36); and not indulging in business talk or in profane pleasures (Isa. 58:13). "These are plainly only casual instances of a much more comprehensive customary law, which was probably extended in course of time to meet changing conditions" (Moore II 25). Indeed, an enormous number of rules and regulations were in the course of time superimposed by talmudical law to implement the biblical command of sabbatical rest; the talmudists themselves aptly described this legislation as like mountains hanging by a hair—very little Bible and a great many regulatory laws (M. *Hagiga* 1:8).

The minute and subtle casuistry of the talmudical laws relating to sabbatical rest created the wrong impression that the Sabbath, in Jewish law and practice, was a complicated science and a heavy burden rather than a time of wistful and pleasurable rest and relaxation. But Jesus' saying that "the Sabbath was made for man, and not man for the Sabbath" (Mark 2:27) in fact reflects an ancient Jewish tradition: the verse "it is holy unto you" (Exod.

31:14) was interpreted as meaning, "unto you is the Sabbath given over, and not you are given over to the Sabbath" (*Mekhilta, Ki-Tissa* 1; B. *Yoma* 85b—as translated by Abrahams I 130). The notion that, notwithstanding those "mountains" of rules, the Sabbath is not an end in itself to which man was subjugated for purposes other than his own welfare and benefit, but is the day of rest created for, required by, and "given over" to the working man, found expression in a good many dicta to the effect that there was no greater blessing ever conferred on man by God than the Sabbath (B. *Shabbat* 10b, B. *Beitza* 16a). "And God blessed the seventh day" (Gen. 2:3)—by making the face of man light up and shine on his day of rest (*Bereishit Rabba* 11).

12

FREEDOM OF THOUGHT, SPEECH, AND CONSCIENCE

At first sight, religious law and freedom of thought and speech are contradictions in terms. The premise underlying all religious (and divine) law, namely, the existence of God, His omnipotence and His omniscience, and the eternally binding force of His will, is by its very nature undebatable and incontestable. But it is noteworthy that neither the Written nor the Oral Law contains any explicit precept to believe in God or not to believe in other deities. Apart from the vast majority of commandments, which are to do or not to do certain acts, you are exhorted to love your God (Deut. 6:5) and fear Him (ibid. 13 et al.), which may, of course, necessarily imply a belief in Him, but the belief is nowhere expressly postulated. The Hebrew term used in medieval and modern usage to denote "faith" or "belief," *emuna*, originally stood for "trust" or "confidence" (e.g., Gen. 15:6, Exod. 14:31). Your religious experience leads you to have confidence in God, as it, indeed, causes you to be aware of God: "Unto thee it was shown, that thou mightest know that the Lord, He is God" (Deut. 4:35). It has been said that true love of God, as well as true fear of Him, must stem from a knowledge of His ways—belief alone would never suffice (Maimonides, *Moré Nevukhim* 3:51).

The cardinal injunction, "Thou shalt have no other gods" (Exod. 20:3, Deut. 5:7), was later interpreted as prohibiting "any notion that there might be a god other than this God" (Maimonides, *Yessodei HaTora* 1:6), a "notion" which is in line with the Maimonidean Principles of Faith, the first of which proclaims the belief in the One and Only God. But however fundamental this "notion" may be, even in the Maimonidean conception no failure to entertain it could ever amount to a criminal offense so long as it was not manifested by some overt act other than mere words (Maimonides, *Sanhedrin* 18:2).

There are, however, capital offenses created already by biblical law outlawing incitement to idolatry, which in a theocracy is tantamount to treason. The false prophet who says, "Let us go after other gods, which thou hast not known, and serve them," shall be put to death (Deut. 13:2–5); and, "If thy brother . . . or thy son or thy daughter, or the wife of thy bosom, or thy friend which is as thine own soul, entice thee secretly, saying, 'Let us go and serve other gods,' . . . thou shalt not consent unto him, nor hearken unto him; neither shall thine eye pity him, neither shalt thou spare, neither shalt thou conceal him: but thou shalt surely kill him" (ibid. 6–10). The many exhortations not to pity or to spare him served as basis for the talmudical law that the case of the inciter to idolatry is the only criminal case in which the normal rules of evidence and procedure may be deviated from, for instance by making use of agents provocateurs (M. *Sanhedrin* 7:10, B. *Sanhedrin* 67a).

While idolatrous and hence treasonable thoughts which had not found expression in inflammatory speech were not judicially cognizable, God's own fury may well be let loose if He sees a soul despise His statutes or abhor His judgments (Lev. 26:15–39). The obstinate urge of a "stiff-necked people" away from God toward idols of gold makes the divine wrath "wax hot against them" (Exod. 32:9–10). And the man who would "bless himself in his heart, saying, 'I shall have peace, though I walk in the imagination of my heart,' " not only adds "drunkenness to thirst," but provokes "the anger of the Lord; and his jealousy shall smoke against that man, and all the curses that are written in this book shall lie upon him, and the Lord shall blot out his name from under heaven" (Deut. 29:19–20).

In the eyes of the prophet, the perversity of questioning the existence of God appears to be self-evident: "Shall the clay say to him that fashioneth it, 'What makest thou?' or, 'Thy work, it hath no hands?' Woe unto him that saith unto his father, 'What begettest thou?' or to the woman, 'What hast thou brought forth?' Woe unto him that striveth with his Maker!" (Isa. 45:9–

10). Tradition has it that this is an anticipatory reference to Habakkuk, who protested God's indifference and iniquity (1:2–3) (Rashi ad Isa. 45:9, *Yalkut Shimoni* 2:324); but we find similar protests often voiced by other prophets.

The Bible abounds with restrictions on the freedom of speech— whether for the sake of God or for the sake of men. "Thou shalt not take the name of the Lord thy God in vain" (Exod. 20:7, Deut. 5:11) is one of the Ten Commandments, reiterated in divers prohibitions against swearing falsely (Lev. 5:4, 19:12) and committing perjury (Deut. 19:16–21). The injunction not to curse the deaf (Lev. 19:14) or the judges and rulers (Exod. 22:27) was later extended to outlaw all cursing (B. *Shevu'ot* 36a; *Mekhilta, Kaspa* 19; *Sifra* ad Lev. 19:14). In contradistinction to the former, which carry no judicial sanctions, special mention is made of two species of cursing that are capital offenses: one is blasphemy (Lev. 24:15–16), the other is cursing one's father or mother (Exod. 21:17, Lev. 20:9). In practice, the most important restriction on freedom of speech is, of course, the prohibition of slander: "thou shalt not go up and down as a talebearer among thy people" (Lev. 19:16) and "thou shalt not raise a false report" (Exod. 23:1).

As in modern systems of law so in biblical law, this kind of restriction underlines rather than undermines the freedom of speech; were it not for the generally valid proposition that everybody is at liberty to speak out as he pleases, the exceptions to such a general rule need not have been particularized. That the general rule is nowhere expressly stated is neither here nor there; we have already observed that Jewish law excels in stating duties and prohibitions and only implying rights.

We find in biblical history several instances of people speaking their minds and thereby arousing divine wrath. Immediately following the exodus from Egypt, the people "tempted the Lord, saying, 'Is the Lord among us, or not?' " (Exod. 17:7), but they appear to have been prompted by their thirst for water (ibid. 3), which was a circumstance mitigating enough for them not to be punished. No such mitigating circumstance could be pleaded in their defense when later the people "complained: it displeased the Lord, and the Lord heard it, and His anger was kindled, and the fire of the Lord burnt among them and consumed them" (Num. 11:1). Miriam and Aaron "spake against Moses because of the Ethiopian woman whom he had married: for he had married an

110 HUMAN RIGHTS IN JEWISH LAW

Ethiopian woman. And they said, 'Hath the Lord indeed spoken only by Moses? hath he not spoken also by us?' And the Lord heard it" (Num. 12:1–2). They were not only slandering Moses because of his Ethiopian wife, they were also questioning God's choice of Moses as His spokesman. "And the anger of the Lord was kindled against them" (ibid. 9), and Miriam, who resented the color and race of her sister-in-law, "became leprous, white as snow" (ibid. 10). The scouts who were sent into Canaan to explore the land "brought up an evil report of the land" (Num. 13:32) and caused the people to murmur against Moses and plot to "make a captain and . . . return into Egypt" (Num. 14:2–4); but there were two dissenters, Joshua and Caleb, who had found the land "exceeding good" (ibid. 7), and it was their report that prevailed: they were allowed to enter and inherit the land, and the others had to perish (ibid. 23–24). And the uprising of Korah and his company, who said of Moses, "Ye take too much upon you, seeing all the congregation are holy, every one of them, and the Lord is among them: wherefore then lift ye up yourselves above the congregation of the Lord?" (Num. 16:3), was quelled by a most drastic divine intervention (ibid. 28–33).

Prophecy is the classical manifestation of biblical freedom of speech. "For Zion's sake will I not hold my peace, and for Jerusalem's sake will I not rest" (lit.: "keep quiet") (Isa. 62:1), is the leitmotif of all prophetic oration. It is said of the prophets that they were poets, preachers, patriots, statesmen, social critics, moralists (Heschel xiv)—and passionate fanatics who put their innate or cultivated pathos to most impressive use. Their main trait was the courage to say no to their society, condemning its complacency, waywardness, and syncretism (ibid. xix); nor had they any inhibition or compunction about telling the kings and princes to their faces exactly what they thought about them. It is true that the prophets preached under divine afflatus, whether because of their true conviction that it was indeed God who used them as His mouthpiece, or because of their statesmanship, knowing full well that their words would have no impact and their threats no effect unless they came from God. But this does not in any way derogate from their courage and undeterrability: on the contrary, the recruitment of God Almighty and His blazing rage to reinforce and fortify their outbursts testifies to their determination to make themselves heard and listened to at all costs.

God had made the people a solemn promise that He would raise up prophets and put His words into their mouths—and He had enjoined the people to hearken to the prophets so raised (Deut. 18:15), an injunction later interpreted as vesting authority in God's prophets even to suspend and change God's law (B. *Yevamot* 90b, *Sifrei Deut.* 175). But the initial problem arose about the differentiation between those prophets who were truly God's prophets and those who purported to be divinely inspired and to prophesy God's words but who in reality were only impostors. The solution proffered in the Bible is unsatisfactory, because it leaves matters in suspense until after the event: "And if thou say in thine heart, 'How shall we know the word which the Lord hath not spoken?' When a prophet speaketh in the name of the Lord, if the thing follow not, nor come to pass, that is the thing which the Lord hath not spoken, but the prophet hath spoken it presumptuously: thou shalt not be afraid of him" (Deut. 18:21–22). In other words, if the prophecy eventually comes true, the prophet was true; if it does not come true, the prophet was false. It may perhaps be said that a prophet—except one who prophesies in the name of other gods and thus conclusively unmasks himself (M. *Sanhedrin* 11:6)—ought to be presumed to be a true prophet until proven false by supervening events. Even this presumption was restricted by Maimonides to apply only to prophecies of blessings; where the prophecies were of misfortunes and afflictions, the fact that in the event they did not come true need not be ascribed to the falsity of the prophecy, but ought rather to be credited to God's unfathomable mercy (*Yessodei HaTora* 9:4).

But there is a biblical record of undoubtedly true prophets whose competence was nevertheless challenged. God had ordered Moses to choose seventy elders and gather them in the tabernacle. "And the Lord came down in a cloud . . . and took of the spirit that was upon him, and gave it unto the seventy elders: and it came to pass that, when the spirit rested upon them, they prophesied, and did not cease. But there remained two of the men in the camp, the name of the one was Eldad, and the name of the other Medad; and the spirit rested upon them . . . but they went not out unto the tabernacle, and they prophesied in the camp. And there ran a young man, and told Moses, and said, 'Eldad and Medad do prophesy in the camp.' And Joshua the son of Nun, the servant of Moses, one of his young men, answered and said, 'My lord Moses, forbid them.' And Moses said unto him, 'Enviest thou for my sake? Would God that all the Lord's people were prophets, and that the Lord would put his spirit upon them,' " (Num. 11:25–29). It had been God's explicit will that the elders should all gather in the tabernacle and prophesy there; but notwithstanding their disobedience in remaining in the camp, Eldad and Medad partook of the divine spirit too, possibly because their decision to stay behind in the camp stemmed from their modesty and humility (B. *Sanhedrin* 17a). While God knew their motives and apparently accepted them, the people observed only their disobedience, and Moses' advisers seem to have thought that such disobedience ought not to be passed over in silence. But whatever sanction Moses might have regarded as appropriate in the circumstances, one thing was quite clear to him: they must not be forbidden to speak out and prophesy; the more prophets the better—would that all the people of Israel were prophets!

The advice which Joshua gave Moses, "forbid them," etymologically also bears the interpretation of "have them imprisoned"— and indeed was so rendered by an early authority (*Sifrei, Beha'alotkha* 96), with explicit reference to the fate of imprisonment that was later to befall the prophet Jeremiah (Jer. 37:18). If that be the true interpretation of the biblical text, this would be the very first instance of imprisonment being suggested as a curb to free speech—and, of course, the very first instance of the suggestion of imprisonment as a curb to free speech being indignantly dismissed out of hand. Not being known in biblical law as a mode of punishment, such imprisonment could only have served as a means either of vengeance or of precaution, neither of which appear to be an adequate reaction to utterances of the divine spirit.

More pragmatically seen, the true prophets were soon found to differ from the "false" ones by the import and contents of their prophecies. The true prophets were highly unpopular, whereas the "false" prophets commanded huge and enthusiastic audiences. The mostly gruesome forebodings of the true prophets fell on unwilling ears, and their uncompromising exposures and rigorous accusations aroused general resentment. Small wonder that they soon became a small minority of dissenters, whereas the great majority of prophets pleased and catered for the masses and accommodated the authorities with their optimistic prophecies and palatable comments. While talmudic tradition puts the total number of duly qualified and divinely inspired prophets at forty-eight males and seven females (B. *Megilla* 14a)—somewhat larger numbers are given by Nahmanides ad Deut. 4:2 and by *Seder Olam Rabba* 21—biblical figures indicate that there were hundreds of prophets ministering at one and the same time to the various sanctuaries and at the royal courts (cf. 1 Kings 18:19, 22:6). The minority of true prophets denounced the majority of their pretentious competitors in no uncertain terms, not only for leading the people astray (Jer. 23:13) and themselves leading dissolute lives (ibid. 14), but also for being the ultimate cause of the fall and destruction of Jerusalem (Lam. 4:13). They were accused of drunkenness and filthiness (Isa. 28:7–8) and of divining for money (Mic. 3:11): they "make my people err, they bite with their teeth and cry, 'Peace' " (ibid. 5). Jeremiah was obviously infuriated when he heard those loyal and optimistic court prophets prophesying "peace, peace, when there is no peace" (6:11, 14). The same freedom of speech that was enjoyed by the prophets whose prophecies were preserved and canonized was in fact enjoyed and exercised no less by the many prophets whose claim to divine inspiration found no such retrospective ratification at the hands of the canonizers. Nor is there a valid reason to assume that those optimistic court prophets were not also "sincere patriots, ardent lovers of the people and zealous in their devotion to state and sanctuary. They as well as the leaders of the state, who had the interest of the country at heart, resented the invectives and exaggerated accusations of Jeremiah and entertained a profound trust in God's attachment to Israel" (Heschel 482). They were blessed with prosperity and success during their lifetimes; the "true" prophets had to content themselves with the glory of immortality.

The majority—backed as it was by the powers that be—succeeded often enough in silencing the minority, however vociferous it may have been. When Amos prophesied that the king of Israel would die by the sword and his people would be led away into captivity, he had to "flee away into the land of Judah, and there eat bread, and prophesy there: But prophesy not again any more at Beth-el, for it is the king's chapel, and it is the king's court" (7:11–13). A more tragic fate befell the prophet Uriah, who had—like Jeremiah—prophesied the downfall of Jerusalem and

Judah and whom the king therefore wished to kill: he fled to
Egypt, but was brought back by force and decapitated (Jer.
26:20–23). Jeremiah himself was repeatedly put in prison (Jer.
26:8, 37:15) and even formally indicted "by the priests and the
prophets" for having "prophesied against this city, as ye have
heard with your ears" (26:11). The defense speech reported of
Jeremiah is worthy of quotation: "The Lord sent me to prophesy
against this house and against this city all the words that ye have
heard. Therefore now amend your ways and your doings, and
obey the voice of the Lord your God; and the Lord will repent Him
of the evil that He hath pronounced against you. As for me,
behold, I am in your hand: do with me as seemeth good and meet
unto you. But know ye for certain, that if ye put me to death, ye
shall surely bring innocent blood upon yourselves, and upon your
city, and upon the inhabitants thereof: for of a truth the Lord
hath sent me unto you to speak all these words in your ears" (ibid.
12–15). This speech resounds through the centuries as a warning cry of the man persecuted for voicing his convictions. In the
event, there "rose up certain elders of the land" who cited in
Jeremiah's defense the precedent of Micah, another prophet who
had prophesied the destruction of Jerusalem but had not been
killed by the king: by killing Jeremiah we might "procure great
evil against our souls" (ibid. 17–19). This defense prevailed, and
Jeremiah's life was spared.

Not only does the prophet unrelentingly speak out himself on
behalf of the oppressed and persecuted (Ezek. 18:18, 22:29; Mal.
3:5; Isa. 10:1–4; et. mult. al.), he also resents oppressed and
afflicted people who remain silent and do not vent their grievances: "as a sheep before her shearers is dumb, so he openeth not
his mouth" (Isa. 53:7)—and God Himself waits for the afflicted to
cry out (Exod. 22:22, 26).

The prohibition against cursing the rulers (Exod. 22:28) was
not allowed to stand in the way of the prophets when they felt
called upon to upbraid the kings. The prophet Nathan did not
hesitate to hurl the gravest accusations in the king's face and to
threaten him with the most atrocious divine retaliations (2 Sam.
12:9–11). When a king had committed judicial murder in order to
enrich himself, the prophet Elijah cursed him publicly. Openly
denouncing royal misconduct was regarded as paramount to any
respect for the king's majesty and even to compliance with the

divine injunction to honor the king. The prophet conjured God's wrath upon princes who misled the people, "for ye have eaten up the vineyard, the spoil of the poor is in your houses. What mean ye that ye beat my people to pieces, and grind the faces of the poor?" (Isa. 3:14–15).

The fact that even among the prophets it was only a minority that exhausted its freedom of speech to the brim and un-abashedly voiced all grievances against the ruling powers seems to indicate that that freedom was in those times the privilege of a select few. This assumption is fortified by the fact that those who did speak out did so under divine afflatus, seeking cover behind God's own inviolability and demanding immunity by virtue of potential divine wrath. Even taking all this for granted, the phenomenon of prophecy as a manifestation of freedom of speech remains of remarkable significance.

It is an old tradition that, with the destruction of the Temple, the gift of prophecy was taken away from the prophets and bestowed upon the scholars (B. *Bava Batra* 12a). Not only did the sages of the Talmud claim for themselves or their immediate predecessors some quasi-prophetic status, but they adduced scriptural authority for the proposition that the words of the sages are weightier than the words of prophets: the prophet must first qualify himself by giving "a sign or a wonder" (Deut. 13:2), whereas sages are to be obeyed solely "according to the law which they teach you" (Deut. 17:11; J. *Berakhot* 1:4, J. *Avoda Zara* 2:8). Small wonder that, once the sages had taken over, nobody ever again dared to claim the gift or competence of divine proph-ecy. Such pretenders to prophetic competency as would from time to time appear (mostly with messianic undertones) were by wide consensus decried and dismissed out of hand.

We have already observed (above, p. 2 ff.) that the hallmark of the creation of the Oral Law was doctrinal controversy, first between the Pharisees and the Sadducees and later between the many sects and schools within the Pharisaic domain. There were also many splinter groups—among them the Essenes, who laid their emphasis on austerity and spiritual purity; the various Dead Sea communities which each developed codes and rites of its own; many Apocalyptic sects with messianic aspirations (from whom the early Christian community emerged); and various Zealot groups concentrating on fighting the Romans and their collabora-

tors underground instead of waiting for a Messiah. It is significant that in this welter of controversy no attempt was ever made
to stifle free discussion. Although the Pharisees looked on Sadducean doctrine as heretical, there is no record of any proceedings
ever taken against the dissemination of such doctrines. However
intolerant one group was of the other insofar as religious dogma
and religious life-style were concerned, they would never contest
their respective rights to preach and propagate their own views.

We are concerned with the law as it developed within Pharisaic
doctrine. As we have seen, the law was developed out of differences of opinion. There is one institution, however, dating back
to biblical law, which does not quite fit into the pattern of free
exchanges and expressions even of dissenting opinions—and
that is the rebellious elder. In the context of the rules governing
the enforcement of judgments, it is written: "And the man that
will do presumptuously, and will not hearken unto the priest that
standeth to minister there before the Lord thy God, or unto the
judge, even that man shall die" (Deut. 17:12). On the face of it, the
capital offense here described is contempt of court and disobedience to judicial orders or priestly rules; but the talmudists were
hard put to give this offense a much more severe character so as
to render capital punishment more plausible. In the event, the
offense was restricted so as to apply to a dissenter from among the
judges who defied the majority—and thus is no longer the offense
it was on the literal interpretation of the text. In order to constitute the new offense it was laid down that the rebellious dissenter's view had first to be overruled on its merits by two
consecutive superior courts, and that it had not only to be held by
the dissenter but also to be acted upon by him (M. *Sanhedrin*
11:2). The dissenter had to have been duly ordained and qualified, "a sage from among the sages of Israel" (Maimonides,
Mamrim 3:4); and while he is allowed to continue holding his own
dissenting view as he pleases, he commits the offense when he
acts upon it or causes others to act upon it *(Sifrei Deut.* 155, B.
Sanhedrin 88b, T. *Sanhedrin* 14:12, J. *Sanhedrin* 11:3). Not
every kind of view gives rise to this offense: only views to the effect
that a certain act is permissible while according to the prevailing
majority that act is a criminal offense, or that a certain act is a
criminal offense while according to the prevailing majority it is
perfectly lawful (Maimonides, *Mamrim* 4:1).

A great talmudic scholar reports a Jerusalemite tradition according to which a rebellious elder was always at the mercy of the court; even if he was convicted, the court could forgive and discharge him. This tradition is reported not to have been followed elsewhere, so as not to multiply differences of opinion in Israel (B. *Sanhedrin* 88b, B. *Sota* 25a), the apprehension presumably being that the court's acquiescence might be interpreted as a license to follow the practice of the rebellious elder, and confusion might ensue as to what really was the practice to be followed. The rejection of this tradition and the rationale for its rejection appear—notwithstanding their endorsement by Maimonides (*Mamrim* 3:4)—to be wholly academic, as the rebellious elder could not be lawfully tried anywhere outside Jerusalem (M. *Sanhedrin* 11:2) and the acceptance or rejection of the procedure followed in Jerusalem by scholars elsewhere would have no practical relevancy.

There is no record of any person ever having been tried on charges of being a rebellious elder (the surmise that Jesus might have been so charged has long been conclusively refuted). But the talmudists sought and found other ways and means of giving some punitive expression to their disapproval of obstinate dissenters.

The most famous heretic of talmudical times was Elisha ben Abuya (who lived in the second century). The story goes that this great sage was one of four who "entered the garden," that is, engaged in theosophical and philosophical studies and in "the science of the unknown," and eventually "demolished the plants." While the three others emerged with their faith unshaken, he came out disillusioned with God, His creation and His laws, and thenceforth openly disavowed them (B. *Hagiga* 14b–15b). His disciple, Rabbi Me'ir, one of the great mishnaic teachers (*tanna'im*), did not sever relations with him, but is reported to have continued showing him reverence, even while witnessing his flagrant breaches of the Sabbath laws (J. *Hagiga* 2:1). The sages later explained Me'ir's conduct toward his teacher by quoting an old proverb: he found an unripe pomegranate—its fruit he ate, its husk he cast away (B. *Hagiga* 15b). But Me'ir appears to have been the only one of Elisha's many colleagues and disciples who did not shun him; the community at large—including, according to talmudic legend, even the harlots—avoided him and went so far in their disdain as to suspect him of treasonable collaboration with the Romans (J. *Hagiga* 2:1).

While in Elisha's case no formal proscription seems to have been called for, several cases are reported in which outspoken and obstinate dissent was visited with *niddui*. This is the term employed in early talmudic literature for the punishment of an offender by his isolation from, and his being held in enforced contempt by, the community at large. Originally, *niddui* was the expulsion of a member from the order of the Pharisees, for it was feared that a continuing association with one who failed to maintain proper standards of conduct would defile the other colleagues (cf. Finkelstein I 77). Later, the *niddui* was limited to a duration of not more than thirty days, with a possible extension for another thirty days if it had been of no avail; if the continuation or aggravation of the sanction was considered necessary, a *herem* could be imposed, which amounted to virtual ostracism (B. *Mo'ed Kattan* 16a). In many cases, the *niddui* was a mere formality expressing disapproval, without any practical effect on the standing of the scholar in the community.

Take, for instance, the case of Akavia ben Mahalalel (who lived in the first century). He was a great teacher of undisputed authority, and it was said of him that there was nobody like him in wisdom and fear of sin (M. *Eduyot* 3:6). In four distinct matters of law he dissented from the majority as a lone dissenter, whereupon the following exchange of speeches is reported to have taken place: "They said to him, 'Akavia, reconsider your view in these four matters, and we will make you president of the court in Israel.' Said he to them, 'I would rather be called a fool all my life than for one moment appear wicked before God, and nobody shall say of me that for the sake of a sinecure I went back on my word' " (ibid.). The Mishna concludes with this laconic statement: "They declared a *niddui* on him, he died during the *niddui*, and the court had his coffin stoned" (ibid.). But this report was then and there denied on high authority: "God forbid that a *niddui* was declared on Akavia, who had nobody like him in wisdom and fear of sin; the *niddui* was declared on Elazar ben Hanokh, who dissented in the matter of the purity of hands, and when he died the court sent a messenger to place a stone on his coffin. Which is to teach that when a man dies during *niddui*, his coffin is stoned" (ibid.).

Whether a *niddui* was in fact declared on Akavia, or whether his name was indeed mistaken for that of the otherwise wholly unknown Elazar ben Hanokh—at any rate it would appear that the *niddui* came to stoning (i.e., placing a stone on) the coffin and nothing more. The rule that the coffin of a man dying during *niddui* is to be stoned by placing one big stone thereon is restated in later sources in the context of the adversities involved in the *niddui* for the living and consisting mainly of having to conduct oneself as if one were in mourning (B. *Berakhot* 19a, B. *Mo'ed Kattan* 15a).

This is well illustrated by the famous story of Rabbi Eliezer. The legend goes that Eliezer tried in vain to persuade the majority that he was right and they were wrong. When they refused to accept his view, he invoked divine intervention on his behalf. He said, "This tree shall prove that I am right," whereupon the tree was uprooted and moved of its own motion for a hundred (others say four hundred) yards. But the scholars rejoined, "Trees are no evidence." Then he said, "Water shall prove it," and the water flowed backwards. They rejoined, "Water is no evidence." He said, "The walls of this house shall prove it," and the walls of the house started to fall down. Rabbi Yehoshua, one of the majority, got angry at the walls and shouted, "When scholars debate the law, it is none of your business," whereupon the walls ceased to fall, out of respect for Yehoshua, but would not stand erect again, out of respect for Eliezer. Then he said, "If I am right, heaven will prove it," whereupon a voice came from heaven and said, "The law is as Eliezer says it is." But Yehoshua stood on his feet and said, "The law is not in heaven: it has been handed down to us from Mount Sinai, and we no longer take notice of heavenly voices; the law which we were handed down provides that decisions are taken by majority vote." The story has two postscripts, one relating the reaction of God, and the other relating the reaction of men. As for the reaction of God, the prophet Elijah is said to have descended from heaven and to have reported that God had smiled and said, "My children have defeated Me." And as for the reaction of men, they held a council and decided to declare a *niddui* on Eliezer. Rabbi Akiva volunteered to notify him of the *niddui,* and having donned mourning attire went to Eliezer's house and sat down at a distance of four hundred yards from him. Asked Eliezer, "Why is today different from other days?" He replied, "My master, it looks

as if your colleagues were isolating themselves from you." Whereupon he rent his clothes, took off his shoes, sat on the earth, and
wept (B. *Bava Metzia* 59b).

The imposition of a *niddui* in this particular case appears
especially inappropriate, as the majority rule could not very well
have been established were it not for the existence and enunciation of a dissenting opinion. Perhaps it was imposed in order to
demonstrate that there would be no discrimination between obstinate dissenters of high repute and of no repute, or that no
divine predilection would be allowed to let any scholar evade his
earthly liabilities.

Among the twenty-four offenses for which a *niddui* could be
imposed, the following may be considered restrictions on freedom
of speech: insulting a scholar, even after his death; calling any
man a slave; adducing God's name or authority in trifling matters; any connection, activity, or speech of a scholar which might
bring him or scholarship into disrepute; disobedience to settled
law on the strength of self-reliant arguments; insisting on minority views overruled by the majority; and imposing a *niddui* without sufficient cause (Maimonides, *Talmud Tora* 6:14; *Yorei Dei'a*
334:44). The offense of misusing the *niddui* had to be created
because not only the courts but also individuals could impose it:
we find creditors imposing it on delinquent debtors (B. *Mo'ed
Kattan* 16a) and individual scholars imposing it for their own
vindication from insults or contempt (ibid., *Maharik* 168–169,
Maharyu 163), though this practice was deprecated in no uncertain terms (Maimonides, *Talmud Tora* 7:13; *Tur, Yorei Dei'a* 334;
Yorei Dei'a 243:9).

Although courts were urged not to pronounce *niddui* against
judges, scholars, or elders (B. *Mo'ed Kattan* 17a, J. *Mo'ed Kattan*
3:1)—and in talmudical times such pronouncements seem to
have been very rare indeed—the ban became the principal instrument for enforcing authority in the Middle Ages. Its prevelance
was in no small degree due to the predominant role which excommunication played in the Church. Some features of the penances
later inflicted on excommunicated Jews were manifestly taken
over from Church practices (Abrahams 66 ff.), but the more
frequently scholars used the *herem* and the lighter *niddui*, and
the more common they became, the less impact and impression
did they make. In the event they became the standard rabbinic

reaction to all forms of deviation or nonconformity considered incompatible with or dangerous to established orthodoxy. As such they are even made use of by orthodox rabbis to the present day, but as neither the person afflicted nor the public at large regard themselves as bound by them, they have ceased to have any practical or deterrent effect.

Mention should be made of the most famous (or notorious) *herem* ever imposed, namely that on Barukh (Benedict) Spinoza in 1656. He was excommunicated by the rabbinical court in Amsterdam for his abandonment of orthodoxy and for his embracing of pantheism, which was held incompatible with traditional Jewish beliefs. Not unlike Elisha ben Abuya, he had tasted of forbidden fruits and mustered the courage to enter a garden of his own making; and not unlike Akavia ben Mahalalel, he was offered—and contemptuously rejected—a huge bribe if he would refrain from publishing his heretical views. It is true that his excommunication followed his voluntary separation from the Jewish community and was not the cause of it; but it had the effect within the Jewish world for many generations of stamping him as a contemptible renegade.

While total excommunication—or civil death—was rightly regarded as the gravest punishment that could—and ought to—be imposed on apostates, we find both lesser sanctions, such as will ensue only in a future world, and even harder punishments, such as physical death, laid down in the law for those who disavowed their God and the divine law.

The general presumption is that all Israel are righteous people (Isa. 60:21) and therefore will be allowed to partake of the blessings of the future life (M. *Sanhedrin* 10:1). Excepted from this general rule is he who denies the resurrection of the dead, or he who denies the divinity of the Torah, or the *epikoros* (ibid.). The Talmud defines an *epikoros* as one who holds the sages, the exponents of divine law, in contempt, or one who interprets divine law according to his own whims (B. *Sanhedrin* 99a–b). Maimonides defines him as one who goes "after the foolishness of his heart and knowingly and brazenly violates the laws of the Torah, saying 'There is no offense in that' " (*Akkum* 2:5). The list of people who have no share in the world-to-come has further been extended to slanderers, who by their speech make other people's faces turn pale (M. *Avot* 3:11). Maimonides also excluded from any prospects of future life the atheists, "who say there is no God and the world has no ruler," those who believe in more than one god or in a god of flesh and blood or other organic substance, those who believe in God but deny His omnipotence or omniscience or the divinity of the Torah or "even of a single word or a single letter" thereof, or who deny the authenticity and binding force of Oral Law (*Teshuva* 1:6–8). Nay, even a believer in the divinity of God's law, if he says, "What good will it do to me to cling to the Jews, that miserable and persecuted people? I had better cling to those who have the might and the power," and he joins them and lives according to their laws, is nothing better than an atheist and his future fate is the same (ibid. 9)—he must indeed be an accomplished apostate to act and speak as he does (Ravad ad loc.).

As we have seen, inflammatory speeches propagating idolatry are a capital offense (Deut. 13:7–12, M. *Sanhedrin* 7:10), but the threat of forfeiting one's life was also extended to informers (to the Inquisition) and *epikorsim*, "because they endanger the community and cause the recreancy of the people from their God" (Maimonides, *Akkum* 10:1). But there is no forfeiting human life outside the realm of criminal law, and the threat there expressed is directed not to organs of law enforcement but rather to the public at large, indicating that the life of such an informer or *epikoros* is not worth living or being saved (ibid.), and reflecting the ultimate disdain of the waste and dissipation of a life devoted to treasonable heresy.

The suppression—by excommunication or other means—of dissenting views, except in extreme cases of apostasy, is, however, quite contrary to and out of tune with the general trend of Jewish law and its philosophy. We have already seen that all the various conflicting opinions in matters of law, including both majority and minority views, were alike considered to have emanated from the One Living God (B. *Eruvin* 13b, B. *Gittin* 6b, J. *Berakhot* 1:4, J. *Yevamot* 1:6). The saying of the Preacher that the words of the wise, the "masters of assemblies," are all given from one shepherd (Eccl. 12:11) was interpreted to refer to the differences of opinion among the sages in matters of law, the "masters of assemblies" being the sages who assemble together to discuss and settle the law: you will find in their assemblies some who permit and some who prohibit the same act, some who declare a person or a thing in given circumstances to be pure and some who declare them in the same circumstances to be impure, some who admit and some who reject certain evidence or certain offerings. Any listener will ask himself, "How can I find out what the law now really is?" But that is what is meant by the words "which are given from one shepherd": one God has given them all, they have all come from the Lord, as it is written: "And God spake all these words" (Exod. 20:1). Therefore "you had better make your ear as a horn to hear and open your heart to understand the words of purifiers and the words of impurifiers, those of permitters and those of prohibiters, of qualifiers and disqualifiers, of admitters and rejectors" (B. *Hagiga* 3b; the version in T. *Sota* 7:12 differs slightly: "make your heart as if into compartments [lit. 'rooms within rooms'] and put therein the words," etc.). No ready-made prescription is offered for the process of understanding here advocated. The only thing which is well settled is that no amount of "understanding" will, as a matter of law, provide sufficient cause for preferring any one view to any other view. The various methods of choosing one view for elevation to the rank of positive law (Halakha) are predetermined by law and have nothing to do with any individual understanding. Perhaps what is meant is just the comprehension of the logical, sociological, and historical processes at work; it is by analyzing these and similar processes that each of the divergent views will be appreciated on its own merits, regardless of how the law is eventually settled.

A third-century sage pronounced that if the law had been given "clear-cut," nothing would have been left for scholars to discuss— fortunately, however, the law was not at all clear-cut, but to every aspect of the law "there were forty-nine shades of pure and forty-nine shades of impure," and on every norm there were many conflicting views, and all likewise the words of the One Living God (*Sopherim* 16:5–7). The verse "God hath spoken once, twice I have heard this" (Ps. 62:11) was taken to mean that every one of God's words was capable of many meanings, but no two words of God have the same meaning (B. *Sanhedrin* 34a). The prophet's allegory that God's word is like fire "and like a hammer that breaketh the rock in pieces" (Jer. 23:29) was elaborated upon to the effect that like blastings of the hammer so does God's word bring forth myriads of sparkles—myriads of sparkling views (ibid.; in B. *Shabbat* 88b the version is that God's word is diffused into seventy tongues). Only very rarely do we find expressions of regret at opinions being divided (e.g., see M. *Bava Batra* 9:10); normally the plurality of views expressed and the possibility of choice between conflicting normative propositions is extolled as a wholly beneficial phenomenon.

Maimonides dismisses as "ugly and indecent" the notion that divergencies of views among the sages could possibly be attributed to disputatiousness or forgetfulness or any other human frailty (Introduction to Commentary on the Mishna). He explains these divergencies as resulting from differences of approach and intellect, justifying them with the biblical predilection for, or indulgence of, the judges and sages that you will find available in your own day (Deut. 17:9 as interpreted in B. *Rosh HaShana* 25b), and whose approach and intellect will naturally differ from those of judges and sages of other ages. If divergent views dating from different generations are each entitled to expression and preservation, there can be no justification for any different treatment of contemporaneous divergencies.

A mishnaic tradition has it that a conflict of opinions will "endure" if the conflict is "for the sake of heaven"; it will not "endure" if it is not "for the sake of heaven" (M. *Avot* 5:17). Conflicts for the sake of heaven are there illustrated by the disputations between the famous schools of Hillel and Shammai; conflicts not for the sake of heaven are, for instance, those engendered by the rebellion against Moses of Korah and his company (Num. 17). The "endurance" or perseverance of scholarly conflicts conducted with the *animus sanctus*, that is, in the course of interpreting and implementing divine law, and for that purpose, signifies not only that all the divergent views were to be placed on record for all posterity (M. *Eduyot* 1:5–6), but also that the holders of the various views, including those whose views would not ultimately prevail, were revered and immortalized for the very views they held and advanced. On the other hand, rebels who failed, like Korah, are remembered mainly for their downfall and punishment, and the conflict which they initiated died with them.

While the free expression of dissenting views in scholarly disputes, or otherwise "for the sake of heaven," was legitimate and, indeed, praiseworthy, the king was given power to visit expressions of rebellion or sedition even with capital punishment. The mandate and authority which the people gave to Joshua, "Whosoever he be that doth rebel against thy commandment . . . he shall be put to death" (Josh. 1:18), was perpetuated to apply to all kings, and was later extended to cover also insults to the royal majesty (Maimonides, *Melakhim* 3:8). Kings were, albeit retrospectively, advised to spare the lives of recreants and content themselves with imprisonment or floggings to vindicate their offended majesty (ibid.).

Freedom of thought and speech is not, however, the privilege of scholars or prophets. The general "human" right to have and express one's own views even though they may differ from all others is attested to in an early aggadic source (though not in normative texts). The legend goes that when Moses was about to die, he addressed God as follows: " 'Creator of all the Worlds, you know the mind of every man, and you know that no man's mind resembles the mind of any other man. Now that my hour comes to take leave of my people, may it please my Lord: if you are going to appoint a leader (or: ruler) over them, do appoint a man who will tolerate (lit: suffer) each and every one of them according to his own particular mind.' And that is why God is called 'God of the spirits of all flesh' (Num. 27:16)—not 'God of the spirit,' but 'God of all the many spirits' " (*Bamidbar Rabba* 21; *Tanhuma, Pinhas* 1). We have here not only the recognition of the diversity of human minds and thoughts, and of the legitimacy of each and all of them, but also—and even more significantly—the explicit postulate that the rulers of the day must so govern their people as to bring that diversity to effective display and allow it to unfold in unfettered expression.

There is also a rule of liturgical law which is based upon the plurality and variety of human thought. When one encounters large masses of people, it is prescribed that the following benediction be said: "Blessed be the Penetrator of Secrets." As everyone knows and sees, each and every individual among those masses of people has a distinctive face and physiognomy different from all the others, but in addition, all of them have different minds and thoughts and views; and that vast diversity of minds and thoughts and views can be penetrated only by God—they are His secrets to cherish (B. *Berakhot* 58a, T. *Berakhot* 7:2).

God is seen as if holding the secrets of men's thoughts in some kind of trust. However well and inescapably He penetrates and

knows them, He will not misuse His knowledge of them, no
matter how bad and wicked they may be, for purposes of incrimi-
nation. No offense is criminal unless it is constituted by an overt
act—and the act is an offense when it violates a prohibition of the
law. But God is said never to "add a thought to an act," that is,
never to take the wickedness of the thought or intent into consideration in order to render an otherwise legitimate act criminal (B.
Kiddushin 39b, B. *Hullin* 142a). Thoughts are free and will never
be punished, even when they violate explicit legal norms, such as
"Thou shalt not hate thy brother in thy heart" (Lev. 19:17) or
"Thou shalt love the Lord thy God with all thine heart" (Deut. 6:5);
but it is not only thoughts that are never punishable because they
cannot amount to overt acts—even speech is not considered an
overt act and therefore not punishable (B. *Makkot* 15b–16a). To
this latter rule there are some exceptions: perjury, for instance, is
considered an overt act, as are cursing and wickedly misusing the
name of God (B. *Temura* 3a–b; Maimonides, *Sanhedrin* 18:1),
and, as already mentioned, incitement to idolatry (Deut. 13:6,
10). But apart from these exceptions, speech and thought alike
are excluded from the operation of the criminal laws.

   The question whether the intent to commit an act can ever give
rise even to civil liability was the subject-matter of one of the
many disputes between the Schools of Shammai and Hillel. The
former held that the biblical term "all manner of trespass" (Exod.
22:9) was wide enough to include inchoate wrongs which were
intended but not completed, while the latter held that mere intent
could never amount to "all manner of trespass" (B. *Kiddushin*
42a, B. *Bava Metzia* 44a). The law was settled to the effect that so
long as the intent had not crystallized at least in instructions
expressly given for carrying it into effect, it could not give rise to
any civil liability (Maimonides, *Gezeila vaAveida* 3:11). As far as
criminal liability is concerned, not even express instructions to
carry a criminal intent into effect would suffice, for criminal
liability attaches only to the perpetrator of the act himself, and
there can be no agent for the commission of a crime (B. *Kiddushin* 42b et al.). The maxim "a matter kept in the heart is no
matter at all" (B. *Kiddushin* 49b–50a) was first enunciated in the
law of contracts but was eventually also applied to negate liability
in general for any thoughts or designs which remained in the
heart and were not transposed into action.

It is a commonplace that, in any legal system, freedom of thought and speech is warranted and characterized by the thought and speech not being criminal offenses or civil wrongs. Where criminal or civil sanction is attached to thought or speech, such freedom is denied; where no such sanction need be apprehended, thought and speech are free. By taking all thought and most speech out of the operation of the criminal law, a lawgiver accords the maximum of freedom which within his competence he is capable of according.

As distinguished from enforceable law, however, Judaism also comprises, of course, theology and ethics. While the prohibition of libel and slander (Lev. 19:16) cannot serve as the cause for criminal prosecutions or civil liability, because only speech and no overt act of wrongdoing is involved, the theological and ethical import and significance of this prohibition cannot be overrated (see above, Chapter 5). There can be nothing as reprehensible in the eyes of Jewish tradition as the exploitation of freedom of speech for the purpose of defaming or injuring another person.

If it is the glory of God to conceal His secrets, the glory of kings on earth is to "search out all matters" (Prov. 25:2). God created all the minds and knows them all, but He created and diversified them for a purpose, and that is, to have all matters on earth investigated in the most variegated and multifarious manner possible.

The notion of the independence of the spirit and the individualization of thought and reasoning made further progress with the evolution of medieval Jewish philosophy. One scholar compared the unquestioning and unthinking believers to a company of blind men who can move forward only by one clasping the hand of the other and all of them "blindly" depending upon the one "seer" who leads the train (Bahya Ibn Pakuda, Hovot HaLevavot 1:2). Anyone whom God has blessed with intellect and with the drive and curiosity to investigate on his own, by rational methods, even into such fundamentals as the very existence and the omniscience and other attributes of God, is in duty bound to make use of the capabilities and talents that God has bestowed on him by embarking on such investigations; a failure to do so shows but lack of wisdom (ibid. 3). In the same vein, a later philosopher held that every man of a wise heart "may freely investigate into all fundamentals of the faith and interpret Scripture in such a way as will, according to his own approach, lead him to the truth" (Joseph Albo, *Sefer HaIkkarim* 1:2).

Let me conclude with the good advice of a famous sixteenth-century sage, Judah Loew of Prague (Maharal): "Even if his words spoken are directed against faith and religion, do not tell a man not to speak and suppress his words. Otherwise there will be no clarification in religious matters. On the contrary, one should tell a person to express whatever he wants . . . and he should never claim that he would have said more, had he been given the opportunity. . . . Thus my opinion is contrary to what some people think. They think that when it is forbidden to speak against religion, religion is strengthened; but it is not so. The elimination of the opinions of those who are opposed to religion undermines religion and weakens it" (*Be'er HaGola* 1, translation by Gordis, 210). If it be said that this, too, is a dissenting view, the more and better the evidence it provides for the freedom of dissenting speech.

13

FREEDOM OF INFORMATION

In curious contrast to the liberality and generosity which the talmudists displayed insofar as freedom of thought and dissent was concerned, they and their successors throughout the ages viewed with well-nigh hysterical fears the dissemination of written material suspected of nonconformity.

There are several allusions in Scripture to the praiseworthiness of accumulating general knowledge, including the wisdom of other nations (e.g., as to King Solomon: 1 Kings 5:10–14; or Daniel 1:17, 9:2; et al.). Of the king of Assyria it is reported that he wrote books "to rail on the Lord God of Israel and to speak against Him" (2 Chron. 32:17), but there is no biblical record of those books having been destroyed even after victory. On the other hand, we find the king of Judah cutting the roll which contained Jeremiah's prophecies with a penknife and casting it "into the fire that was on the hearth, until all the roll was consumed in the fire" (Jer. 36:23), probably the first recorded instance of book burning.

Oddly enough, talmudical law provides for the burning of books not only, and not primarily, where heathen books are concerned. The rule is that a book containing the Torah, the Holy Law, may not be used or read if it was written by a heathen or even held in his possession (B. *Gittin* 45b). This rule was in the third century elaborated to the effect that while a Torah written by a heathen must be stored away and ought not to be used, a Torah written by a *min* must be burned (ibid.). *Min* is ordinarily interpreted as meaning a Christian, and there are indications to show that the danger posed to the true faith by Christians was worse and

129

greater than that of the heathen, if only because the former "know better and turn apostate," while the latter "are ignorant and apostate" (B. *Shabbat* 116a); and the burning of holy books written by Christians may have been intended to prevent them from writing those books for their own missionary purposes. However that may be, the rule was changed again by Maimonides, who restated it as follows: "It is prohibited to burn or destroy any holy books or their commentaries or annotations. Whosoever destroys them is liable to be flogged. This applies to holy books written by Jews in holiness. But a Jewish heretic (*epikoros*), when he wrote the book of the Torah, it must be burned notwithstanding all the Holy Names therein, because he did not believe in the holiness of God and did not write it to His glory, but did regard it as any other book. And as this was his attitude, the Holy Name was not consecrated—and it will be a good deed to burn his book so as not to leave any remembrance either to *epikorsim* or to their works. But Holy Names (in holy books) written by non-Jews are to be stored away, as are all holy books written by non-Jews" (*Yessodei HaTora* 6:8). An *epikoros* is, in the view of Maimonides, comparable to a heathen, because like the idolater he denies God and the divinity of the law; but while the heathen has no obligation to God and is not bound by His law, the *epikoros* is a traitor to God's cause and must be barred from any intercourse or communication (*Akkum* 2:5). This ostracism logically extends to everything written by him. A later authority expressed the view that if such a heretic writes a holy book, it must be presumed that he writes it for purposes of idolatry (*Beit Yossef* ad *Yorei Dei'a* 281).

The jealousy with which the talmudists watched over the monopoly to write the holy books is easily explained by the fact that these books served not only purposes of study but more particularly purposes of ritual and liturgy. They had to be "pure" and "holy" to serve their purposes, and impure hands would impurify them. Considerations of this kind do not apply to books intended for study or pleasure—but it would stand to reason that books suspected of propagating idolatry or apostasy would be dealt with by the law differently from books which appear to be innocuous.

Reading profane or "external" books was regarded by some sages as an impediment to having a share in the world-to-come (M. *Sanhedrin* 10:1), and opinions were divided as to what the profane books may be. There is early authority to the effect that the books of Homer (presumably in the Greek original) are legitimate reading material (J. *Sanhedrin* 17:1). The admonition from the mouth of the wisest of men that "of making many books there is no end, and much study is a weariness of the flesh" (Eccl. 12:12), was taken as a clear indication of the difference between such books as provide sheer pleasure and such as require hard study; it was only books which were apt to cause "weariness of the flesh" by hard study that were to be advised against. Reading Homer was "like reading a letter" and required no exertion—and was therefore permissible.

The books of Homer are mentioned in another early source as the subject of a dispute as to whether they "impurify the hands." The law is that books which are constantly or frequently used are apt to impurify, whereas books used or handled only rarely are not. The Sadducees held that the books of Homer impurify—an indication to the effect that at least among the Sadducees Homer was rather popular. The Pharisees, on the other hand, held that impurity follows the liking: the better-liked books are, the more are they impurifying; the holy books are very much liked, therefore impurifying; Homer's books are very much disliked, therefore not impurifying (M. *Yadayim* 4:6). It would thus appear that the matter had been reduced to a question of taste—unless the Pharisaic view is taken as normatively determining which books are to be liked and which are to be disliked. Not all the holy books as now canonized in the Bible were always treated alike for this purpose. Opinions were divided as to whether the books of Esther, Ecclesiastes, and even the Song of Songs were not essentially too unhallowed to impurify (M. *Yadayim* 3:5, B. *Megilla* 7a). In the same vein, doubts were expressed as to whether books like Ecclesiastes or the Proverbs ought to be canonized (B. *Shabbat* 30b).

Books which were not canonized, even though their canonization was considered and debated, are in talmudic parlance called "external" books. The admonition against reading them may have stemmed from the apprehension that they might be mistaken for holy books. Although the reader of external books is said to jeopardize his share in the world-to-come, we find the sages themselves relying on external books and quoting them as authority for the most pious statements (the book of Ben Sira, for instance, is singled out as prohibited reading in B. *Sanhedrin* 100b, but quoted as authority in B. *Hagiga* 13a, B. *Yevamot* 63b, B. *Ketuvot* 110b, B. *Bava Batra* 98b and 146a, B. *Nidda* 16b, and B. *Bava Kamma* 92b). It has been suggested that the prohibition related only to "reading" the external books in the same way in which the holy books are "read," namely, as part of the liturgy; in the same way in which God is said to be grieved when He hears the holy Song of Songs sung in bars and taverns (B. *Sanhedrin* 101a, T. *Sanhedrin* 12:10), so will He be grieved to hear unholy books read in places of worship.

The rule permitting the reading of Homer was stated to include also "all books written from now on" (J. *Sanhedrin* 17:1). In another source, "all books written from now on" are lumped together not with Homer but with Ben Sira—as not impurifying the hands (T. *Yadayim* 2:13). Indeed, like both Homer and Ben Sira, books written from now on cannot be "holy books," the redaction of the canon being final and completed; and as far as impurity of the hands is concerned, the canonized books occupy an exclusive position. But whether "all books written from now on" will also, in common with both Homer and Ben Sira, make innocuous reading, the one for pleasure and the other for wise instruction, is quite another question: it could not, in the nature of things, be foreseen what "all books written from now on" might look like. And when it eventually became evident what some of those books were about, the rule permitting their reading was soon superseded by an elaborate net of prohibitive norms.

The transition from the permissive to the prohibitive norm is strikingly echoed by later corruptions of the name of Homer. Originally the name of Homer stood, of course, for the archetype of famous authors of belles-lettres (cf. *Arukh*, s.v. *merom*, and addendum by Mussafia: "the head of Greek poets is Homerus, and his books are until the present day considered important among the nations; they contain talks and quarrels between the gods"), and "Homeric books" became synonymous with fiction (Krochmal XI 5). But when the books had been outlawed, commentators started to misread the Greek "Homer" by deriving it from Hebrew or Hebraized roots to which appropriate meanings were then attributed, such as "*Hamira* books, so named because they convert the true religion for lies" (Bartenura ad M. *Yadayim* 4:6), or "*Meram* books, which contest the holy law, so named because they are rejected by God and due to be eliminated" (Maimonides, Commentary ad M. *Yadayim* 4:6). The books which were mentioned only as not impurifying although read and used, ended up by being—wrongly—identified with prohibited books. And it is no longer ascertainable whether the true Homer would still be included in what have now become *Hamira* or *Meram* books.

In fact there is a clear differentiation between Homeric books (the reading of which is permitted) and books of the *minim* (the reading of which is prohibited) even in one of the texts relating to impurity of hands (T. *Yadayim* 2:13). That the prohibition did indeed apply only to books of the *minim* is manifest from the rule that if a fire breaks out on a Sabbath, they are not to be saved but let to burn; and on working days they must actively be thrown into the fire (T. *Shabbat* 13:5, B. *Shabbat* 116a). On the occasion of the enunciation of this rule, R. Tarfon (end of 1st cent.) is reported to have asserted that if ever such a book came into his hands, he would burn it himself (ibid.). There is no record of any such burning of books ever having taken place, either by R. Tarfon or at all, but the talk of burning in connection with books seems to have been widespread—we even find one great scholar propounding that in Scripture itself there are many passages which ought to be burned (B. *Hullin* 60b).

On the question of what kind of books the books of the *minim* really were, opinions are divided. The earliest and most authoritative definition was given by R. Yishma'el (2d cent.) to the effect that they are books which "arouse hatred, envy, and rivalry between Israel and their Father in Heaven" (T. *Shabbat* 13:5, B. *Shabbat* 116a)—and in respect of such books the psalmist said, "Do not I hate them, O Lord, that hate Thee? and am not I grieved with those that rise up against Thee? I hate them with perfect hatred: I count them mine enemies" (Ps. 139: 21–22). By this definition, the books of the *minim* would be those which incite, or are intended or calculated to incite, defection from God and His law. Among later commentators we find one confining "books of the *minim*" to holy writ written by non-Jews for purposes of idolatry (Rashi ad B. *Shabbat* 116a), another restricting them to Sadducean books in which the binding interpretation of the law is heretically rejected (Asheri ad *Sanhedrin* 11:3). The meaning of *minim* does not in fact lend itself to a definition which would be valid for all periods and all contexts; each period had *minim* of its own. In some contexts *minim* is synonymous with idolaters (e.g., B. *Avoda Zara* 26b); in another, *minim* denotes Christians as distinguished from idolaters (e.g., B. *Shabbat* 116a); in yet another, *minim* is used as describing Jewish transgressors and heretics (e.g., B. *Berakhot* 29a, B. *Hullin* 13b, B. *Horayot* 11a).

The ultimate statement of the law is to be found in the Maimonidean code and reads as follows: "Many books have been written by idolaters for purposes of idolatry, what its principles are and what its practices and its laws. God has commanded us not to read in those books at all. . . . It is forbidden even to look at the pictures. . . . All these prohibitions have one purpose, and that is not to turn to idolatry. . . . And not only idolatry proper is what one may not turn to even in thought, but every idea which may cause a person to uproot any of the principles of the Torah. We are admonished not to entertain it and not to consider it, lest we be drawn after the contemplations of our hearts, for human reason is short, and not everybody is capable of discovering the whole truth; and if every person goes after the imaginations of his heart he might end up by destroying the world owing to the deficiency of his reason. . . . A man may, for instance, contemplate the singularity of the Creator, thinking maybe He exists, maybe not; what is above and what is below, what in front and what in back; or he may think of prophecy, maybe it is true, maybe it is false; or of the Torah, maybe it is divine, maybe it is not—but he does not know what measures to apply and what tests to use in order to arrive at the truth, and hence might arrive at *minut*. This is what the Torah warned us of, 'that you seek not after your own heart and your own eyes, after which ye use to go awhoring' (Num. 15:39)—that is to say, that not each of you should go after his own heart and indulge in the illusion that his reason is apt to attain the truth. The sages said, 'after your heart'—leads to *minut;* 'after your eyes'—leads to whoring . . ." (*Akkum* 2:2–3).

The rule thus formulated has an express negative aspect and an implied positive one. As a negative injunction it prohibits the reading of idolatrous literature; but there is implied in the reasoning an exhortation to read—and possibly to read exclusively—only such literature as is calculated to strengthen the true faith. Any reading material that is liable to arouse any doubts as to any of the dogmatic principles of the true faith will have to be relegated to the realm of idolatrous—or quasi-idolatrous—literature and ought to be caught in the prohibition. The danger of defection—which is the rationale of the prohibition—is present not only where there is a direct incitement to idolatry, but also where devotion and loyalty are undermined by more subtle means. It is literature which is inimical to an unflinching adherence to the true faith and to an unswerving obedience to divine law which the law must—quasi in self-defense—suppress.

It is perhaps one of the ironies of legal history that the philosophical work of Maimonides himself was eventually caught within the ambit of the prohibition he had formulated. The immediate cause for such scholars as Yonah Gerondi, Solomon ben Abraham, and Meir Halevi Abulafia (all in the thirteenth century) banning the Maimonidean book and prohibiting its study was his preoccupation with, and expertise in, Greek and particularly Aristotelian philosophy; but the book could well have also fallen under the Maimonidean heading of reading material likely to foster independent reasoning and hence arouse all sorts of possible doubts.

As far as Greek philosophy is concerned, it was laid down, at a time when hellenization became an acute danger to Judaism, that the Greek language and Greek wisdom should not be taught to children (M. *Sota* 9:14). It is very doubtful whether this rule was ever observed; at any rate we find reports of schools in which Greek language and Greek wisdom were taught (B. *Sota* 49b, B. *Bava Kamma* 83a). A disciple is reported to have asked his master whether he might be allowed to study Greek wisdom now that he had completed the study of the whole of the Torah; he got an affirmative answer, with the reservation that, as you must engage in the study of the Torah day and night (Josh. 1:8), you have to find for the study of Greek a time that is neither day nor night (B. *Menahot* 99b). The logistic difficulties involved do not necessarily detract from the substantive affirmation.

The notion that you must first master the whole of the Torah before you can be allowed to engage in external studies lies at the root of a ban proclaimed by the rabbis of Barcelona, early in the fourteenth century, against anybody studying "the books of the Greeks on natural sciences and theology" who has not yet attained the age of twenty-five years and not yet "filled his belly with the delicacies of the Torah" (Rashba, *Responsa* 1:416, 715). It is noteworthy that medical books were expressly excluded from the ban, because the Torah allowed physicians to heal, and they ought not to be denied the instruction they need to carry out their profession (ibid.). On the other hand, books of instruction for magicians and books inciting to idolatry were to be burned (ibid.).

Whether it was in pursuance of the wisdom of which the Preacher said, "Wisdom is good with an inheritance: and by it there is profit to them that see the sun. . . . the excellency of knowledge is that wisdom giveth life to them who have it" (Eccl. 7:11–12), or whether it was that the prohibition against alien philosophy was not taken too seriously—the fact is that many great Jewish thinkers, from the tenth century onwards, were well versed in Greek and Arab philosophy and freely acknowledged their indebtedness to alien sources. Many of them were attacked and some even banned on account of their xenophilia, many others (foremost among them Saadia Ga'on) escaped unscathed into the galaxy of uncontested authorities. In the course of the centuries, the emphasis appeared to shift more and more from extraneous to intrinsic defects in books; bans were prompted by suspected inherent perniciousness rather than by the objection-ability of any source material.

A striking example is the ban on Karaite literature. The Karaite doctrine held that the only binding law was that laid down in Scripture, and that the Oral Law tradition, as reflected in the Talmud, was but a presumptuous trespass on divine prerogative. The books of the Karaites were banned in order to prevent the dissemination of their heretical doctrine. Similar fates befell the books of persons suspected of apostasy (like Uriel da Costa and Spinoza), of false messianism (like Shabbatai Zevi and Jacob Frank), and of creating schisms in Judaism (like the Hassidim), not to mention the many bans which were declared on books believed to be pernicious because of their erotic or otherwise immoral impact (for details see Carmilly-Weinberger, passim).

It is refreshing and reassuring to find that all the books that were ever banned or prohibited for any reason and at any time have—insofar as they have been preserved—safely survived all the bans and prohibitions. No one seriously contends any longer that the liability of a book to be banned or prohibited still forms part of Jewish law. Nor does anyone seriously contend that bans pro-claimed on any book in the past are still binding even on the Orthodox. The decision to abstain from reading heretical or otherwise pernicious books has become a matter for individual self-restraint rather than legislative intervention.

14

THE RIGHT TO EDUCATION AND PARTICIPATION IN CULTURE

In no branch of the law is the right to receive embedded so much in the duty to give as in the law relating to education. The obligation incumbent on fathers to teach their sons diligently is reiterated three times in the Bible (Deut. 4:9, 6:7, 11:19), while the *right* of the young or uneducated to seek guidance and information from their elders can only be inferred, either from the good advice to go and seek it (Deut. 32:7), or from specific questions put in their mouths, with or without readily provided answers (Exod. 12:26, 13:14; Deut. 6:20), or from statements to the effect that they were in fact told and taught (Ps. 44:2, 78:3). The younger generations were singled out as particular beneficiaries of mass education (Deut. 31:13), which appears to have been introduced at an early stage if only for the purpose of divine revelation (Exod. 19:9, 20:18) and which was later institutionalized to acquaint all the people with their law and with their history (Deut. 31:10–12).

A wise king would regard as one of his main tasks "to teach the people knowledge" (Eccl. 12:9). We know of a king who sent out itinerant teachers and priests who went from town to town throughout the country "and taught the people" (2 Chron. 17:7–9). Ezra the Scribe was charged, inter alia, with teaching the people (Ezra 7:25), and he established quite a faculty to assist him (Neh. 8:7–8).

The blessings of education find abundant expression in the many proverbial exhortations to acquire knowledge and to heed the teachings of parents and elders. The very purpose of writing the Book of Proverbs was "to impart instruction of wisdom, justice, judgment, and equity; to give subtilty to the simple, to the young man knowledge and discretion" (1:3–4). Everybody is well advised to heed the instructions of his father and the reproofs of his mother as "a way of life" (1:8–9, 6:20–23), and the wise will hear and learn and always persist in deepening his education (1:5–6). "Happy is the man that findeth wisdom, and the man that getteth understanding: For the merchandise of it is better than the merchandise of silver, and the gain thereof than fine gold. . . . The Lord by wisdom hath founded the earth; by understanding hath He established the heavens" (3:13–19, 8:10–11, 20:15). Wisdom and understanding must be acquired (4:5), but once you acquired wisdom, understanding will follow as a matter of course (4:7). If you give instruction to a wise man, he will be yet wiser, and all instruction will make for an "increase in learning" (9:9). The more knowledge you accumulate, the better and more prudently will you be able to avoid and overcome hardships (11:9, 13:6). "Poverty and shame shall be to him that refuseth instruction; but he that regardeth reproof shall be honored" (13:18); therefore "apply thine heart unto instruction, and thine ears to the words of knowledge" (23:12).

Talmudical law specifically elaborated on particular aspects of the right and duty of education. It is an early tradition that (parental) instruction in the Bible has to start when the child is five years old, to be followed by instruction in the Mishna at the age of ten and in the other parts of the Talmud at the age of fifteen (M. Avot 5:21). The parental duty of education and instruction in general was, however, said to start as soon as the child began to speak (B. Sukka 42a; Maimonides, Talmud Tora 1:6). Public schools appear to have existed originally only in Jerusalem—and it is reported that there were 480 of them (J. Pei'a 1:1, J. Megilla 3:1); pupils residing elsewhere appear to have come up to Jerusalem and attended classes only at the age of sixteen or seventeen (B. Bava Batra 21a). This unsatisfactory state of affairs prompted a high priest by the name of Joshua ben Gamla (in the last pre-Christian century) to have schools established all over the country, where children started to attend classes at the age of six or seven (ibid.). The law was settled to the effect that no child was to attend school before the age of six; but whether he was to start at the age of six or at the age of seven depended upon the strength of the child and his physical condition (Maimonides, op. cit. 2:2). The law follows the advice tendered by one of the great sages to a schoolteacher, that he should not accept a pupil under the age of six, but "accept one from the age of six onwards and stuff him like an ox" (B. *Ketuvot* 50a). In the discussion which ensued on this piece of advice, apprehensions were expressed lest "stuffing him like an ox" might be too much of a treat for a child of such tender age; and it was ultimately agreed that the curriculum was to be settled with due regard to the child's age and receptivity (ibid.).

The great reform of Joshua ben Gamla by which parents were enabled—and, indeed, required—to delegate their duty of education, insofar as formal education and instruction were concerned, to professional teachers, resulted in the rule of law that schools had to be established in every town and community; and where a town had no school for children, the townspeople were to be ostracized until a school was established—"for the world does not subsist but for the babble of schoolchildren" (Maimonides, op. cit. 2:1). We hear of countrywide inspections being carried out to ensure that every township had its properly functioning school (J. *Hagiga* 1:7). The psalmist's verse, "Except the Lord build the house, they labor in vain that built it; except the Lord keep the city, the watchman waketh but in vain" (127:1), was interpreted to mean that no city could subsist without teachers and scribes to instruct in the Lord's law (J. *Hagiga* 1:7).

Nothing, not even building God's own Temple, was allowed to interfere with or interrupt the instruction of children (B. *Shabbat* 119b); nor was the teaching of children suspended even on the Sabbath (ibid. 150a). But while the rule was that instruction was to continue "throughout the whole day and some portion of the night, so as to train them to study day and night" (Maimonides, op. cit. 2:2), children were mercifully let off at least on the eves of Sabbaths and holidays and on holidays proper (ibid.). The fate of the children had, of course, to be shared by their teacher, who had to stay with them throughout (ibid. 3); still, a teacher should not be unmarried, "because of the mothers who come to see their children," and hence was supposed to lead a marital life in his own home; nor should the teacher be female, "because of the fathers who come to see their children" (M. *Kiddushin* 4:3; B. *Kiddushin* 82a; Maimonides, op. cit. 2:4). Later authorities warned that teachers should not be made to excessively exert themselves, lest they be too tired to do their work properly (Rema ad *Yorei Dei'a* 245:17). One single teacher should not be entrusted with more than twenty-five pupils at a time; if there were between twenty-five and forty pupils, the teacher was entitled to an assistant; if there were more than forty, they were to be split into two separate classes (B. *Bava Batra* 21a; Maimonides, op. cit. 2:5).

The duty to teach and impart instruction was incumbent not only on professional teachers but on everybody who had the necessary qualifications, that is, on every scholar in Israel (Maimonides, op. cit. 1:2); but while professional teachers were entitled to wages, scholars were not entitled to remuneration, for as God has taught you gratuitously, so you must teach others gratuitously (B. *Berakhot* 29a; Maimonides, op. cit. 1:7). The original notion was that each father hired a teacher for his children and paid him his wages, either as agreed upon or in the amount that was customary (Maimonides, op. cit. 1:3); with the introduction of public schools the expenses of education fell upon all parents jointly and would normally be defrayed out of the general revenue of the town or community (Rema ad *Yorei Dei'a* 245:15 and ad *Hoshen Mishpat* 163:3).

Education of children by professional teachers and in public schools did in no way relieve the father of his parental responsibility; the duty of teaching and instructing one's son rests upon the father always (B. *Kiddushin* 29a, T. *Kiddushin* 1:11). Nor is the duty of education confined to teaching and instructing one's children; no less important is the duty of self-education. It has been ruled that self-education has priority even over the education of children, unless a particular child is exceptionally gifted (B. *Kiddushin* 29b; Maimonides, op. cit. 1:4). Opinions were divided as to whether a man should first study the Torah and then marry a wife, or rather first marry and then study—and usages in this respect appear to have differed in the various provinces (B. *Kiddushin* 29b, and Rashi and Tossafot ad loc.). Maimonides decided the issue by holding that you may marry first and study later only if your sexual desires urge you to such an extent that "your heart is not free" for anything else (op. cit. 1:5). The duty to study the Torah is incumbent on everybody, regardless of age, health, poverty, marital or other status; and verses glorifying meditation in the law of the Lord "day and night" (Josh. 1:8, Ps.

1:2) are quoted as authority for the rule that the study must continue both during daytime and during nighttime (Maimonides, op. cit. 1:8). Everybody is advised to find himself a teacher from whom to learn and with whom to study (M. *Avot* 1:6, 16), and there is a dictum to the effect that one such teacher is not enough but that one should have as many teachers as possible (B. *Avoda Zara* 19a). While in earlier times people were apparently fit enough intellectually to perform the duty of studying and meditating in the Written and the Oral Law, provision had to be made in later periods for people who were intellectually unfit to perform this duty. First it was laid down that "in case of necessity" you might fulfil your duty of studying the Torah by duly saying the morning and evening prayers, in which whole chapters from the Torah are included (B. *Menahot* 99b; Rema ad *Yorei Dei'a* 246:1); and then it was held that he who could not study himself would duly perform his duty by enabling others to study (*Tur, Yorei Dei'a* 246:1), a provision later widely used by rich men who wished to look after their business rather than study the Torah, and who were held to make up for their own lack of education by supporting the educated poor.

A bastard who is a scholar has precedence over an uneducated high priest (M. *Horayot* 3:8; Maimonides, op. cit. 3:2). It is said that the study of the Torah is paramount to all other duties (M. *Pei'a* 1:1; Maimonides, op. cit. 3:3), and that God Himself looks upon the failure to study, and occupy oneself with, His laws as an offense worse than disobeying them by committing crimes (J. *Hagiga* 1:7). The first account man will have to give his Creator will be of his accomplishments in studying and educating himself (B. *Kiddushin* 40b; B. *Sanhedrin* 7a; Maimonides, op. cit. 3:5), wherefore man is well advised to study the Torah, even if he does so for some ulterior purpose and not for the sake of performing his duty (B. *Pessahim* 50b, B. *Sota* 47a, B. *Sanhedrin* 105b). On the other hand, no one should indulge in study for his own pleasure only, or with a view to finding an elixir to get rich or successful (B. *Shabbat* 83b, B. *Berakhot* 63b; *Yorei Dei'a* 246:21). "This is the way of the Torah: you will have to eat bread and salt, drink little water, sleep on the floor, live a life of suffering, and exert yourself in studying" (M. *Avot* 6:4). But not every student or scholar is really expected to take upon himself privations of this kind. Great sages have praised the combination of study with the pursuance of a trade or profession, that is, "the way of the world," as the best synthesis (M. *Avot* 2:2); and never should one indulge in study to the extent of becoming dependent for one's livelihood on the charity of others (Maimonides, op. cit. 3:10; Rema ad *Yorei Dei'a* 246:21).

As for methods of study, it is said that the bashful and hesitant will never learn, and the impatient and irritable will never teach (M. *Avot* 2:5). Elaborate rules were laid down to guide students in putting questions and teachers in provoking and answering them (B. *Eruvin* 54b, B. *Berakhot* 38b, T. *Sanhedrin* 7:7, *Yorei Dei'a* 246:9–15). Nobody should despair of learning and understanding: the Torah is not in heaven nor beyond the seas, but "very nigh unto thee, in thy mouth, and in thy heart" (Deut. 30:11–14). That the Torah is neither in heaven nor beyond the seas was hermeneutically taken to indicate that it is not accessible to, or acquired by, those who are as haughty as if they reached unto heaven or as diffuse as if the whole world belonged to them (Maimonides, op. cit. 3:8).

On the other hand, it was early recognized that even within the four corners of the Torah there are matters which not everybody is qualified and hence allowed to inquire into. "Do not search into what is too miraculous for you, and do not investigate into what is hidden from you—there is plenty for you in what God has opened up for you. What good can come from inquiring into the secret things and running after the strange things, if what you can see with your eyes you do not understand" (Ben Sira 3:21–22). The law was indeed laid down that in matters of sex, i.e., the laws relating to sexual offenses and impurities, discussions should take place in a quorum not exceeding three, in matters of apocalyptics in a quorum of two, and in matters relating to visions of the chariot even a single man should not engage unless he was a sage and of ripe understanding; "and he who looks at four things, what is above, what is beneath, what is in front, and what is behind, would better not have been born" (M. *Hagiga* 2:1). The limitation of discussions in matters of sex to very small circles is due to apprehensions that wider discussions might stimulate sexual desires (Ovadia of Bartenura and Maimonides ad loc.; B. *Hagiga* 11b); whereas the limitations pertaining to discussions of esoteric matters are intended to prevent "the masses who cannot understand these matters" from dealing with them (Maimonides ad M. *Hagiga* 3). The four things above, beneath, in front, and behind are those that no mortal sees with his eyes, and they are matters of clairvoyance or speculation (Maimonides and Ovadia of Bartenura, loc. cit.). Once you have reached the stage where the subject-matter of your inquiry (excluding, presumably, God Himself) is no longer physically tangible and conceivable, you no longer have "liberty to speak" (B. *Hagiga* 13a). These restrictions were based (*inter alia*) on the text of the question which Moses let the people ask of God: "ask now of the days that are past, which were before thee, since the day that God created man upon the earth, and ask from one side of the heaven unto the other . . . " (Deut. 4:32)—your inquiries may extend to everything as from the day man was created, and as between one side of heaven and the other, but not beyond (B. *Hagiga* 11b, T. *Hagiga* 2:7). It is submitted that these rules and utterances may possibly reflect the general horror of jurists at the then widespread preoccupation with occultism and esotericism, manifold traces of which are preserved to us in apocryphal literature and the writings of the Qumran sect.

Both education and self-education are, of course, to be concentrated on God's law and the holy books—or, in the language of the Universal Declaration, participation "in the cultural life of the community" (Art. 27.1). There are, however, indications showing that even the duty, and certainly the right, of education could be, and in actual practice was, extended beyond religious culture. It is, for instance, a rule that a man is in duty bound to teach his son a craft or trade so as to enable him to earn an honest living (B. *Kiddushin* 29a, T. *Kiddushin* 1:11), as well as to teach him to swim so as to enable him to save his life (B. *Kiddushin* 30b). As for the crafts and trades, what a man should choose for his son is a clean and easy trade (M. *Kiddushin* 4:14), and there is quite a catalogue of trades considered unclean or unsavory or difficult (B. *Kiddushin* 82a–b). While it is true that mankind needs men of all trades, happy is he whose father was prudent enough to teach him a clean and easy one (ibid.).

There is some discussion in the Talmud as to the propriety of studying Greek. After a sad experience the people had with "an old man who knew the wisdom of the Greeks," a curse was pronounced on anybody who taught his son "the wisdom of the Greeks" (M. *Sota* 9:14, B. *Sota* 49b, B. *Bava Kamma* 82b, B.

Menahot 64b). Nevertheless we find that Rabbi Yishma'el was asked by his nephew, who had already "studied the whole of the Torah," whether he might study "the wisdom of the Greeks." And Yishma'el replied, "This book of the law shall not depart out of thy mouth, but thou shalt meditate therein day and night" (Josh. 1:8)—now, if you find an hour which is neither day nor night, you may go and study Greek wisdom (B. *Menahot* 99b). It would appear from this story that there was nothing inherently wrong with studying Greek philosophy; the impediment was of a technical nature, there being no time left for studies other than the prescribed and holy ones. The deprecation of "the wisdom of the Greeks"—which one commentator confined to Greek mystics and esoterics (Ovadia of Bartenura ad M. *Sota* 9:14)—did not extend to the Greek language, the study and use of which were considered legitimate (B. *Bava Kamma* 83a, B. *Sota* 49b).

The talmudical depreciation of "Greek wisdom," however, took rather unfortunate roots in the thinking of medieval Jewish authorities. Some of Maimonides' books were banned and burned because of the "Greek wisdom" therein contained, Aristotle being quoted there time and again. Eventually the error of discarding and prohibiting "Greek wisdom" outright had to be admitted and recognized, the more so as "Greek wisdom" had become the collective name for all nonreligious disciplines. In 1305 an authoritative decision was handed down to the effect that medical books were permitted for study to everybody, but other non-Jewish philosophical or scientific books were open for study only to persons aged twenty-five or above, who could be presumed to have already studied enough religion to be firm in their faith (*Responsa Rashba* 1:715). In the same vein it was later laid down that it was permissible to study all sciences and disciplines, provided you engaged in those studies not regularly and systematically but only at random, and provided you had already filled your "belly with the meat and wine" of Jewish theology (Rema ad *Yorei Dei'a* 246:4).

While "Greek wisdom" was looked upon askance as full of dangers and pitfalls, Greek poetry was originally more graciously treated. There is early authority to the effect that "the books of Homer and such like books to be written in future" may freely be read, their reading being compared not to studying a serious discipline but to reading private letters (J. *Sanhedrin* 17:1). Had not the Preacher admonished against making too many books only because "much study is a weariness of the flesh" (Eccl. 12:12), meaning that it was books for study that may be too many and may be prohibited, but not books for pleasure. That the writings of Homer are also mentioned in another mishnaic context may serve as evidence that they were indeed available and actually read (M. *Yadayim* 4:6). It was only in recent times that scholars wondered whether the books of Homer, if they had in fact been read, would indeed have passed the test of admissibility (e.g., see Kohut III 254; Krochmal XI 5).

The privilege accorded to Homer and books of pleasure was soon allowed to fall into oblivion. The first prohibition we find is of illustrated books—"paintings of strange animals or of men and their deeds, as, for instance, the battle of David and Goliath, with captions underneath describing the pictures" (Rashi ad B. *Shabbat* 149a)—which were originally prohibited for reading on Sabbaths only, but then classified with forbidden images and idols (B. *Shabbat* 149a). In medieval law, the prohibition was extended to books of allegories, wars, and love stories, to heed the psalmist's advice not to sit "in the seat of the scornful" (lit. "the frivolous") (Ps. 1:1), there being no essential difference between these and illustrated books (Asheri ad *Shabbat* 23:1, Tossafot ad *Shabbat* 116b, *Orah Hayim* 307:16). An exception proposed to this rule, that any book written in the Hebrew language may be read because of the linguistic edification involved (Rema ad *Orah Hayim* 307:16, *Darkei Moshe* ad *Tur*, *Orah Hayim* 307:7), was not generally accepted, there being no inherent holiness in the Hebrew language (*Ba'er Heiteiv* and *Turei Zahav* ad *Orah Hayim* 307:16). From the point of view of education, however, it must be stressed that these prohibitions—which were never universally obeyed or strictly enforced—were all intended to secure concentration on holy studies and to prevent the waste of precious time with unedifying and useless reading.

PART

II

RIGHTS OF EQUALITY

15

ALL MEN ARE BORN EQUAL

"And God said, Let us make man in our image, after our likeness.
. . . So God created man in His own image, in the image of God
created He him; male and female created He them" (Gen. 1:26–
27). Thomas Paine observed that if "this be not divine authority,
it is at least historical authority, and shows that the equality of
man, so far from being a modern doctrine, is the oldest upon
record" (*The Rights of Man*, 1791). Indeed, the equality of men is
necessarily implied in the belief—fundamental in Judaism—that
God created man in His image. One distinction only is alluded to
by Scripture, and that is the distinction between the sexes; and
even this distinction is stressed only for the purpose of equating
male and female as having been both created in the image of God.

Another verse in which the creation of man in the image of God
is reiterated gave rise to a famous debate between two first-
century scholars as to what the golden rule of Jewish law may be.
Rabbi Akiva said it is "Love thy neighbor as thyself" (Lev. 19:18),
and Ben Azzai said it is "This is the book of the generations of
Adam: On the day that God created man, in the likeness of God
made He him" (Gen. 5:1) (*Sifra, Kedoshim* 4:12; *Bereshit Rabba*
24:7; J. *Nedarim* 9:3). Akiva appears to have limited the prescription of neighborly love to one's own people only, so near and dear
that the epithet "neighbor" can properly be applied to them;
holding, presumably, that extending love to perfect strangers was
more than normal human beings could be expected to be capable
of, but extending such love to "neighbors," with whom one was in
constant or regular contact, and with whom one had common
interests and customs, was a requirement fundamental enough

to be selected for the golden rule of the law. Ben Azzai, on the other hand, while not necessarily excluding some discrimination between nearer and farther people insofar as actual "neighborly love" was concerned, preferred for the golden rule of the law a much more fundamental and much farther reaching proposition, namely, that all the generations of Adam, that is, all men, equally bear the imprint of divine creation and divine likeness, and must be treated accordingly.

The elevation of the principle of the equality of all men to the status of the golden rule of Jewish law did not, however, result in the enactment of any specific legal rules. There is not, for instance, any explicit prohibition of discrimination, nor are there any norms setting up standards of behavior to ensure respect for the equality of men in general. The only legal norm in Scripture based expressly on the creation of man in the image of God is the law making the taking of human life a capital offense (Gen. 9:6); and it was Akiva who taught that killing a human being is tantamount to diminishing the image of God (*Bereshit Rabba* 34:326).

It is perhaps typical of Jewish law, however, that the creation of man in the image of God should have been adduced as the *ratio legis* for a rule of hygiene of an eminently practical nature—that one ought to wash every day: man owes to the image of God which he reflects at least the duty of meticulous cleanliness (B. *Shabbat* 50b and Rashi ad loc.; *Avot deRabbi Natan*, Version II, 30; *Vayikra Rabba* 34).

The creation of man in the image of God can be traced as one of the sources of the rules exhorting man to imitate God. The biblical exhortation "to walk in all the ways of God" (Deut. 8:6, 10:12, 11:22, 13:5) was interpreted as follows: "How can man walk after God? Is it not written, 'For the Lord thy God is a devouring fire' (Deut. 4:24)? What is meant is, to walk after God's attributes: as He clothes the naked (Gen. 3:21), so do thou clothe the naked; as He visits the sick (Gen. 18:1), so do thou visit the sick; as He comforts mourners (Gen. 25:11), so do thou comfort mourners; as He buries the dead (Deut. 34:6), so do thou bury the dead" (B. *Sota* 14a). Or, it was said that man glorifies God and exalts Him by imitating Him: "As He is gracious and merciful, so be thou gracious and merciful" (B. *Shabbat* 133b). Indeed, Scripture itself exhorts, "Ye shall be holy, for I the Lord your God am holy" (Lev. 19:2). It has been said that if such human epithets as "merciful and gracious, long-suffering and abundant in goodness" (Exod. 34:6), can be applied to God at all, it is only in order to indicate that those are the ways in which *men* should walk (Maimonides, *Dei'ot* 1:6). God's "humility" in caring for humble people like widows and orphans, strangers and the poor (Exod. 22:20–23, Deut. 10:18, B. *Megilla* 31a), and in reviving the spirit of the humble and the heart of the contrite (Isa. 57:15), and in general, God's "personal concern for the humble, the needy, the distressed," and His goodness, charity and "interest in the common joys and sorrows of men," are but patterns for man's imitation (Moore I 440–441).

The most important echo which the creation of man in the image of God has found in Jewish law is the reference to it in the warning administered by the court to witnesses in capital cases. Before allowing a witness to testify, the court has to warn him in the following terms: "If you are going to testify what your opinion is, or what you know from hearsay, or if you think that you are not going to be cross-examined, you had better know beforehand that a criminal is not like a civil case: in a civil case, a man (who has unjustly been deprived of property) can be compensated and satisfied; but in a criminal case, his blood and the blood of his children depend on him (i.e., the witness) until the end of the world. . . . Man was created single, to teach you that whoever destroys one human life is regarded as if he had destroyed a whole world. (But man was created single also) For the sake of peace among men, that no one may be heard to say to another, 'My father was greater than yours.' And also in order that the *minim* (Christians) should not be heard to say, 'There are many authorities in heaven.' And also to show God's greatness: if a man imprints many coins with the same seal, all coins will come out identical; but the King of Kings imprints every man with the seal of the first man He created, and not one of them is identical with any other. Therefore each one ought to say, 'It is for me alone that the world was created' " (M. *Sanhedrin* 4:5).

It is when the fate of a common criminal is at stake that the equality of all men becomes a living issue. Nobody—and, more particularly, no witness testifying against him—can claim any right or dignity or lineage distinguishing him from any other human being, including the criminal at bar; nobody may be heard to say that one human life is worth more or is better than any other—and the life of the lowest criminal is, qua human life, as essential and valuable in the eyes of God as your own. It is reported that when a man came before a judge telling him that the (alien) governor of his city had ordered him to kill a certain man or else he would be killed himself, he was told not to kill but rather be killed: "Who says that your blood is redder than his? Maybe the blood of that man is redder than yours?" (B. *Sanhedrin* 74a, B. *Pessahim* 25b, B. *Yoma* 82b, J. *Shevi'it* 4:2, J. *Sanhedrin* 3:6). To bring home the equality of all men and the equal value of all human lives in situations like these, where a man stands to forfeit his life because he committed a capital offense, or where he is in peril of losing his own life unless he takes the life of another, is to give such equality a meaning far beyond idealistic theorizations.

There is one other thing to be noted in the warning administered to witnesses, and that is the emphasis laid on the equality of men notwithstanding the natural differences between them. It is pointed out there that the differentiation between individuals is the highlight of divine creation; it is this differentiation, in spite of the identical mold employed in the creation of all, that distinguishes God's work from human handicraft. But instead of the differences being stressed as such and elevated to a primary object of awareness and imitation, they are called in aid as just another proof of the equality of men: each man being different, each has the same cause to claim that for him alone was the world created; no such claim could be made by the individual if there had been nothing to differentiate him from other men. If it is true that every man has the right to claim, "for me alone was the world created," then it is no less true that no man can have any such claim better than any other's. It is the differences between men that render their respective rights to individuality equal; hence the equality of the value of all human lives.

When the accused had been found guilty and had, according to law, to be executed, it was said that God would go into mourning; and if He grieves for the blood of the wicked that had to be shed, all the more must He grieve for the blood of the righteous (M. *Sanhedrin* 6:5). Legend has it that when the people rejoiced at the downfall of their Egyptian persecutors, God lamented, "My creatures are drowning in the sea—and you are singing songs!"

(B. *Sanhedrin* 39b). Apropos of the biblical law that a criminal sentenced to death and hanged may not be left hanging overnight but must be buried the same day (Deut. 21:23), the parable was told of two twin brothers who were exactly alike: one became a brigand, the other was made king; when the brigand was hanged, everybody cried, "Look! the king is hanging!"—whereupon the king ordered the corpse to be taken down and buried immediately (B. *Sanhedrin* 46b, T. *Sanhedrin* 9:7). Every criminal has a king for his brother, and every king a criminal; no deviation from the path of the law can derogate from the right to equal membership in the family of man.

The equality and dignity of men found classical expression in the prophetical books of the Bible. Every man is called by God's name and was created and formed to His glory (Isa. 43:7). God's goodness knows no persons; He is good to all, and satisfies the desires of every living thing (Ps. 145:9–16). The prophet Jonah, who had been charged with prophesying the downfall of Nineveh, "that great city," was "displeased exceedingly, and he was very angry" (4:1), when God saw that the people of Nineveh had turned from their evil ways and decided to spare them (3:10)—and God had to teach him the lesson that the "more than sixscore thousand persons . . . and also much cattle" (4:11) are the objects of God's mercy and pity no less than of His wrath (even though, in addition to their being "wicked," they were heathens). A later prophet put the poignant albeit rhetorical question: "Have we not all one father? Hath not one God created us? Why do we deal treacherously every man against his brother?" (Mal. 2:10). We find the same rhetorical question repeated in talmudical times, when Jewish scholars put it to their Roman oppressors (B. *Ta'anit* 18a, B. *Rosh HaShana* 19a).

Human worth and dignity were never put on a higher pedestal than by the words of the psalmist that man is just a little lower than God Himself, crowned by God with glory and honor, and with dominion over all things in the world (Ps. 8:3–6)—echoing God's own blessing to man, "be fruitful, and multiply, and replenish the earth, and subdue it, and have dominion over every living thing that moveth upon the earth" (Gen. 1:28).

16

DISCRIMINATIONS ON ACCOUNT OF RACE

It has been said that Jewish law is color-blind (Rackman, in Konvitz 45). While it is true that there is no mention anywhere in Jewish law of any such factor as race or color, we have in the Bible a very strong indication of God's own attitude to racial prejudice. It is reported that "Miriam and Aaron spake against Moses because of the Ethiopian woman whom he had married: for he had married an Ethiopian woman" (Num. 12:1). The Lord heard it (ibid. 2), and "the anger of the Lord was kindled against them" (ibid. 9); and, behold, "Miriam became leprous, white as snow" (ibid. 10); it was as if "her father had spit her in the face" (ibid. 14). As is usual with slanderers, Miriam and Aaron did not stop at their original subject, the "Ethiopian woman," but took the good opportunity and vented themselves in an outburst of protest at Moses' monocratic pretensions (ibid. 2). The Lord retorted that Moses was His faithful and trusted servant (ibid. 7–8); not only was his leadership willed by God, but there was also nothing wrong or blameworthy or unlawful in his choice of an "Ethiopian woman" for a wife. It would appear that his brother and sister did not like to have a black woman marry into the family. Racial prejudice as a sideline to family pride seems as old as mankind (cf. Gen. 24:3). When Moses, nonetheless, married "beneath" his family, he was maligned by them as being no longer worthy of his political standing and exalted status. God's reaction was swift and unequivocal: Miriam had offended a woman because she was black, so God made Miriam white as snow. Had it not been for

154

Moses' desperate cry, "Heal her now, O God, I beseech thee" (Num. 12:13), God's fury at this racial calumny might have resulted in the most enduring and painful punishment.

The many wars in which the ancient Israelites were engaged and which—unless they were in the nature of punishments meted out to them by God (e.g., 2 Kings 24:2–3)—were fought by God's command, gave rise to some discriminatory laws. The most explicit is that prescribing the blotting out of "the remembrance of Amalek from under heaven—thou shalt not forget it" (Deut. 25:19). This was first interpreted as a command of physical extermination (1 Sam. 15:3), and it cost Saul, who—apparently out of humanitarian compassion—did not comply with it to the prescribed extent, his kingdom (ibid. 26, 28:18). His successor, David, did not much better, but contented himself with smiting the one company of Amalekites which had attacked him (ibid. 30:1–17); the rest of the Amalekites were not smitten until the days of King Hezekiah (1 Chron. 4:43). Later, the command not to forget blotting out the Amalekites from under heaven was homiletically reduced to the command not to forget but to remember: "Israel stood before God and said, 'Master of the Universe, you told us to remember to blot out the remembrance of Amalek, but we are flesh and blood, we live only short lives; maybe You, who live for ever, do the remembrance Yourself?' And God said, 'My children, if you only remember once every year, I shall count your remembering as if you had blotted them out from the world' " (*Pessikta Rabbati* 12:8).

Another such discriminatory law relates to the "seven nations" enumerated in the Bible (Deut. 7:1): "thou shalt smite them and utterly destroy them; thou shalt make no covenant with them, nor show mercy unto them; neither shalt thou make marriages with them" (ibid. 2–3). The grave humanitarian problem posed by this divinely ordained ruthlessness was solved by talmudical law with the simple expedient of asserting that none of the seven nations are any longer in existence: "their remembrance has been lost" (Maimonides, *Melakhim* 5:4). Similar but not so ruthless laws with regard to the Ammonites and the Moabites (Deut. 23:3–6) were declared obsolete, since the king of Assyria had "removed the bounds of the peoples" (Isa. 10:13) and brought about their irretrievable intermixture and transmutation, so that those particular nations are no longer recognizable (M. *Yadayim* 4:4).

On the other hand, there are nations which have gravely
wronged you, like the Edomites and the Egyptians, but the law is
that you may not "abhor" them on that account (Deut. 23:8). This
is the general rule: "Rejoice not when thine enemy falleth, and let
not thine heart be glad when he stumbleth: Lest the Lord see it,
and it displease Him, and He turn away His wrath from him"
(Prov. 24:17–18), a rule solemnly reiterated in talmudical law (M.
Avot 4:19). And if "thine enemy be hungry, give him bread to eat,
and if he be thirsty, give him water to drink" (Prov. 25:21).

The enemy nations against whom biblical law discriminates for
historical reasons are indeed an exception to the general rule.
This exception is best illustrated by the postulated equality of all
nations as of all men: God's "hand is stretched out upon all the
nations, and His purpose is purposed upon the whole earth" (Isa.
14:26); God's prophets are sent to the nations at large (Jer. 1:5);
and all nations alike will glory in God's truth, judgment, and
righteousness (ibid. 4:2). The God of the prophets being a God of
justice and righteousness, His purpose is universal, and He
addresses Himself to all men. Israel is distinguished from other
nations only in that she already owes allegiance to God, whereas
the other peoples must yet recognize Him: "Look unto me, and be
ye saved, all the ends of the earth" (Isa. 45:22); but ultimately all
nations will partake of bliss and salvation (Jer. 3:17) and will
exalt in prayer to God on His holy mountain (Isa. 2:2, 56:7). Even
as the differences between men will never disappear, so will
nations remain different and separate, though ultimately united
in the worship of God. The messianic prophecy is one of peaceful
coexistence of all nations on earth. When God "shall judge among
the nations," they will "beat their swords into plowshares and
their spears into pruning hooks: nation shall not lift up sword
against nation, neither shall they learn war any more" (Isa. 2:4). It
is in the best Jewish tradition that "neither the prophets nor the
sages" ever contemplated "that in messianic times Israel would
rule the world or would subdue the heathens"; it is only that
"there will no longer be hunger, or war, or envy, or rivalry, but that
the good will be overflowing, and all the world will be full with the
knowledge of God" (Maimonides, *Melakhim* 12:4–5).

17

DISCRIMINATIONS ON ACCOUNT OF RELIGION

It is in the nature of Jewish law qua religious law that it will not suffer any religion beside its own. On the score of the belief in, and the service and worship of, the one single God, Jewish law is relentless and uncompromising. The premise from which all Jewish law flows, that there is no true and right faith other than the Jewish, necessarily implies an intolerance of contradictory and incompatible religions. This intolerance has found most articulate expression in the laws concerning idolaters and idolatry—polytheism being the prototype of religions incompatible with Jewish monotheism.

The fundamental precept of the Jewish faith is that "thou shalt have no other gods" beside the Lord (Exod. 20:3, Deut. 5:7); "thou shalt worship no other god, for the Lord, whose name is Jealous, is a jealous God" (Exod. 34:14). Turn to other gods, and you will "utterly perish" from your land, bring hell and destruction upon yourself (Deut. 32:16–26) and be scattered among the nations (Deut. 4:26–27). In order to prevent people from going after pagan gods, it was prohibited to covenant and intermarry with pagans (Exod. 34:15–16; and see p. 81 ff.); their altars were to be destroyed, their images broken, and their idols burnt (Deut. 7:25). In later law detailed provisions were made regulating the intercourse with pagans, with a view to preventing, on the one hand, any direct or indirect contact with or benefit from any idolatrous practices or rituals, and, on the other hand, any physical danger from uninhibited barbarians who were not sub-

157

ject to God's laws. Thus, a woman was not allowed to be alone in
the company of one or more pagans lest she be raped, and a man
was not allowed to be alone with them lest he be killed (M. *Avoda
Zara* 2:1; Maimonides, *Issurei Bee'a* 23:4 and *Rotzei'ah* 12:7),
nor were small children allowed to be left in their care lest they be
harmed (Maimonides, *Issurei Bee'a* 22:5). The sale to pagans of
arms or weapons and other dangerous things was prohibited (M.
Avoda Zara 1:7; Maimonides, *Akkum* 9:8), as was the sale to
them of certain products and livestock that could serve as implements of pagan rituals (M. *Avoda Zara* 1:5). The injunction
"Neither shalt thou bring an abomination into thine house"
(Deut. 7:26) was held to apply to all requisites of pagan ritual
(Maimonides, *Akkum* 7:2). The prohibition on enjoying implements of pagan ritual was extended also to such pagan products
as wine and vinegar, milk, bread, oil, and cheese (M. *Avoda Zara*
2:3–6), partly because they serve for pagan ritual, and partly
because of suspected adulteration. Within the land of Israel it was
not allowed to sell houses to pagans; leases were to be granted
them only for commercial and not for dwelling purposes (M.
Avoda Zara 1:8–9; Maimonides, ibid. 10:3–4). Looking at and
enjoying images of gods and goddesses put up for purposes not of
worship but of decor was allowed, however. When a philosopher
found a rabbi enjoying his bath in front of a sculpture of Aphrodite, he asked him how doing so could be compatible with the
injunction "there shall cleave nought of the cursed thing to thine
hand" (Deut. 13:17), whereupon the rabbi replied, "I did not come
within the domain of Aphrodite, it was she who came within
mine; the bath was not installed as a decor to Aphrodite, but
Aphrodite was put up as a decor to the bath" (M. *Avoda Zara* 3:4).

The biblical injunction "thou shalt show no mercy unto them"
(Deut. 7:2), referring to the "seven nations" only, was at one time
interpreted as relieving from the duty of rescue where the life of
an idolater was in peril (M. *Sanhedrin* 8:7, Maimonides, ibid.
10:1), though there is also early authority to the contrary effect (T.
Sanhedrin 11:11). But where the life and livelihood of pagans
were concerned, these laws fell into obsolescence; instead it was
laid down, "for the sake of peace," that the poor from among the
idolaters were to be supported together with the Jewish poor, that
pagans ought to be greeted and treated like any other man, and
that pagan dead should be buried together with Jewish dead (M.

Gittin 5:8–9; B. *Gittin* 61a). There is a dictum to the effect that you ought not to mock or ridicule any man other than an idolater (B. *Megilla* 25b); but this license was later restricted to the derision of heathen deities only, as distinguished from their human worshippers (*Yorei Dei'a* 147:5).

While all these discriminations applied only to idolaters, some scholars held that sectarians and heretics might be worse than idolaters and thus should be treated at least as if they were; for while pagans can be presumed to act out of ignorance, sectarians and heretics, who were brought up in Judaism, ought to know better than to deny or disobey God (B. *Shabbat* 116a, J. *Shabbat* 16:9). Thus, Jewish idolaters are worse than pagan idolaters not only in the sense that by practicing idolatry they, unlike the pagans, commit a criminal offense punishable with death (Maimonides, *Akkum* 2:5–6), but because, even without practicing it, a Jew incurs capital punishment if he "reproacheth the Lord" (Num. 15:30) by only advocating idolatry (Maimonides, loc. cit.). However much discriminated against in civil life—whether as a precaution against religious enticements or as a police measure—pagans are not subject to the criminal law relating to idolatry and will not be disturbed in their own religious practices so long as they conduct them among themselves.

Christian Jews were originally regarded as sectarians and heretics (*minim*); but when Christianity became a separate religion and conquered the gentile world, it could not be and was no longer regarded as a Jewish sect, and Jews adhering to the Christian faith were now apostates and liable to be punished as such. Non-Jews of the Christian faith, like pagans, were never subject to Jewish criminal law. Nor were non-Jewish Muslims; and as Islam could never be regarded as a Jewish sect, the provisions of the criminal law relating to sectarians and heretics never applied to Jews who adhered to Islam. We find a solitary opinion expressed that such Christian sects as still practiced iconolatry should be regarded as idolaters (Eliezer ben Natan in his *Even Ha'ezer* 291); but iconolatry does not come within the legal ambit of idolatry, the icons not being themselves worshipped as deities. There is a talmudic dictum to the effect that there can be no idolaters at all outside the land of Israel, but only foreigners who still practice the ancient customs of their forefathers (B. *Hullin* 13b). The law was eventually settled that adherents of the monotheistic religions, like Christianity and Islam, are to be classified as "strangers" (*gerim*), and strangers "thou shalt love as thyself" (Lev. 19:34, Deut. 10:19). All the rules which govern your conduct toward Jews must govern your conduct toward monotheistic non-Jews (Num. 15:16; Nahmanides, *Sefer Hamitzvot* 16; *Responsa Rivash* 119; *Beit Yossef* ad *Tur, Hoshen Mishpat* 266; *Ba'er Hagola* ad *Hoshen Mishpat* 425; et al.); and such discriminations as still remained (and as to which see the next chapter) had nothing to do with their different religion.

18

DISCRIMINATIONS OF ALIENS

Biblical law distinguished, for certain purposes, between Israelites and "foreigners." The release of debts in the seventh year did not apply to foreigners (Deut. 15:3); only a foreigner could be charged with interest on a loan (Deut. 23:20); a foreigner could not be made king (Deut. 17:15); a foreigner was not allowed to eat of the Passover sacrifice (Exod. 21:8), but foodstuffs prohibited to Israelites could be given to strangers or sold to foreigners (Deut. 14:21). These explicit exceptions seem to indicate that unless expressly otherwise provided, all laws applying to Israelites apply also to foreigners. King Solomon expressly included foreigners in his prayer at the inauguration of the Temple; even those who "came out of far countries" would be welcome in the congregations that pray to God and whose prayers are heard (1 Kings 8:41–43).

Talmudical law introduced a good many additional provisions concerning aliens, mostly with a view to keeping the Jewish people apart and its faith and rites intact. A child born to a non-Jewish woman will be a non-Jew even if the father is a Jew; a child born to a Jewess will be Jew even if the father is a non-Jew (M. *Kiddushin* 3:12; B. *Yevamot* 17a). A non-Jew is not bound to obey all God's laws: he fulfills his duty if he performs the seven laws said to be binding upon the descendants of Noah ("Noachides"), namely, the prohibitions of idolatry, blasphemy, incest and adultery, homicide, larceny, and of eating live animals; and the administration of justice (B. *Sanhedrin* 56a, B. *Berakhot* 31b, B. *Kiddushin* 17b, T. *Avoda Zara* 8:4); and having duly performed them, he ranks as a "righteous gentile" and has a share in the world-to-come (Maimonides, *Teshuva* 3:5 and *Me-lakhim* 8:11); it has even been said that he is regarded as if he were a high priest (B. *Sanhedrin* 59a).

Where any particular provision of the law is expressly restricted in the Bible to Israel or to "your people" or "your neighbor," and the like, talmudical scholars interpreted it as not applying to aliens. The injunction, for instance, not to avenge or bear any grudge "against the children of thy people" (Lev. 19:18) was held not to prohibit grudges against non-Jews (*Sifra* ad loc.). Similarly, the law obliging the finder of "all lost things of thy brother's" (Deut. 22:3) was said not to apply to lost chattels of a non-Jew (B. *Bava Kamma* 113b); but while in strict law the finder may be under no obligation to the loser, failure to return lost property to a non-Jew was branded as unlawful enrichment unworthy of a conscientious and law-abiding Jew (Me'iri ad *Bava Kamma* 113b; Maimonides, *Gezeila vaAveida* 9:3). In the same vein, the scriptural liability for damage done by one man's ox to the ox of "his neighbor" (Exod. 21:35) was held to extend only to damage caused to the property of a Jew and not to damage caused to the property of a non-Jew (M. *Bava Kamma* 4:3). The story goes that two imperial Roman officers were dispatched to find out what good things the laws of the Jews had to offer. They came to Rabbi Gamliel and studied under him the Written and the Oral Law; and taking leave of him they said, "We have made a very thorough study of your laws and found them good and true—except for what you hold that lost or stolen property of a non-Jew need not be returned" (*Sifrei, Haberakha* 344), or, according to another version, "except for what you hold that a Jew is not responsible for damage done by his ox to the ox of a non-Jew" (B. *Bava Kamma* 38a). Whereupon Rabbi Gamliel abolished those rules, so as to avoid the desecration of the name of divine law (J. *Bava Kamma* 4:3). Whether this story is a legend or the report of an actual happening, it is highly significant that discrimination of this kind was already in the first century singled out for deprecation by legal observers.

Another discrimination which found its way into the law books would be bad indeed had it in fact ever been practiced: while the murderer of a Jew was liable to capital punishment, the murderer of a non-Jew was said not to be so liable (Maimonides, *Rotzei'ah* 2:11), his punishment being left to the discretion of the king or of the court (ibid. 2:4 and *Melakhim* 3:10). The authority and only source for this ruling is a dictum of one Issi ben Akiva to the effect that "before the Torah was given, the shedding of blood was forbidden generally; after the Torah was given, instead of aggravating the law they mitigated it: in truth they said, he who slew a non-Jew was not punishable at the hands of an earthly court but his punishment was left to heaven" (*Mekhilta, Mishpatim* 4). The reference to pre-Mosaic law is to God's admonition to Noah and his sons, "Whoso sheddeth man's blood, by man shall his blood be shed" (Gen. 9:6), which cannot possibly be, and never was, interpreted as differentiating between Jewish and non-Jewish blood. However, Issi ben Akiva found a verse in which homicide is described as slaying one's "neighbor" (Exod. 21:14), and hence jumped to the conclusion that the offense was restricted to slaying a Jew. There is one other mention of "his neighbor" in the context of homicide, "if any man hate his neighbor and kill him" (Deut. 19:11), but here the "neighbor" has rightly been related to the hatred rather than to the killing: the nearer the victim is to you, if you hate him, then you find yourself eventually resolving to kill him (*Sifrei, Shoftim* 187). But all the other biblical prohibitions of murder are either clothed in general language ("thou shalt not kill": Exod. 20:13, Deut. 5:17) or expressed to relate to all men without distinction ("he that killeth any man shall be put to death": Lev. 24:17; "whoso killeth any person, the murderer shall be put to death": Num. 35:30). And following the biblical pattern, talmudical law, too, speaks in general terms of the murderer who is liable to decapitation (M. *Sanhedrin* 9:1), without in any way qualifying murderers with reference to their victims. It is only when dealing with the law of mistake that it is provided that where a person intends to kill an idolater and actually kills a Jew, he is not punishable (ibid. 2), a provision to be read and applied only in the particular context of exculpatory mistakes, and as such possibly applying also to the killing of an idolater or other non-Jew in mistake for a Jew. Never was the original biblical law (as laid down in Gen. 9:6, Lev. 24:17, Num. 35:30, quoted above) in any way abrogated or "mitigated": Jewish law has always, in my submission, been and remained the same, that killing any man, whether Jew or non-Jew, with premeditation, is a capital offense. The statement of Issi ben Akiva was made at a time when the capital jurisdiction of the Jewish courts had already ceased, that is, after the destruction of the Temple in 70 C.E. (B. *Sanhedrin* 52b, B. *Ketuvot* 30a), and was in the nature of purely theoretical hermeneutics; no rule of law could reasonably be based on or deduced from it. If it was taken up and restated, it was in view of the general principle that in criminal matters the accused would always be entitled to the benefit of every doubt (B. *Bava Kamma* 44b, B. *Sanhedrin* 79a), hermeneutical and legislative doubts included. It should be added that though Issi's dictum was adopted by one of the codifiers, other authorities maintained throughout that the prohibition of homicide and the provision for its punishment extended to the killing of any man, be he Jew or non-Jew (cf. Eliezer ben Natan in his Commentary to *Bava Kamma* 113).

Cities where unintentional killers found refuge from revenge were by explicit biblical law open to Jews and non-Jews alike (Num. 35:15). Talmudical law restricted the availability of cities of refuge only to non-Jews who had killed non-Jews and denied the benefit of refuge to a non-Jew who had killed a Jew (M. *Makkot* 2:3; B. *Makkot* 9a, Maimonides, *Rotzei'ah* 5:4). On the other hand, a Jew who had accidentally killed a non-Jew was entitled to refuge (Maimonides, op. cit. 5:3), implying, of course, that he was indeed in need of refuge and liable to revenge and prosecution for having killed a non-Jew.

Non-Jews are exempted from sanctifying their firstborn animals (M. *Bekhorot* 2:1, Maimonides, *Bekhorot* 4:3), as they are not from "among the children of Israel" (Exod. 13:2). Nor are non-Jews liable to contribute to priests' dues (*Sifrei, Shoftim* 165), to the poor and the strangers (B. *Hullin* 135b; *Sifra, Kedoshim* 1:11), or to pay taxes (M. *Shekalim* 1:5).

A non-Jew is not qualified to act as agent for a Jew, and his acts cannot be considered as those of his Jewish principal (B. *Bava Metzia* 71b; Maimonides, *Sheluhin* 2:1), nor can a Jew act as agent for a non-Jew (J. *Demai* 6:1; Maimonides, loc. cit.). Opinions differed as to whether a non-Jew could under Jewish law act as agent at all, even for another non-Jew (J. *Terumot* 1:1). It appears, however, that non-Jews could be, and actually were, under Jewish law, appointed attorneys for Jews (*Mordekhai* ad *Bava Kamma* 7:71).

A non-Jew is not, as a general rule, qualified to testify as a witness even in civil matters (M. *Bava Kamma* 1:3; Maimonides,

Eidut 9:4). The words of the psalmist about "strange children whose mouth speaketh vanity and their right hand is a right hand of falsehood" (144:7–8) were thought to apply to non-Jews in general (B. *Bava Batra* 45a). Hence where there is no real danger of "falsehood," as where non-Jews had signed as witnesses manumission deeds for slaves or divorcement bills for women, or any document under non-Jewish law, their evidence was admissible (M. *Gittin* 1:5). Similarly, the testimony of a non-Jew is admissible and credible if he spontaneously relates what he has seen, without having any stake in the cause at issue (M. *Yevamot* 16:5; Maimonides, *Geirushin* 12:16). And non-Jewish experts, such as physicians, are qualified witnesses in their special fields of professional knowledge (Asheri ad *Yoma* 8:13; *Orah Hayim* 618:1).

An alien is disqualified not only from being made king (Deut. 17:15), but also—by analogy—from being appointed to any other public, judicial, military, or aministrative office (Maimonides, *Melakhim* 1:4).

There is a sharp dichotomy as to the concept of strangers or aliens between biblical and talmudical law. The former speaks of strangers (*gerim*) in the sense in which the children of Israel were strangers in the land of Egypt (Exod. 23:9, Lev. 19:34, Deut. 10:19), that is, aliens who dwelt and worked, voluntarily or involuntarily, in the land and in the midst of another people exercising suzerainty over them, and who did not give up their own ancestral faith and customs. In the definition of a great commentator, *gerim* are persons who settle to live in a country in which they were not born (Rashi ad Exod. 22:20). Talmudical law, however, introduced the distinction between a stranger who had converted to Judaism (*ger tzedek*) and a stranger who had not (*ger toshav*) (B. *Avoda Zara* 64b), applying the biblical injunctions to love the strangers and treat them as your equals only to the former category, and the various discriminations of aliens only to the latter. While talmudical law thus achieved an almost perfect equality between indigenous and converted Jews, it practically obliterated the provisions of biblical law which had been intended and expressed to apply particularly to unconverted aliens. Whatever may have been the theological or sociological motivation for this drastic and retrogressive change, biblical law still stands out, not only in the ancient world but among the legal systems of all times, as pioneer and paragon of the nondiscrimination of strangers: God Himself loves them (Deut. 10:18) and protects them (Ps. 146:9), and their oppression is a grave offense and abominable sin (Exod. 22:20, 23:9; Lev. 19:33; Jer. 7:6, 22:3; Zech. 7:10). Judges are warned to dismiss from their minds any possible prejudice against strangers (Deut. 24:17), and the divine curse falls upon him "that perverteth the judgment of the stranger" (Deut. 27:19). Like widows and orphans and the poor, strangers must be amply supported (Lev. 19:10, 23:22; Deut. 10:18), at least so long as they are not allotted their own lands (Ezek. 47:22–23). In general, "if a stranger sojourn with you . . . as ye do, so shall he do: One ordinance shall be both for you of the congregation and also for the stranger that sojourneth with you . . . as ye are, so shall the stranger be before the Lord. One law and one manner shall be for you and the stranger that sojourneth with you" (Num. 15:14–16). Not only have we ourselves been strangers in the land of Egypt—and, indeed, where not?—and hence know well enough "the heart of a stranger" (Exod. 23:9) and can feel and sympathize with him, but we ourselves are but strangers and sojourners with God (Ps. 39:13, 1 Chron. 29:15), and we cannot ask for nor expect from God any treatment better than that which we ourselves accord the stranger in our midst.

19

DISCRIMINATIONS OF WOMEN

The general rule of Jewish law is that, unless expressly otherwise provided, all laws applicable to men are applicable to women: the laws "which thou shalt set before *them*" (Exod. 21:1) are to be set before men and women alike (B. *Kiddushin* 35a), and men and women are expressly designated as subjects of criminal laws and liable to the punishments prescribed if found guilty (Num. 5:6). The rather numerous exceptions to this general rule are conditioned either by the physiological peculiarities of females, as for instance the duties incumbent on women after childbirth or during menstruation, or by psychological (or pseudopsychological) considerations; into the latter category fall all disabilities arising out of the woman's place in ancient society and, in particular, in a patriarchal household. Both such physiological and psychological factors make for discriminations in favor of women as well as for discriminations against them; indeed, much of what today would be regarded as a discrimination against them, e.g., their disqualification as witnesses, was originally conceived as a discrimination in their favor (see below).

The most striking discrimination of women is their exemption from positive duties which are to be performed at a specified time (M. *Kiddushin* 1:7). The reasons originally adduced for this exemption are purely hermeneutical, for instance, that the appearance before God "three times in the year" is expressly limited to males (Exod. 23:17), and hence all duties to be performed at a specified time are limited to males (B. *Kiddushin* 34b). Not so the negative duties: the prohibition of working on the Sabbath, for instance, applies to women also, if only because they are expressly

167

included (Exod. 20:10, Deut. 5:14), though this prohibition, too, is bound up with a specified time—the Sabbath day. Or, the negative duty to refrain from eating leavened bread on Passover (Exod. 22:15) is incumbent also on women, although restricted to certain days in the year; and while, in theory, the positive duty to eat unleavened bread on Passover (ibid., Lev. 23:6, Deut. 16:3) is not binding on women, it was held to be so interconnected with the prohibition of leavened bread that it must apply to women, too, as otherwise they might get nothing to eat on Passover (B. *Pessahim* 43b, B. *Kiddushin* 34a). In post-talmudical sources we find the exemption of women from positive time-bound duties explained by the consideration that all of the woman's time belongs to her husband, and her household duties appear at all times to have preference over any other (*Kolbo* 73). But a woman is always at liberty to perform such duties as are not binding upon her, if she so desires (B. *Eruvin* 96b, B. *Rosh HaShana* 33a and Tossafot ad loc.).

God's first command to man, "Be fruitful and multiply and replenish the earth" (Gen. 1:28), is addressed in plural form to both male and female; nevertheless opinions were divided as to whether this was a duty incumbent also upon women. If it was in the nature of a divine command, it would be so binding, as it was expressly addressed to women too; if it was only in the nature of a divine blessing, it need not be interpreted as imposing any duty (Tossafot ad *Yevamot* 65b q.v. *valo*). The law was settled that the duty was incumbent on men only and not on women (M. *Yevamot* 6:6; Maimonides, *Ishut* 15:2), the reason being not only that in another verse (addressed to Jacob) the duty to "be fruitful and multiply" was expressed in the singular masculine tense (Gen. 35:11), but also that in the act of procreation the man is the active and the woman only a passive party (B. *Yevamot* 65b; and cf. B. *Sanhedrin* 74b, where Esther's submission to the pagan king is excused with the assertion that she let herself be trod upon like "a piece of land"). Though there is thus no legal duty on a woman to beget children, she may claim a divorce from her husband for not having conceived, because she is entitled to the comfort of children of her own—as the husband may divorce a wife who has not, after at least ten years of marriage, given birth to a child (B. *Ketuvot* 72a and 75b; Maimonides, *Ishut* 15:8–10). And although the woman is considered the passive partner in sexual intercourse, she is criminally liable for sexual offenses committed upon her with her consent (M. *Keritot* 1:4; B. *Yevamot* 84b–85a; Maimonides, *Issurei Bee'a* 17:5), her sexual enjoyment being regarded as the *actus reus* (Tossafot ad *Bava Kamma* 32a, s.v. *eehu*).

Women are also exempt from duties imposed on a parent toward his son, such as circumcising him, teaching him, training him for a trade, and giving him a woman in marriage (M. *Kiddushin* 1:7, B. *Kiddushin* 29a); and as women are exempt from the duty of teaching, so are they exempt from the duty of studying and learning (B. *Kiddushin* 29b; Maimonides, *Talmud Tora* 1:1)—they are perfectly entitled to study and learn to their hearts' content if they so wish, but they cannot expect the divine reward assured to those who duly perform a duty binding on them (B. *Sota* 21a; Maimonides, op. cit. 1:13). Duties owed by a child to his parents are incumbent also on women, such as honoring and maintaining them; but this duty, too, has been said to be subject and subordinated to a wife's overall duties to her husband: "the husband has ample time to devote to his parents, but the wife has no time left" (T. *Kiddushin* 1:11).

While as a general rule women incur all civil liberties and enjoy all civil rights to the same extent as men (B. *Kiddushin* 35a; *Mekhilta, Mishpatim* 10), there are some noteworthy exceptions. A defaulting debtor was liable to be sold in bondage for his debt (Exod. 22:2; Lev. 25:39), but if the debtor was a woman she was not allowed to be so sold (M. *Sota* 3:8; T. *Sota* 2:9), nor could a woman, in contradistinction to a man, voluntarily sell herself into bondage (*Mekhilta, Mishpatim* 3). A woman was not allowed to acquire a male slave (T. *Sota* 2:9), presumably to save her from getting into ill-repute (B. *Bava Metzia* 71a).

The vast majority of discriminations on account of sex apply to married women only. Though a married woman is, like anybody else, liable in damages for any injury she has done to persons or property, no compensation can be recovered from her during coverture (M. *Bava Kamma* 8:4), for all her property vests in her husband for the duration of the marriage, and he is under no obligation to pay her debts even out of her own property in his hands (Rema ad *Hoshen Mishpat* 96:6), unless the debts were incurred by her with his express or implied authority (cf. M. *Shevu'ot* 7:8). If she injured her husband, he must divorce her before he can recover from her (Maimonides, *Hoveil uMazik* 4:18); but, even after divorce, the wife is not liable for any injury done to his property, as distinguished from his person, if the injury was caused by her in the course of her marital duties—or else there would be no peace in any household (J. *Ketuvot* 9:4; Maimonides, *Ishut* 21:9). On the other hand, if a husband injures his wife, even in the course of coitus, she may recover damages from him at once, and he cannot lay his hands on this compensation money (B. *Bava Kamma* 32a; Maimonides, *Hoveil uMazik* 4:16–17).

An infant girl could be sold into bondage or given in marriage by her father but not by her mother (M. *Sota* 3:8; *Mekhilta, Mishpatim* 3). Once she reached the age of puberty she could not be married without her consent (Maimonides, *Ishut* 3:12, 4:1). Later authorities deprecated the marriages of girls who had not reached the age of consent and hence could not have validly consented (*Even Ha'ezer* 37:8).

The marriage ceremony is performed by the husband "consecrating" the woman to himself as his wife; any such "consecration" by the woman of the man to herself as her husband is a nullity (Maimonides, *Ishut* 3:1–2; *Even Ha'ezer* 27:7; and cf. B. *Kiddushin* 5b). This notion of "consecration" has replaced the original notion of "acquisition" of the wife by the husband (M. *Kiddushin* 1:1); but there was nothing in the acquisition, and there is nothing in the consecration, to deprive the wife of her personal liberty and subjugate her to her husband, except in the sense that by consenting to be married to him she is deemed to have pledged herself irrevocably for sexual intercourse with him in any way he desires (B. *Nedarim* 15b, 20b). Sexual intercourse, however, is not only a right which the husband acquires by marriage as against his wife, but even more so a right which the wife acquires as against her husband (Exod. 21:10; B. *Ketuvot* 47b, 56a; Maimonides, *Ishut* 14:7).

This consecration of the wife to the husband, and not of the husband to the wife, led to discriminations of various kinds, the gravest of which is that a man may marry as many wives at a time as he desires (B. *Yevamot* 65a; M. *Kiddushin* 2:6–7; Maimonides, op. cit. 14:3; *Even Ha'ezer* 1:9), while a woman can be married only to one husband at a time (cf. Lev. 18:20, 20:10; Deut. 22:22; M. *Sanhedrin* 9:6; Maimonides, op. cit. 1:3). Polygamy has not always been actually practiced and has even been prohibited for certain sects (Damascus Document 4:20–5:5) or dignitaries (1 Tim. 3:2, 12); but it was only in the tenth century c.e. and for one section of the Jewish people that it was effectively outlawed by the *herem* of Rabbenu Gershom, the "Light of the Diaspora"; and while the *herem* is nowadays generally observed, the original discrimination does in practice still survive, more particularly in those cases in which dispensations from the *herem* are permissible.

As the husband is the only actor in bringing the marriage into being, as it is he who "consecrates" the wife, so is he the only actor in bringing the marriage to an end: "When a man hath taken a wife and married her, and it come to pass that she find no favor in his eyes, because he has found some uncleanness in her: then let him write her a bill of divorcement, and give it in her hand, and send her out of his house. And when she is departed out of his house, she may go and be another man's wife" (Deut. 24:1–2). It is the husband in whose eyes the wife finds, or ceases to find, favor—whether the husband finds favor in the eyes of his wife is legally irrelevant. Originally it was only the husband who determined which "uncleanness" was appropriate or sufficient to justify divorce; it was, in fact, his caprice which could determine the matter. Later law rectified this situation and laid down objective causes of divorce applicable to all (B. *Gittin* 89a, 90a; M. *Ketuvot* 7:6; Maimonides, *Ishut* 24:11–19). But it is still the husband alone who writes and delivers the bill of divorcement, either himself or by his agent, and sends the wife away. Any bill of divorcement written by the wife or her agent, or delivered by her or her agent into the husband's hand, would be a nullity, nay an absurdity, and the expulsion by the wife of her husband would be without any legal significance, except perhaps to deprive her of her claims of alimony and maintenance against him. While to the celebration of the marriage the wife's consent was required, the husband could divorce his wife without her consent (M. *Yevamot* 14:1; Maimonides, *Geirushin* 1:2; *Even Ha'ezer* 119:6), but as nobody can be deprived of any right in his or her absence, the wife could not be divorced unless she was present herself or through an agent appointed by her for that purpose (B. *Gittin* 11b, 77b; Maimonides, op. cit. 5:2). Her personal or vicarious presence, however, was considered of no avail when she was insane—not

that her husband could not send her away, but he had to provide
for her maintenance (Maimonides, op. cit. 10:23), and the fact
that she had not become a divorcee but remained a married
woman would protect her from unfair exploitation (B. *Yevamot*
113b, B. *Gittin* 71b). On the other hand, when the husband
becomes insane, he is automatically incapacitated to divorce his
wife, and she is stuck with him forever (M. *Yevamot* 14:1;
Maimonides, op. cit. 2:17). The reason given for the rule empo-
wering the husband to send away his insane wife, to wit, that
"sane people have not the strength to live with an insane in the
same house" (Maimonides, op. cit. 10:23), surprisingly does not
hold good when the wife is sane and has to live with an insane
husband.

Again Rabbenu Gershom intervened and by his *herem* outlawed divorces without the wife's consent. Having already outlawed polygamous marriages, he now had to allow for exceptions
or dispensations from the *herem*. It was thought unjust, for
instance, to render the divorce of an adulterous or "rebellious" or
otherwise sinful wife impossible without her consent, and still
prevent the husband from at least marrying another wife. Courts
were therefore empowered to license bigamous marriages, notwithstanding the *herem*, whenever a wife refused to accept a
divorce although a court had found that her marriage ought to be
dissolved, more particularly where it ought to be dissolved because of her misconduct (Rema ad *Even Ha'ezer* 119:6); and so
would a bigamous marriage be allowed to a man whose wife was
by insanity incapacitated to consent to a divorce (Rema ad *Even
Ha'ezer* 1:10). The old discrimination is thus perpetuated: bigamous marriages can never be allowed to women, even if the
insanity or other disease or invalidity of the husband is incurable
and whatever may have been his misconduct; it is solely the
husband who can ever be allowed to remarry even though his first
marriage still subsists. Where, however, husband or wife suffers
from a disease or invalidity not affecting the capacity to consent to
a divorce, and the disease or invalidity is such that the other
spouse cannot fairly be expected to continue marital life, the
court may "compel" the husband to give, and the wife to accept, a
bill of divorcement—the reason being adduced that Rabbenu
Gershom could not have intended by his *herem* to discriminate
between the sexes, as if the husband could be compelled to give a

divorce and the wife could not be compelled to accept it (*Responsa Asheri* 42:1). "Compulsion" could be effected by flogging the husband (B. *Ketuvot* 77a; Maimonides, *Ishut* 15:7); but not only would flogging never be administered to a woman, but even with men the opinion prevailed that he should be compelled by means of exhortations and stern warnings rather than by violence (*Even Ha'ezer* 154:21 and Rema ad loc.). Flogging, however, was of no avail unless it led the husband to proclaim, "I will now divorce her" (B. *Kiddushin* 50a; Maimonides, *Geirushin* 2:20), and if he did not make this declaration, no amount of flogging could bring about the divorce. With women it was different; they need not be directly "compelled," but instead of any direct compulsion, the bill of divorcement could be thrown into the wife's room or courtyard and would then be regarded as if it had been delivered into her hand (B. *Gittin* 77a–b).

Another discrimination of the woman is that where a marriage is dissolved because of the wife's adultery, she may not thereafter be married either to her former husband or to her partner in adultery (M. *Sota* 5:1; Maimonides, *Sota* 2:12); whereas a man who committed adultery may, after divorce, remarry his former wife or marry his adulterous partner—the underlying reason being, of course, that while the wife by her adultery committed a capital offense (Lev. 20:10, Deut. 22:22), the husband committed no offense whatever by taking another (unmarried) woman in addition to his wife. And while a divorced wife who remarried was not allowed thereafter to be married to her first husband again, the husband could marry as many wives in succession as he liked and could always remarry his former wives (cf. Deut. 24:4).

While the husband is the sole heir of his wife, a widow does not inherit her husband at all (M. *Bava Batra* 8:1; B. *Bava Batra* 111b; Maimonides, *Ishut* 22:1). A widow is entitled to maintenance out of her husband's estate so long as she lives (M. *Ketuvot* 9:1), unless she chooses to take her *ketuva*, that is, her property which had been in her husband's custody plus the stipulated accretions thereto, instead of maintenance (Maimonides, op. cit. 18:1). This kind of discrimination is shared by the widow with the daughters (whether married or unmarried) of the deceased. It is the male descendants who inherit their father; only "if a man die and have no son, then ye shall cause his inheritance to pass unto his daughter" (Num. 27:8). Unmarried daughters, like widows, are entitled to be maintained out of the estate of their father until they marry (M. *Bava Batra* 8:4). It was observed very early that in many cases this discrimination may well work out to the benefit of the female supportees and to the detriment of the male heirs; where the estate is small, the widow and the daughters will be maintained out of it even if the sons are left with nothing (M. *Bava Batra* 9:1). A man could, of course, leave the whole or part of his estate to his widow or daughters by will; but so deep-rooted was the notion that widows do not inherit that it was laid down that a will bequeathing the whole estate to the widow was to be interpreted as vesting the estate in her as executrix and trustee for the legal heirs (B. *Bava Batra* 131b). Where the testator's intention was unmistakably expressed to the effect that the widow should take the estate for herself and in her own right and not as executrix or trustee, she would inherit her husband's estate but lose her right to her *ketuva*, i.e., her own property (ibid. 132b; Maimonides, *Zekhyia uMatana* 6:6–8); *Even Ha'ezer* 107:1–3), provided the husband made the bequest in good faith and not only in order to cheat her out of her property (*Even Ha'ezer* 107:5). On the other hand, the disposition by a woman of her own property in favor of a third party, made prior to her marriage, was held invalid as defrauding her husband of her property (B. *Ketuvot* 79a; Maimonides, op. cit. 6:12). We have already noted that the wife's property vests in her husband until their marriage is dissolved, either by death or by divorce; the same applies to property acquired by the wife during coverture (B. *Sanhedrin* 71a, B. *Kiddushin* 23b), and any disposition by the wife of any such property is null and void (B. *Yevamot* 66b; Maimonides, *Ishut* 22:15–17; *Even Ha'ezer* 90:13), unless such property was given her on the condition that she herself use or dispose of it for a specific purpose (Maimonides, *Zekhyia uMatana* 3:14; *Even Ha'ezer* 85:11). The husband may not, on the other hand, dispose of his wife's real property without her concurrence (B. *Yevamot* 66b and Rashi ad loc.; Maimonides, *Ishut* 22:20; *Even Ha'ezer* 90:13).

A woman is disqualified from testifying as a witness in court (M. *Shevu'ot* 4:1; B. *Shevu'ot* 30a; *Sifrei, Shoftim* 190; Maimonides, *Eidut* 9:2). Apart from hermeneutical reasons given for the rule, such as the use of the masculine gender when speaking of witnesses (e.g., in Deut. 17:6), it was also asserted that "the king's daughter is all glorious within" her house (Ps. 45:14), and no woman should be required to leave her house and attend court (B. *Shevu.'ot* 30a). There are, however, exceptions to this rule: women are competent witnesses in all matters outside the realm of strict law, like criminal law, where every relevant fact has to be established by the evidence of at least two duly qualified witnesses (B. *Bava Kamma* 114b, B. *Yevamot* 39b); they are also competent to testify in matters within the particular knowledge of women, such as customs and events in places frequented by women (Rema ad *Hoshen Mishpat* 35:14), and on their own or other women's purity (M. *Ketuvot* 2:6, B. *Ketuvot* 72a). In posttalmudic times, the evidence of women was often admitted where no other evidence was available on a given issue (*Responsa Maharam of Rotenburg* 920; *Responsa Maharik* 179), or in matters not considered important enough to bother male witnesses (*Kolbo* 116; *Responsa Maharik* 190).

A consequential disqualification of the woman is her incompetency to act as a judge (J. *Sanhedrin* 3:9; *Hoshen Mishpat* 7:4). The rule is that whoever is disqualified as a witness is disqualified as a judge (M. *Nidda* 6:4). It is true that in biblical times we find at least one woman, the prophetess Deborah, acting as a "judge of Israel" (Judg. 4:4), but her judgeship is regarded as being of a governmental and exhortatory rather than of a judicial character (cf. Judg. 2:16–18). The opinion was later voiced that notwithstanding her disqualification as a witness, a woman is fully qualified to act as a judge (Ritba ad *Kiddushin* 35a; Tossafot ad *Bava Kamma* 15a, s.v. *asher*, and ad *Nidda* 50a, s.v. *kol*).

A woman should not be appointed guardian over the persons or properties of others, because women are not accustomed to administering properties and representing the interests of other people (B. *Gittin* 52a; Maimonides, *Nahalot* 10:6; *Hoshen Mishpat* 290:2). In contradistinction to many other discriminations likewise flowing from the position of women in ancient society, this particular disqualification from guardianship was allowed to become obsolete (*Sha'arei Uziel* 8:2).

A woman is disqualified from being made king (or queen), for the king has to be chosen from among "thy brethren" (Deut. 17:15). This biblical language is quoted as authority for the rule that "for all offices in Israel only men and not women are to be appointed" (Maimonides, *Melakhim* 1:5). There was, however, a queen who reigned over Israel, Salome Alexandra (76–67 B.C.E.), and she was praised and admired by scholars and authorities of her own and later generations: her reign was hailed as a period of prosperity and divine blessing (*Sifra, Behukotai* 1; *Vayikra Rabba* 35:10).

The prohibition that a woman may not wear "that which pertaineth unto a man" (Deut. 22:5) was interpreted as disqualifying women from wearing arms, and hence from military service (B. *Nazir* 59a). While women have the reputation of being easily frightened and terrified (Isa. 19:16, Nahum 3:13), and may on this ground become eligible for exemption from military service (Deut. 20:8), the law is that in a war of defense both men and women are to be called up—even bride and bridegroom, from under their canopy, are expected to join up (M. *Sota* 8:7, T. *Sota* 7:24).

The fact that there were women prophetesses (Exod. 15:20, 2 Kings 22:14, 2 Chron. 34:22, Isa. 8:3, Neh. 6:14), women counselors (2 Sam. 14:2, 20:16), and women scholars (T. *Keilim Metzia* 1:6, B. *Pessahim* 62b), though few in number, would indicate that women could, even in a patriarchal society, reach dignities normally reserved to men.

Where a man and a woman ask for charity, the woman is to be preferred to the man (T. *Ketuvot* 6:8; Maimonides, *Matnot Anyim* 8:15; *Yore Dei'a* 251:8), because of her greater embarrassment and more urgent needs. If a man and a woman can be released from prison or redeemed from captivity, the woman is to be released first (M. *Horayot* 3:7; Maimonides, loc. cit.). Where a man and a woman die at the same time, the woman is to be buried first (*Semahot* 11). When a man and a woman are waiting to be heard in court, the woman is to be heard first (B. *Yevamot* 100a; Maimonides, *Sanhedrin* 21:6; *Hoshen Mishpat* 15:2).

A daughter cannot commit the offense ascribed to the "stubborn and rebellious son" (Deut. 21:18)—not only because the text speaks of "sons" and not of daughters (M. *Sanhedrin* 8:1, *Sifrei, Teitzei* 218), but also because by their nature women are not "gluttons or drunkards" (Deut. 21:20), however stubborn and rebellious they might conceivably be (B. *Sanhedrin* 69b; T. *Sota* 2:8; Maimonides, *Mamrim* 7:11).

An infant girl reaches puberty at the age of twelve, while an infant boy reaches puberty only at the age of thirteen—because

God imbued women with more intelligence than men (B. *Nidda* 45b), or because women live shorter lives than men (Maimonides, Commentary ad M. *Nidda* 5:6).

As women are normally heavier than men, an animal hired for the carriage of a man may not be used to carry a woman, but an animal hired to carry a woman may be used to carry a man (B. *Bava Metzia* 79b; Maimonides, *Sekhirut* 4:5).

20

DISCRIMINATIONS ON ACCOUNT OF BIRTH

Jewish law does not know the distinction between "legitimate" and "illegitimate" children. A child born to an unmarried mother is as legitimate as a child born in wedlock, but where the mother is married to a man other than the child's father, or is the father's sister or other near relative to whom the laws of incest apply, then the child is a bastard (*mamzer*) (M. *Yevamot* 4:13). A child born to an unmarried Jewish mother who is not disqualified from marrying the child's father enjoys all the rights both against his mother and against his father, as well as all rights to their respective estates after their deaths, that a child born in wedlock enjoys (B. *Yevamot* 59b–60a, *Even Ha'ezer* 6:8), the only difference being that while a child born in wedlock need not prove his father's paternity, it being presumed that the mother's husband is the father of her children, a child born out of wedlock has to prove his father's paternity, where the father denies it, before he will succeed in any claim against his father or his father's estate (B. *Yevamot* 69b, *Even Ha'ezer* 4:26 and Rema ad loc.).

On the other hand, a *mamzer* is discriminated against insofar as he or she is disqualified from marrying a non-*mamzer* (Deut. 23:3; Maimonides, *Issurei Bee'a* 15:1; *Even Ha'ezer* 4:22), except a proselyte (B. *Yevamot* 79b; Maimonides, op. cit. 15:7; *Even Ha'ezer*, loc. cit.); but in respect of property rights, including rights of inheritance, there is no discrimination between the *mamzer* and any other child (B. *Yevamot* 22b; Maimonides, *Nahalot* 1:7; *Hoshen Mishpat* 276:6). A *mamzer* is eligible to any,

178

even the highest, office (B. *Yevamot* 45b); and in settling the ranks of precedence the law provides that, generally, "the priest precedes the Levite, the Levite the Israelite, the Israelite the *mamzer*, the *mamzer* the proselyte, and the proselyte the manumitted slave—provided they are equal in all other respects; but a *mamzer* who is a scholar takes precedence over a high priest who is uneducated" (M. *Horayot* 3:7, T. *Horayot* 2:10; and see p. 141).

Difficulties have arisen and given rise to discriminations where the incidences of birth were unknown or undisclosed or where the prescribed divorce procedures were not observed, thus raising doubts as to whether a child might not in law have to be regarded as a *mamzer*. Where, for instance, a child was found abandoned and his parents were unknown, or where the child's mother was unmarried and refused to disclose the father's identity (M. *Kiddushin* 4:2), opinions were divided as to whether the child, as a potential or "doubtful" *mamzer*, ought not to be treated as such rather than be allowed to marry into the community, or whether he should be accorded the benefit of the doubt and treated as a non-*mamzer*. The law was eventually settled to the effect that the prohibition of intermarriage extended also to a "doubtful" *mamzer* (Maimonides, *Issurei Bee'a* 15:21–23; *Even Ha'ezer* 4:24). But where a foundling was found in circumstances that would not raise any reasonable suspicion of *mamzerut* nor indicate any intention to conceal the birth, the child will be treated as a non-*mamzer* (B. *Kiddushin* 73b–74a; Maimonides, op. cit. 15:31; *Even Ha'ezer* 4:31). The same applies to a child whose mother declares that the father was not disqualified from marrying her but does not disclose his identity; unless the circumstances of the birth provide a clear indication to the contrary, the mother's statement is accepted (M. *Ketuvot* 1:8; Maimonides, op. cit. 15:32; *Even Ha'ezer* 6:17–18). A woman whose marriage was purported to be dissolved in a manner not recognized under Jewish law, e.g., by a divorce decree of a secular court, or even by divorce proceedings not wholly in conformity with rabbinical precepts, such as a Karaite divorce, is in law regarded as being still married to her former husband; if she remarries, any child she bears to her second husband is regarded as a *mamzer* (*Beit Yossef* ad *Tur, Even Ha'ezer* 4; Rema ad *Even Ha'ezer* 4:37). This rule was extended to disqualify qua "doubtful" *mamzer* each member of those communities in which such invalid divorces were or are practiced, provided the marriages performed in such communities were valid under Jewish law (*Responsa Radbaz* 73 and 796).

Normally, the status of a child is determined by the status of his or her father; if the father is a priest, and the mother is of a nonpriestly family, the son will be a priest. But this rule holds good only so long as there is no legal defect in either of the parents; any such defect as would constitute an impediment to marriage is transmitted to the child, irrespective of whether the defect rests in the father or in the mother. Thus, a child will be regarded as *mamzer* when either his father or his mother, even if they are not married to each other, is a *mamzer*. Where the parents of a child are not only disqualified or prohibited from marrying each other, but have no capacity to marry at all under Jewish law, as is the case with non-Jews, the status of the child always follows the status of the mother (M. *Kiddushin* 3:12).

There is no legal discrimination on account of birth other than against real or "doubtful" *mamzerim*. "All families are presumed eligible for intermarriage; but notwithstanding this rule, if you see two families in constant enmity with each other, or if you see a family quarreling and fighting with all and sundry; or if you see a man who is exceedingly quarrelsome and overbearing—better keep away from them, for these are indications of defectiveness. And a man who always finds defects in others, as, for instance, says of others that they are *mamzerim*, is suspected of being a *mamzer* himself; or if he says of others that they are slaves, is suspected of being himself a slave: he who discredits another, discredits him with his own faults and defects" (Maimonides, *Issurei Bee'a* 19:17).

Although the status of *mamzer* devolves from parents to children throughout the generations and is thus never extinguished, it has been laid down that families are to be regarded as having absorbed all defective elements to the extent that defects are no longer identifiable or traceable (B. *Kiddushin* 71a); and it has been said by weighty authority not only that no investigation should be conducted into the "purity" of families from defects of this sort, but even that a person who has positive knowledge of any such defective element in any family should not be allowed or heard to disclose it (*Beit Yossef* ad *Tur, Even Ha'ezer* 2; Rema ad *Even Ha'ezer* 2:5).

The "right of the firstborn" (Deut. 21:17) may be regarded as another discrimination on account of birth. This right appears to have been practiced and recognized throughout the ancient world, and biblical law only refers to it as if it were self-understood (ibid.), without laying it down expressly: a man who has sons from a beloved wife and from an unbeloved wife may not prefer the son of the beloved and appoint him "firstborn" for the purpose of having the double portion of his inheritance devolve upon the son of the beloved (ibid. 21:15–17). The case here propounded of sons from beloved and unbeloved wives was in talmudical law parabolized to indicate that firstborn sons born in sin, like *mamzerim*, may not be deprived of their rights of primogeniture, for there are no beloved or unbeloved wives in the eyes of God (B. *Yevamot* 23a; *Sifrei, Teitzei* 216). The law is that the firstborn son of the father, not the firstborn of the mother, is entitled to a double portion in his father's but not in his mother's estate (M. *Bava Batra* 8:4), and that a father may not deprive his firstborn son of his right to a double portion (ibid. 8:5). In earlier times the right of primogeniture appears to have been negotiable as between the firstborn and the other sons, for otherwise Jacob could not have acquired that right from Esau (Gen. 25:31–33); and there is a tradition to the effect that Reuben, Jacob's firstborn son, lost his primogeniture to Joseph because of his misconduct (1 Chron. 5:1–2). Jacob himself, however, blessed his firstborn Reuben as his might and the beginning of his strength, "the excellency of dignity, and the excellency of power" (Gen. 49:3); and it appears indeed that the firstborn son occupied a position of honor and dignity within the family—if only because all the firstborn were regarded as sanctified to God (Exod. 13:2). It was all the firstborn who were chosen for Temple service (Num. 3:45, 8:18) until the Levites took over and the firstborn were redeemed (ibid. 3:51, 8:16). The redemption of the firstborn from God's service by a token payment to a priest (Exod. 13:13) has remained a customary rite throughout the ages (M. *Bekhorot* 8:1; Maimonides, *Bekhorot* 1:1–2; *Yorei Dei'a* 305:1).

Primogeniture appears to have been the determining factor also in the succession to the throne (cf. 1 Kings 1:5, 2:22; 2 Chron. 21:3), unless the king decreed otherwise during his lifetime (1 Kings 1:30, 33–35; 2 Chron. 11:22). God's blessing that the king "may prolong his days in his kingdom, he and his children, in the midst of Israel" (Deut. 17:20) is the source for the law that the succession to the throne devolves upon the king's "children"; but "whoever is first to inherit is first to succeed to the throne, and therefore each elder son has preference over a younger son" (Maimonides, *Melakhim* 1:7). This rule was extended to "all the offices and appointments in Israel." All of them are hereditary from generation to generation, the elder sons having precedence over the younger ones; provided, however, that the son is qualified to "fill the place of his fathers with wisdom and the fear of God" (ibid.). The heredity of the priesthood is laid down already in the Bible (Exod. 28:1, 40–43; 29:4, 24, 28, 29, 30, 32, 35, 44), and the high priest appears to have always been the eldest son (Lev. 6:15, 16:32; Num. 3:32, 25:13; Maimonides, *Klei HaMikdash* 1:7).

In later law, ways and means were found and legitimized to enable such rights of the firstborn as related only to property to be waived by them or to be withheld from them by testamentary or other disposition (cf. B. *Bava Metzia* 49a; B. *Bava Batra* 126b, and Rashbam ad loc.; T. *Kiddushin* 3:7–8; Maimonides, *Ishut* 6:9, *Nahalot* 6:5).

21

DISCRIMINATIONS ON ACCOUNT OF PROPERTY

While the ideal state of society and the ultimate divine blessing is achieved "when there shall be no poor among you" (Deut. 15:4), the sad reality we have to face is that "the poor shall never cease out of the land" (ibid. 11).

The poor are the object of a twofold duty imposed by law: positively, that they must be aided, assisted, and maintained (Lev. 25:35, Deut. 15:7–8), and negatively, that they may not be oppressed (Exod. 22:24, Deut. 24:14–15) or otherwise discriminated against. We are mainly concerned with the negative injunction; but it may be noted in passing that talmudic jurists made an emphatic point of the manner in which the positive duty of charity should be performed; you may not embarrass the poor by letting him feel that he is receiving charity (B. *Ketuvot* 67b, B. *Bava Batra* 10a–b), but must give him your alms secretly and anonymously (Prov. 21:14, B. *Hagiga* 5a) or in such a way that he is given the feeling that he is doing a favor to you (J. *Shekalim* 5:4), as indeed he is by enabling you to sanctify God's name in providing livelihood to His creatures (*Vayikra Rabba* 34, *Ruth Rabba* 5:9, 19). The duty is not fulfilled by giving some alms, but you must "open thine hand wide unto him, and shalt surely lend him sufficient for his need, in that which he wanteth" (Deut. 15:8), that is, according to the living standard to which he was accustomed in better times (B. *Ketuvot* 67b; Maimonides, *Matnot Aniyim* 7:3).

The Lord is the maker of rich and poor alike (Prov. 22:2), and the one who is rich today may be made poor tomorrow, as the

poor of today may tomorrow be rich (B. *Temura* 16a); so let the
rich man not "glory in his riches" (Jer. 9:23). The earthly might
which riches may confer is more than counterbalanced by the
special love and protection that God Himself extends to the poor
(Exod. 22:26, Deut. 24:13–15, Isa. 25:4, Ps. 146:7, Prov. 22:23).
Some particular propensities are attributed to the poor; for instance, that it is in a life of poverty and self-denial that wisdom
and learning are acquired (M. *Avot* 6:4; and see p. 141), that it is
the children of the poor from whom the Torah will emanate (B.
Nedarim 81a), and that the greatest masters of the law came,
indeed, from among the poor (B. *Yoma* 35b). It is the poor who are
"of a contrite spirit and trembling at God's word" (Isa. 66:2); they
will be raised up out of the dust and set among princes, for they
are the pillars of the earth (1 Sam. 2:8, Ps. 113:7–8); and the
Messiah, who will bring salvation to the world, will be lowly and
riding upon an ass (Zech. 9:9).

It is not without significance that the first explicit prohibition
of discrimination of the poor to be found in the Bible forbids
countenancing "a poor man in his cause" (Exod. 23:3), that is,
according him any preference or showing him any deference
because he is poor, whether in order to encourage and comfort
him (Rashi ad loc.), or in order to award him the money which he
needs and which his adversary might anyhow have to give him by
way of charity (*Sifra, Kedoshim* 4). But then it is no less forbidden to "wrest the judgment of the poor" (Exod. 23:6), that is, to
subvert his rights and find against him only because he is poor
and hence unprotected and uninfluential. Such potential or actual prejudice against the poor was decried by the prophets in no
uncertain terms (Isa. 10:2, Jer. 5:28), God Himself assuming the
role of "judge of the poor" (Isa. 11:4, Jer. 22:16) where human
judges may fail.

The rule against discriminations in favor of poor and rich alike
found its classical expression in these verses: "Ye shall do no
unrighteousness in judgment: thou shalt not respect the person
of the poor, nor honor the person of the mighty; but in righteousness shalt thou judge thy neighbor" (Lev. 19:15)—"righteousness" being nondiscrimination between rich and poor, and "unrighteousness" any bias for or against one or the other.

The ransom that every man must give "for his soul unto the
Lord" (Exod. 30:12) is a living testimony to the equality of man.
"The rich shall not give more, and the poor shall not give less"

(ibid. 15), there being no difference in value between human souls. And where gifts or sacrifices to God are left to the discretion or ability or generosity of the individual donor, the least gift of the poor is as highly valued as the largest of the rich (M. *Menahot* 13:11). God accepts the humblest donation of the poor as if he had given Him his soul (B. *Menahot* 104b).

In order to avoid even the appearance of a discrimination, the duty to assist and maintain the poor is itself imposed on the rich and on the poor alike. (B. *Gittin* 7b); the poor man will perform his duty either by contributing whatever he can afford to the general charitable fund or by contributing to the maintenance of somebody still poorer than himself (*Yorei Dei'a* 248).

It is reported that in early talmudical times rich decedents were brought to their funerals in caskets of silver and gold, and the poor were brought in wicker baskets made of willow. When it was observed that the poor people were thereby "put to shame," it was laid down that all dead, rich and poor, were to be brought to their funerals in wicker baskets "for the honor of the poor" (B. *Mo'ed Kattan* 27a). Also, formerly the rich drank on public occasions from white glasses, while the poor drank from colored glasses; when it was observed that the poor people were thereby "put to shame," it was laid down that everybody should on those occasions drink from colored glasses "for the honor of the poor" (ibid.). For the same reason it was later ruled that only such modestly priced wines should be served on public occasions as were the customary fare of the poor (Maimonides, *Eivel* 13:7). The cloth with which the dead are to be covered before burial should be so inexpensive as to be also within the means of the poor, and must be the same for rich and poor alike (ibid. 4:1).

Specific prohibitions of oppression of the poor relate to withholding wages overnight (Deut. 24:14–15), to usury on loans (Exod. 22:24, Lev. 25:36), and to retaining pledges, especially raiments (Exod. 22:25–26, Deut. 24:12–13)—all considered illegal and immoral exploitations of the precarious situation of the impoverished. Later the concept of oppression was extended to cover any defraudation or deception (Maimonides, *Gezeila vaAveida* 1:4), especially when practiced clandestinely (Ibn Ezra ad Lev. 19:13), and even just intimidations and importunities (B. *Bava Metzia* 59b), such as "vexing the poor and needy" (Ezek. 22:29).

It has been said that the epithet "poor" should not really be used in respect of the indigent but rather in respect of the fool: "there is no poor but the poor of mind" (B. *Nedarim* 41a). Conversely, "rich" often serves as a synonym for "evil": the rich are "full of violence" (Mic. 6:12), wicked transgressors to be cut off the land of the living (Isa. 53:8–9), and ever increasing their riches by oppressing and robbing the poor (Prov. 22:16). In the good sense of the word, the truly rich are those who are happy and satisfied with whatever they have (M. *Avot* 4:1), and the wise have their wisdom for a crown of riches (Prov. 14:24).

PART

III

RIGHTS OF JUSTICE

22

EQUALITY BEFORE THE LAW

"Ye shall have one manner of law" (Lev. 24:22), meaning not only that the same due processes of law are required in civil as in criminal matters (M. *Sanhedrin* 4:1; *Sifra, Emor* 20:9), but also laying down the general rule that all law must be the same for all (B. *Ketuvot* 33a, B. *Sanhedrin* 28a, B. *Bava Kamma* 83b–84a). This rule is reiterated with special emphasis on the stranger: "One law and one manner shall be for you and for the stranger that sojourneth with you" (Num. 15:16). The force and the protection of the law both extend to everybody, citizen and stranger, man and woman, freeborn and slave, alike. It is true that talmudical law restricted the binding force of legal obligations to Jews only and held non-Jews bound to obey solely the seven Noachide commands (above, p. 161); but the protection of the laws was always extended to non-Jews who chose to avail themselves of it. Thus, Jewish courts will entertain suits of non-Jews who voluntarily submit to their jurisdiction (Maimonides, *Melakhim* 10:12); but a non-Jewish litigant cannot be compelled to submit to the jurisdiction of a Jewish court, even if his non-Jewish adversary has already submitted to it (ibid.). Where non-Jews submit to the jurisdiction of a Jewish court, their causes will be determined according to their own non-Jewish law or custom, unless they expressly opt for Jewish law to be applied (Responsa attributed to Nahmanides, 225; Ritba ad *Bava Metzia* 71b).

Equal protection of the law means, first and foremost, equality in the administration of justice. The biblical injunction "in justice shalt thou judge" (Lev. 19:15) is further elaborated by the Deuteronomist as follows: "Hear the causes between your brethren, and

189

judge righteously between every man and his brother, and the stranger that is with him. Ye shall not respect persons in judgment; but ye shall hear the small as well as the great; ye shall not be afraid of the face of man" (Deut. 1:16–17). Entering from the general into particulars, Maimonides answers the question "What is justice in the process of law?" in the following terms: "It is the equalization of both parties for all purposes: not that one should be allowed to speak as he pleases and the other be cut short; not that one be treated with courtesy and the other with irritation; and if one is dressed well and the other is dressed poorly, the well-dressed is to be asked either to dress as the other or to dress the other as himself, before the case is heard; not that one should stand and the other be seated, or that one should sit above and the other sit below, but both should stand or sit next to each other" (Maimonides, *Sanhedrin* 21:1–3, restating *Sifra, Kedoshim* 4; T. *Sanhedrin* 6:2; B. *Shevu'ot* 30a). The rule of the equality of litigants was later pushed to the extreme of disallowing several plaintiffs to sue a single defendant, or one plaintiff to sue several defendants, in the same action (*Mordekhai* ad *Shevu'ot* 4:761).

The biblical commands not to be a respecter of persons and not to discriminate between rich and poor (above, and Deut. 16:19, Exod. 23:3) are, of course, but another aspect of the same rule of equality. But as nature has made men unequal, the doctrine of equality had to be modified to fit realities: the equality of all men before the law can only mean that, *ceteris paribus*, nobody is to be preferred and nobody is to be slighted. The necessary reservation, "all other things being equal," opens the door to legitimate inequalities, but each such departure from equality is derived from other rules of justice likewise equally valid for all. Thus we find, immediately following the rule of the equality of litigants, the exception that when there are many litigants in court waiting for their cases to be heard, priority is to be given first to orphans, second to widows (cf. Isa. 1:17), third to scholars; and as between male and female litigants, priority is given to women (Maimonides, *Sanhedrin* 21:6; *Hoshen Mishpat* 15:2). Later jurists held these priorities to be subject to an overriding priority of the litigant who came first and waited longest (Rashi ad *Sanhedrin* 8a; *Hoshen Mishpat* 15:1). In the cases of orphans and widows, the priority accorded to them stems from considerations of charity; in the case of scholars, from the public interest in minimizing the loss of time from their holy studies; and in the case of women, from the desire to spare them the embarrassment of having to wait in court (Maimonides, loc. cit.); and as to the waiting list, the priority stems, of course, from considerations of efficiency and fairness.

A derivative of the equality rule is the parties' equal right of audience. From King Solomon's art of administering justice (as reported in 1 Kings 3:23), we learn that a judge must first attentively listen to the arguments and evidence on both sides and then carefully repeat them to himself before he comes to a decision (Maimonides, *Sanhedrin* 21:9; *Hoshen Mishpat* 17:7). Even where he thinks the matter is quite clear and leaves no room for doubt, he must make due inquiry and may not cut short any argument. Witness God Almighty, who certainly knows everything there is to be known, but before passing judgment He is heard to ask: "Who told thee that thou wast naked? Hast thou eaten of the tree?" (Gen. 3:11); or: "Where is Abel, thy brother? What hast thou done?" (Gen. 4:9–10); nay, God even went down to earth "to see whether they have done altogether according to the cry of it which is come to Me, and if not, I will know" (Gen. 18:21)—showing that even omniscience (or what we may call divine "judicial notice") does not relieve the conscientious judge of the duty to listen and, where necessary, to inspect (*Responsa Rema* 108). Nor would it be commendable for a judge to rely on interpreters to translate the proceedings to him (Maimonides, op. cit. 21:8; *Hoshen Mishpat* 17:6); the ideal judge is polyglot, understanding the different languages spoken by the people under his jurisdiction. For the same reason that the judge ought to hear, and be impressed by, the words and demeanor of the parties themselves—as it is written: "Then both the men, between whom the controversy is, shall stand . . . before the judge" (Deut. 19:17)—the practice of legal representation did not take root in Jewish courts until a very late stage (Assaf 95 ff.). The deprecation of the man who "did that which is not good among his people" (Ezek. 18:18) was held to apply to attorneys (B. *Shevu'ot* 31a); they are fierce men, full of arguments, who get excited over litigation that does not concern them (Tossafot ad loc., s.v. *zeh*). But another reason for looking askance at legal representation may well have been that the equality of the parties might be infringed by the qualities or standing of their respective attorneys, or by one party being represented and the other not (and what the Jewish courts in talmudical times may have known of forensic pleadership in Athens and Rome would hardly have encouraged them to change their own practice: see Jones 120–126; Schulz 108). Parties could be allowed to present their arguments in writing, instead of or in addition to oral argument, only if both agreed and both remunerated the scribes in equal shares (*Hoshen Mishpat* 13:3, elaborating on M. *Bava Batra* 10:4).

Another derivative of the principle of equality is the rule that you may not hear one party in the absence of the other. Not only may you not make a decision without having heard "the other party" first, but you must hear both parties in the presence and hearing of each other (B. *Sanhedrin* 7b; B. *Shevu'ot* 31a; Maimonides, *Sanhedrin* 21:7; *Hoshen Mishpat* 17:5), or else you lend, or look as if you are lending, a hand to slander (Exod. 23:1: "thou shalt not raise a false report"; Lev. 19:16: "thou shalt not go . . . as a talebearer"), or even to fraud (Exod. 23:7: "Keep thee far from a false matter"). At the root of this rule lies the scriptural injunction "Hear the cause between your brethren," immediately followed by the words "and judge righteously" (Deut. 1:16), to indicate that in order to do justice you have to hear the parties together, "between them." This hermeneutical reasoning was supplemented by quasi-psychological considerations. It was believed that people would not easily lie in matters concerning each other when they are confronted with each other; more particularly, a debtor would not lie in the face of his creditor (B. *Bava Metzia* 3a). This kind of—rebuttable—presumption presupposes that in their ordinary dealings people are frank and candid with each other, and that he who seeks to defraud another would do so normally behind his back. The presence of judges sitting in court might not only deter litigants from scandalizing the court but also encourage them to put forward exaggerated claims or blown-up charges against adversaries who are not present there and then to contradict and deny (Sema ad *Hoshen Mishpat* 17:5; *Kessef Mishne* ad Maimonides, *Sanhedrin* 21:7). A party is always apt to lie in the absence of the other party and try to impress the judges unduly with his own version of the case (*Sefer HaHinukh* 90). But a litigant who exploits the absence of his adversary in such an unfair manner is called a "sly evildoer" and counted among those who bring the world to ruin (M. *Sota* 3:4 and Bartenura ad loc.). In contrast to the apparent judicial experience with these "sly evildoers" stands the presumption that gives every plaintiff the credit of good faith; a man is presumed not to institute proceedings if he has no valid claim at all (B. *Shevu'ot* 40b), nor will a defendant contest a claim if he cannot put up a *bona fide* defense (B. *Bava Metzia* 3a). This presumption of good faith would seem to apply only if and when the other party is present; in the absence of the other party, the court is apparently to expect the worst of, and be on guard against, any litigant (M. *Avot* 1:8). But the *ratio legis* is not so much the apprehension of fraudulent or slanderous abuse of the judicial process as rather the notion that everything to be done in the course of the proceedings must be done in such a way that each of the parties concerned will at all times, from his own observation, be fully aware of what has come before the court and of how the court dealt with it. Thus, a court may hear no witness and take no other evidence except in the presence of both parties (B. *Bava Kamma* 112a–b; Maimonides, *Eidut* 3:11; *Hoshen Mishpat* 28:15). In systems that allow the parties to examine and cross-examine witnesses, a rule of this kind is meant to implement that right; but in systems like the Jewish, where all examinations of witnesses are carried out by the court only (M. *Sanhedrin* 3:6, 4:1 and 5, 5:1–4), the object of the rule surely is to let the parties see and hear and satisfy themselves that justice is being done. The danger inherent in *ex parte* hearings, and the necessity of hearing and examining both sides, is alluded to in Proverbs: "He that is first (heard) in his own cause, seemeth just; but his neighbor (i.e., his adversary) cometh and searcheth (lit. interrogates) him" (18:17), suggesting that it is the adversary who does the searching cross-examination; but this has never been the rule of practice.

Even the rule that no man may be a judge in his own cause (B. *Shabbat* 119a et al.) is, from the point of view of Jewish law, to be derived from the principle of the equality of the parties. By having or acquiring an interest in the subject-matter the judge disturbs the equilibrium, whether by identifying himself with one of the parties or by adding to them another interested party and thus detracting from their own prospects. A judge who has accepted a gift or a bribe from one party has thereby disqualified himself—

not necessarily because of the illegality of his conduct, but because of the "interest" he has acquired, albeit possibly unwittingly, in the cause of the party from whom he accepted it (B. *Ketuvot* 105b). Nay, even if he accepted bribes from both parties, he has acquired a personal interest that disqualifies him, not because he is apt to identify himself with either party, but because he has superadded to theirs his own interest to satisfy both of them and thus disturbed their exclusive equality before the law (*Responsa Havat Ya'ir* 136). The apprehension of the judge's potential monetary interest went so far as to preclude his claiming or receiving any court fees (B. *Ketuvot* 105a; M. *Bekhorot* 4:6; Maimonides, *Sanhedrin* 23:5; *Hoshen Mishpat* 9:5), and it would not matter that such fees were to be paid by all litigants alike. Nor was a judge allowed to levy fees or other emoluments for his scribes or clerks, it being assumed that the better paid his clerks and scribes were, the more esteemed and the more efficiently served the judge would be, and thus he would have an interest in their being remunerated (B. *Shabbat* 56a; Maimonides, op. cit. 23:3; *Hoshen Mishpat* 9:4). This was that "turning aside after lucre" in which the judges of Beersheba are reported to have indulged, apart from taking bribes (1 Sam. 8:3). The disqualification of judges was extended not only to borrowing some chattel from one of the parties (B. *Ketuvot* 105b; Maimonides, op. cit. 23:4; *Hoshen Mishpat* 9:1), or to having in any other way, however insignificant, benefited from him (ibid.), but also to liking or disliking personally anybody involved in the case (B. *Ketuvot* 105b, *Hoshen Mishpat* 7:7): "the just judge is the one who does not know either of the parties and has never heard of them before" (Maimonides, op. cit. 23:6). Nor need the disqualificatory interest of the judge be a personal one; he would be disqualified even if his interest was an indirect one, for instance as a member of the community, where the safeguarding or recovery of community property was at stake (B. *Bava Batra* 43a), or as a taxpayer, where he would have an interest in the equal and equitable distribution of tax burdens (*Responsa Asheri* 6:18, *Hoshen Mishpat* 7:12). In these and similar cases proceedings should be transferred to the courts of another town or country where all the judges are wholly disinterested.

The equality of the parties has its counterpart in the impartiality of the judge. "When the litigants stand before you, consider both equally wrong; when they have heard and accepted your judgment, consider them both equally right, and never make yourself the advocate of either of them" (M. *Avot* 1:8; Maimonides, op. cit. 23:10; *Hoshen Mishpat* 17:10). Consider them wrong in the sense that nothing they aver or allege should be taken for granted unless and until duly admitted or proved; and consider them right in the sense that with their submission to the judgment pronounced, all defects in the position of either of them have been cured. No judge ought to take upon himself the role of an advocate, as if he had any stake or interest in the outcome of the proceedings. But, here again, justice suffers no hard-and-fast rule. It is the duty and function of the judge to cross-examine witnesses, and he is exhorted to cross-examine most searchingly and thoroughly so that the truth may come to light (M. *Sanhedrin* 5:2; B. *Sanhedrin* 32b and 41a; Maimonides, *Eidut* 1:1–8), but when he does so, he may well appear to the party who produced the witness as if he had made himself the advocate of the other party. Moreover, there occur exceptional cases in which the judge is in duty bound to help one party plead and present his case against the other. "Where the judge sees that one of the parties has a good point and wishes to enunciate it but cannot put the words together, or that the truth is on his side but he is so enraged or angered or intimidated that he cannot speak, or that he is too stupid to say what he ought to say, the judge may assist him a little and get him started on his argument, in order to 'open thy mouth for the dumb' (Prov. 31:8); but he must be very careful so as not to act like an advocate" (Maimonides, *Sanhedrin* 21:11). Conversely, where the judge suspects any fraud on the court, though the cause of action has ostensibly been proved, for instance where nothwithstanding all cross-examination the witnesses stick to their story but the judge is not satisfied that they are telling the truth, he should disqualify himself and let another judge retry the case (B. *Shevu'ot* 30b–31a; B. *Sanhedrin* 32b; Maimonides, op. cit. 24:3; *Hoshen Mishpat* 15:3). But a later jurist thought that justice required such a judge, if indeed he was satisfied that there had been an attempt to mislead the court, to furnish the innocent party with a certificate to the effect that no other judge should entertain the suit against him (*Responsa Asheri* 68:20). The rule was that where the witnesses were duly qualified and wholly consistent with each other (cf. Mark 14:59), the relevant facts were deemed to be established by their testimony (Deut. 19:15)—hence the importance of some legal machinery to enable judges to detect and disavow "fraudulent actions."

The difficulty of attaining real justice in the judicial process is reflected in the wise warning given by one of the sages, that whoever succeeded in avoiding appointment as a judge kept himself aloof from enmity, larceny, and perjury (M. Avot 4:7)—enmity, because the party found liable or guilty will always bear a grudge against the judge; larceny, because there is always the danger that a party was held liable to pay money which was not really due from him; and perjury, because an oath may have been tendered unlawfully or unnecessarily (Bartenura ad loc.). Indeed, it has been said that if a judge by his judgment takes away money from one party and bestows it on the other party contrary to law or justice, God will take his soul, for it is written: "Rob not the poor . . . For the Lord will plead their cause, and spoil the soul of those that spoiled them" (Prov. 22:22–23; B. Sanhedrin 7a; Maimonides, op. cit. 23:9). Whether it was suchlike hazards of the judicial office, or reluctance to assume judicial responsibility, or a desire to avoid honor and power, the sages, we are told, shunned judicial appointment, even by the subterfuge of disappearing and hiding from the authorities who wished to appoint them (B. Sanhedrin 14a, Hoshen Mishpat 8:3); but it was eventually settled that judicial responsibility ought not to be shirked: "no judge should say, 'Why should I of all people have to bear the burden?' "—he should act and proceed to the best of his own conscience, "according to what his eyes behold' (Maimonides, loc. cit.). The judge's eyes are, of course, to be focused on the parties before him; and the foremost prescript of justice and fairness is that no man should judge his fellowman without first attempting to put himself in that man's place (M. Avot 2:4), that is, to see him through his own eyes.

The equality of all before the law is well illustrated also by the rules restricting the taxation powers of the king. It is one of the king's prerogatives "to impose taxes on the people for his own needs or for purposes of warfare," and any royal decree by which taxes are imposed has the force of law and must be obeyed by all; the king may impose punishments for disobedience, even including the death penalty (Maimonides, Melakhim 4:1). But "a king who takes away the land of any of his citizens not in accordance with the decrees he has enacted, is a robber," and he does not acquire a good title to any property so sequestrated (Maimonides, *Gezeila vaAveida* 5:13). "This is the rule: any decree which the king enacts and which is applicable to all (is valid); if it applies not to all but to particular persons only it is (invalid and) a robbery" (ibid. 14). The term "robbery" is used in this context not only by way of deprecation of unequal taxation, but mainly to indicate that no title to property can be acquired by the exercise of powers derived from law, where a violation of the principle of universality and equality is involved. In later times, when taxes were imposed by community regulations (*takkanot hakahal*), the rule was retained that any taxation was valid and enforceable only if applicable to each and every member of the community alike (*Responsa Rashba* 1:788 and 5:178, *Responsa Rivash* 477). The very power of communal legislation was conditioned upon the premise that all members of the community were alike affected by the cause which rendered the regulation necessary and were alike interested in and in need of it (*Sha'arei Zedek* 4:4, 16). While such regulations could validly be enacted by a vote of a majority of the community elders, such majority had always to be satisfied that the regulations were needed by and applicable to all members of the community alike (Ritba ad *Avoda Zara* 36b). Equality was not necessarily lacking, however, if a given regulation applied only to a particular trade or a particular locality or a particular class of persons, provided it applied equally to all persons within that trade, locality, or class (*Responsa Havat Ya'ir* 81).

While the principle of equal applicability to all was also postulated for the binding force of non-Jewish laws of the lands where Jews lived (*dina demalkhutta*), it was recognized that such laws might discriminate between Christian (or Muslim) and Jewish people, and they were held to be binding upon the Jews provided they did not discriminate between Jew and Jew but were at least equally applicable to all Jews (*Responsa Maharik* 194). The reason underlying this concession seems to be that the king has the power to legislate for a class of persons, for instance, the strangers (Jews) in his lands, provided his laws apply equally to all persons within that class (*Hokhmat Shelomo* ad *Hoshen Mishpat* 369:8).

23

JUDICIAL STANDARDS

God, the Judge of all the earth (Gen. 18:25), exercises His judicial power by doing justice; He would not "slay the righteous with the wicked, that the righteous should be as the wicked" (ibid.), but gives every man his due "according to his ways and according to the fruits of his doings" (Jer. 17:10). Even the heathen are warned that on the day of the Lord, "as thou hast done, it shall be done unto thee; thy reward shall return upon thine own head" (Obad. 1:15). God's fury exhausts itself and His anger is "accomplished" by punishing the offender "according to thy ways" (Ezek. 7:8), and "the vengeance of the Lord" is to do unto her "as she hath done" (Jer. 50:15). But then, on the other hand, God is "merciful and gracious, long-suffering and abundant in goodness and truth, keeping mercy for thousands, forgiving iniquity and transgression and sin" (Exod. 34:6–7); and as the Judge, God "regardeth not persons, nor taketh reward; He doth execute the judgment of the fatherless and widow, and loveth the stranger" (Deut. 10:17–18). God's own judicial attributes are to be imitated by the human judge: "the spirit of the Lord shall rest upon him . . . and he shall not judge after the sight of his eyes, neither reprove after the hearing of his ears; but with righteousness shall he judge the poor, and reprove with equity for the meek of the earth. . . . And righteousness shall be the girdle of his loins, and faithfulness the girdle of his reins" (Isa. 11:2–5). God's "judgments" and "righteousness" shall be given to the judge to judge the people, to "save the children of the needy, and break in pieces the oppressor" (Ps. 72:1–4). The verse "Ye shall walk after the Lord your God" (Deut. 13:4) has been interpreted, out of context, to

198

require the *Imitatio Dei* (B. *Sota* 14a): "as He is merciful, so must you be merciful; as He is compassionate, so must you be compassionate" (B. *Shabbat* 133b).

It is not only the imitation of God's justice and mercy that distinguishes the human judge; it is said that the judge who passes true judgment is like God's partner in the creation of the world (B. *Shabbat* 10a), brings God's presence down unto the world (B. *Sanhedrin* 7a), and radiates light like heaven (B. *Bava Batra* 8b).

On the more terrestrial level, Moses was advised by his father-in-law, the Midianite priest, to select "out of all the people able men, such as fear God, men of truth, hating covetousness," to "judge the people at all seasons" (Exod. 18:21–22). Moses himself recalled later that he had appointed "wise men, and understanding, and known among your tribes" (Deut. 1:13), and charged them to "hear the causes between your brethren, and judge righteously between every man and his brother, and the stranger that is with him. Ye shall not respect persons in judgment: but ye shall hear the small as well as the great; ye shall not be afraid of the face of man; for the judgment is God's: and the cause that is too hard for you, bring it unto me, and I will hear it" (ibid. 16–17).

The law was laid down in the following terms: "Judges and officers shalt thou make thee in all thy gates which the Lord thy God giveth thee, throughout thy tribes: and they shall judge the people with just judgment. Thou shalt not wrest judgment; thou shalt not respect persons, neither take a gift; for a gift doeth blind the eyes of the wise and pervert the words of the righteous. That which is altogether just shalt thou follow, that thou mayest live . . . " (Deut. 16:18–20). (What is here rendered as "that which is altogether just" is, literally, "justice, justice shalt thou follow.")

Originally, hierarchies of judges were appointed over a thousand people, hundreds, fifties, and tens, with Moses as the supreme judge of last resort (Exod. 18:21, Deut. 1:15). These judges judged the people "at all seasons," even before laws had been given. It is therefore probable that in ancient Israel judicature preceded legislation and that some of the later law may have originated in judicial precedents. When the people settled in the land of Israel, the allocation of jurisdiction on a purely numerical basis was replaced by allocation on a geographical basis, and judges were appointed in every town (Deut. 16:18; *Sifrei, Shoftim*

144; B. *Sanhedrin* 16b). It is disputed whether the injunction to establish a court in every town applied only in the land of Israel or also in the Diaspora; some hold that outside the land of Israel a court must be established in every district but need not be established in every town (B. *Makkot* 7a). The biblical restriction to "all thy gates which the Lord giveth thee" (Deut. 16:18) was eventually held to warrant the limitation of applicability to the land of Israel (Maimonides, *Sanhedrin* 1:2); but it was nevertheless regarded as a rule of law that every Jewish community must have its own law court (*Arukh HaShulhan* ad *Hoshen Mishpat* 1:18).

The jurisdictional powers vested in the various courts varied according to their composition. A court of three exercised general civil jurisdiction, while courts of twenty-three exercised general criminal (including capital) jurisdiction (M. *Sanhedrin* 1:1–4). In towns with less than 120 inhabitants, i.e., householders, there was only a court of three judges (B. *Sanhedrin* 3b; Maimonides, op. cit. 1:10); towns with more than 120 inhabitants should also have a court of twenty-three (M. *Sanhedrin* 1:6). The figure of 120 is explained in the Talmud as being the minimum number needed for the proper functioning of the court of twenty-three—and it may be for this reason that nobody should make his home in a town in which there is no criminal court (B. *Sanhedrin* 17b).

While no regular court could consist of less than three judges, recognized experts in the law (*mumhe larabbim*) were already in talmudical times admitted as single judges in civil cases (B. *Sanhedrin* 5a), albeit not without reservations, there being no true single judge other than God alone (M. *Avot* 4:8; Maimonides, op. cit. 2:11). No litigant can be compelled to submit to the jurisdiction of a single judge (*Hoshen Mishpat* 3:2).

Judicial qualifications were enumerated by Maimonides as follows: "Judges must be wise and sensible, learned in the law and full of knowledge, and also acquainted to some extent with other subjects, such as medicine, arithmetic, astronomy and astrology, and the ways of sorcerers and magicians, and the absurdities of idolatry and the like, so that they should know how to judge them. . . . A judge should not be too old in years, nor may he be a eunuch or childless—the eunuch is cruel, and the father of children is compassionate. . . . And as judges must be pure with justice, so must they be pure from all bodily defects; and efforts should be made to find men of stature and imposing appearance, well-groomed and high-minded; and they should be conversant in many languages so as not to stand in need of interpreters. . . . The seven fundamental qualities of a judge are wisdom, humility, fear of God, disdain of money, love of truth, love of men, and a good reputation. . . . They will earn the love of the people by generosity and modesty, by being pleasant in company and by speaking to and dealing with people in kindliness. . . . They must be exemplary in the observance of the laws and painstakingly strict with themselves, conquering their impulses; and their bearing should be fine always. They must have a courageous heart to rescue the oppressed from oppressors. . . . They should not be greedy and never get agitated over their own money. . . . It is justice that they are supposed to pursue, not fortunes. Men of integrity (they should be) who pursue justice for its own sake, lovers of truth and haters of injustice, who run away fast from the least iniquity" (op. cit. 2:1–7).

The injunction not to be respecters of persons appears twice (Deut. 1:17 and 16:19) and was interpreted in one place to enjoin judges from discriminating between rich and poor or between litigants of high and low repute (Sifrei, Shoftim 144), and in the other place as being directed to those who appoint judges: one should not prefer a man for judicial appointment because of his good looks, or because he is a hero, or because he is one's relative, or because of having once borrowed money from him, or because he is proficient in languages (Sifrei, Devarim 17; Maimonides, op. cit. 3:8). While the knowledge of languages is elsewhere listed as a desideratum for judges (B. Menahot 65a; Maimonides, op. cit. 2:6), this earlier source seems to suspect linguistic proficiency as apt to create wrong impressions of intellectual caliber.

And the injunction not to be afraid (of the face) of any man (Deut. 1:17) has been interpreted as a warning to the judge never to suppress his words because they might be resented by others (B. Sanhedrin 8a). One authority expressly renders "any man" of whom not to be afriad as any "rich man or potentate" (Yonatan ben Uziel ad loc.). The biblical assertion that any judgment you may give is indeed God's judgment, and therefore that you need not and may not be afraid of any man or ruler—based as it is on the assumption that you gave your judgment according to God's law to the best of your knowledge and conscience—amounts to the charter in Jewish law of the independence of judges.

There are some further disqualifications to be noted. In general, a man is disqualified from judicial office if he is a habitual gambler or moneylender or a dealer in illicit goods (M. *Sanhedrin* 3:3). It has also been said that a judge should not engage in manual work, lest he expose himself to contempt (B. *Kiddushin* 70a). In particular cases, a judge is disqualified if one of the parties is related to him or if, although unrelated, either party is liked or disliked by him (M. *Sanhedrin* 3:4–5).

A judge must show patience, forbearance, and respect for persons, when sitting in court (Maimonides, op. cit. 25:1; *Hoshen Mishpat* 8:2–5). He may not act under actual or potential pressure or undue influence—the most dreaded potential influence being caused by bribes, including even "bribes of words" (B. *Ketuvot* 105a–b et al.). He must so conduct himself that justice is not only done, as commanded by God, but is also manifestly seen by the people to be done; a judge must satisfy men no less than God (M. *Shekalim* 3:2), for it is written: "Ye shall be guiltless before the Lord and before Israel" (Num. 32:22). The exhortation to do what is "right and good in the sight of the Lord" (Deut. 6:18 and 12:28) gave rise to a dispute between the sages: one said that "good" is what is good in the eyes of heaven, and "right" is what is right in the eyes of man; and the other said that "right" is what is right in the eyes of heaven, and "good" is what is good in the eyes of man; but both were agreed that it was not enough to stand the test of "the sight of the Lord"—you also have to satisfy human standards by adjudicating that which is right or good in the eyes of man (Rashi ad Deut. 12:28; *Sifrei, Re'ei* 79; T. *Shekalim* 2:2).

No judge ought to sit in court together with another judge whom he dislikes (B. *Sanhedrin* 29a), there always being the danger that he might be tempted to decide not according to law and his conscience but so as to disagree with and annoy his colleague (Maimonides, op. cit. 23:7). The "pure of mind" of Jerusalem would not sit down in court unless they knew exactly who all the other members of the court were; and in order to keep himself "far from a false matter" (Exod. 23:7), no judge ought to sit together with any judge suspected of greed or malevolence (Maimonides, op. cit. 22:10).

There is not in Jewish law—as distinguished from most other ancient systems of law—any specific criminal sanction attached to bribery of judges. Josephus wrongly contends that a judge who took a bribe was by Jewish law liable to capital punishment (*Contra Apionem* 2.27). The law is that a judge's disqualification for having taken a bribe invalidates any proceedings he has taken and any decision he has rendered (cf. M. *Bekhorot* 4:4, B. *Bekhorot* 28b), and not only is he liable to restore the money he received by way of bribe to the party who paid it to him (Maimonides, op. cit. 23:1; *Hoshen Mishpat* 9:1), but he may be liable in damages to the other party if any decision against that other party has been acted upon to his detriment (M. *Bekhorot* 4:4 and Maimonides' Commentary ad loc.). The invalidation of the proceedings with the ensuing civil liability of the judge was regarded as a quasi-penalty (*kenass*) imposed on the judge (*Sema* ad *Hoshen Mishpat* 9:5), and Jewish law refuses to attach more than one sanction to any given offense, even though the one sanction attached to it may be civil and not criminal in nature (M. *Makkot* 1:2; B. *Makkot* 4b, 13b; Maimonides, op. cit. 18:2).

The civil liability of judges is not limited to cases of bribery and suchlike grave misconduct; on the contrary, the law was originally laid down for cases of judicial negligence, omissions or errors which need not amount to misconduct at all: "a judge who passed judgment imposing liability on the nonliable or discharging the liable from liability, the judgment is final, and the judge shall pay the damage out of his own pocket" (B. *Sanhedrin* 6a, 33a; B. *Bava Kamma* 100a, 117b). The standard of justice required and expected of a judge was such that any deviation therefrom, however slight, was presumed to be such negligence as would render the judge liable in damages.

Thus it was much less dangerous to come before a bad judge under Jewish law than it was (and is) under other systems of law. For where a judge erred in law, his judgment was a nullity, without having to be set aside on appeal; whenever any of the parties so desired, the case had to be retried (B. *Sanhedrin* 32a, 33a). Some difficulty arose in defining what an error of law amounted to for this purpose; it was eventually settled that a decision conflicting with the law as laid down in the later codes disclosed an error of law on the face of it (Maimonides, op. cit. 6:1; *Pithei Teshuva* ad *Hoshen Mishpat* 25:1). And a judgment bad in law which had already been enforced or complied with, or which for any other reason could not be set right in a new trial, rendered the judge liable in damages (Maimonides, op. cit. 6:3—ignorance of the law, or the inability to properly apply the law, apparently being regarded as professional negligence.

Apart from "errors of law" there were "errors of discretion." A judge was deemed to have committed an error of discretion not only where he erred on the facts, but also where the law had not yet clearly been laid down or finally settled on any given issue; in such cases an error which we would nowadays consider an error of law was considered an error of discretion only (B. *Sanhedrin* 33a; Asheri ad *Sanhedrin* 4:6; Me'iri ad *Sanhedrin* 23a). While in matters of law already settled in the codes any error was easily detectable and there was no difficulty in persuading a court of the necessity for, and the right to, a retrial, in matters of law not yet so settled the issue depended on judicial opinions which—though other judges might disagree and hold different opinions—could never be held to be wrong on the face of them. As between the litigants at bar, therefore, the issue was regarded as having been finally determined, even if it afterwards transpired that an "error of discretion" might have occurred—subject to the provision that every case could be reopened whenever new material evidence as to facts came to light (M. *Sanhedrin* 4:1: criminal cases could be reopened only if new facts had come to light which might prove the innocence of the accused; Maimonides, op. cit. 11:1; *Hoshen Mishpat* 16:1 and 20:1).

While as between the litigants and the judge no more could or need be done to have the scales of justice restored, the erroneous judgment could still work injustice at large, if it were allowed to stand as a judicial precedent (cf. M. *Avot* 1:11: judges ought to be very careful with their dicta, lest they mislead others and eventually cause divine law to fall into disrepute). It is in order to avoid any possible injustice in any particular case that, in spite of the immutability and unconditional validity of divine law, no binding force is accorded in Jewish law to the judicial prcedent. There is a talmudic dictum to the effect that a judge who, instead of using his own discretion and reason in a matter not yet clearly settled by law, relies on the previous decision of some other judge, is doing wrong and not fulfilling his judicial duty (B. *Yevamot* 109b, *Hoshen Mishpat* 10:2). Reliance on a previous decision is defined by the commentators as comparing the case before him with another case that had come before another judge, instead of consulting his teacher or master or an expert in the law available in his city, on the particular case before him (Rashi and Me'iri ad *Yevamot* 109b). Consultations with teachers or experts are recommended in cases where the judge is in any doubt as to what the law is (ibid.); and where a judge "hangs himself" on a precedent without first ascertaining that the previous decision was, indeed, right and just, "he brings upon himself great evil, and his conduct shows a coarseness of mind which leads to miscarriages of justice" (Maimonides, op. cit. 20:8). Even the precedent of the most outstanding and eminent judge may not be blindly followed: "It is an error of law not to follow the earlier decision of a great authority, only where that decision was, in your own eyes, the right decision to take; but even the greatest of jurists, of most ancient fame, may have arrived at decisions which, for reasons of your own, you would not have taken; it is then your duty to decide contrary to their decisions, for there is no judge except 'the judge in his own days' (Deut. 17:9); and so long as a point is not settled in the codes, you have to build or to demolish as you think just, even contrary to the rulings of great scholars" (Asheri ad *Sanhedrin* 4:6). As to the scriptural reference to the judge "that shall be in those days" (Deut. 17:9), the question was posed, how could anybody come before a judge other than the one living and acting in his own days? The seemingly redundant words were interpreted to imply that no one should be heard to say, "How good were the old days, and what a pity that the judges of old are no longer!" The judge that is in your days is the best and only judge for you: Dan in his generation, and Jephthah in his, and Samuel in his, were judges as good and competent as Moses himself was in his own generation; and no judge need pretend to the knowledge and competence of others in different times (B. *Rosh HaShana* 25a–b). In other words, there can be no true justice if it is out of touch with, and not conditioned by, the changed and changing circumstances of time and place; it is the judge of your own days, unfettered by chains of precedents from times past, who must discern for you the nature of your rights and the availability and effectuality of your remedies.

Justice requires not only that you do not "hang yourself" on precedents, but also that you form your own opinion independently, and not just go along with the decision of the majority of the court or with the considered and well-reasoned view of any of its members. Especially in criminal cases, the scriptural injunction not to "speak in a cause to decline after many to wrest judgment" (Exod. 23:2) was applied to a judge who adopts the opinion of his colleagues on the bench, without giving his own mind to the issue before the court (Maimonides, op. cit. 10:1). Conversely, and however self-reliant and independent each individual judge is required to be, it was thought that proper administration of justice would presuppose consultation and conference among the judges. Talmudical legend has it that even God Himself would not sit alone in judgment: "all the hosts of heaven stand around Him, to His right and to His left, and take sides before Him" (J. Sanhedrin 1:1). In capital cases, where the life of the accused was at stake, proceedings had to be adjourned after conclusion of the evidence and would not be resumed until the following day, so that the judges could consult with each other the whole night (M. Sanhedrin 5:5). Criminal law being assuaged by mercy, the law was that a judge who had spoken for convicting the accused could then in conference be persuaded to vote for acquittal; but a judge who had already expressed himself in favor of an acquittal could not be heard the next day to vote for conviction (ibid.). In noncapital cases, the collegiate court appears to have been established for this very purpose of conference and consultation, and in criminal and quasi-criminal causes it had to be composed of professional judges ("experts") so as to render the consultation meaningful (Maimonides, op. cit. 5:8). In cases of contracts and debts, courts could be composed of laymen, the reason being that creditors might not be willing to lend money if they had to look for courts of experts to sue for recovery (B. Sanhedrin 3a).

The efficacy of legal remedies depends not only on their availability but also on the promptness of their adjudication. There are two rules which apparently contradict each other: one, that judges ought to proceed with caution and without haste (M. Avot 1:1; Maimonides, op. cit. 20:7; Hoshen Mishpat 10:1), and the other, that judges should not delay their judgments (B. Sanhedrin 35a; Maimonides, op. cit. 20:6; Hoshen Mishpat 17:11). On the one hand, justice may be jeopardized by an overhasty and premature judgment of judges who "leap forward and cut the case short before having considered it inwardly and thoroughly until it has become clear to them like the sun," conduct which earned them epithets like "idiots, wicked, and coarse-minded" (Maimonides, op. cit. 20:7). On the other hand, delays of justice were known already in ancient times to make for denials of justice. A special term was coined in Jewish law to denote "afflictions of justice" (*innuj din*) by protracted or oppressive litigation, by way of complement to "perversions of justice" (*ivvut din*) denoting wrong and misguided judicial decisions—both being regarded as the prohibited "unrighteousness in judgment" (Lev. 19:15) and as the true, if hidden, causes of war (M. *Avot* 5:8), famine, pestilence, and suchlike disasters (B. *Shabbat* 33a). The story goes that when Rabbi Yishma'el and Rabbi Shimeon were led to be executed by the Romans, Shimeon wondered why he should have deserved so cruel a punishment at the hands of God; and Yishma'el asked him: "Did ever come a man before you with a legal suit, and you delayed him until you had finished your meal or put on your shoes or your dress?" Whereupon Shimeon said, "You have comforted me, my master" (*Mekhilta, Mishpatim* 18).

As between undue haste and undue delay, it would seem that the path of justice is in the middle: you ought not to deliver judgment until you have taken time to consider it, but the time you take to consider it may not be such as to cause any "affliction" or hardship to either party. The ideal judge is the one whose seat is founded on compassion and who sits thereon in truth, administering and expounding the law and hastening justice (Isa. 16:5, my translation).

A talmudical tradition deplores the decline of judicial standards and achievements: Judges having now become respecters of persons, they are no longer really independent, and "not to be afraid of any man" has become an empty phrase; and having foremost in their minds not the concerns of others but their own fortunes ("for with their mouth they show much love, but their heart goeth after their covetousness": Ezek. 33:31), they are in peril of the prophecy coming true, "Woe unto them that call evil good, and good evil . . . that are wise in their own eyes, and prudent in their own sight . . . that justify the wicked for reward, and take away the righteousness of the righteous from him" (Isa. 5:20–23); and having become arrogant and corrupt, all goodness and justice have gone from the world (B. *Sota* 47b).

24

PROCEDURAL SAFEGUARDS

In criminal cases, the courts sit only during the day and adjourn at sunset (M. *Sanhedrin* 4:1; Maimonides, *Sanhedrin* 11:1). If the proceedings have been concluded during the day, acquittal will be announced forthwith, but a judgment of conviction and sentence may not be announced until the following day (ibid.), since there may be a chance that the judges will change their minds during the night (Rashi ad *Sanhedrin* 32a). No criminal sessions may therefore be held on the eves of Sabbaths and holidays (M. *Sanhedrin* 4:1; Maimonides, op. cit. 11:2); and either because the trial is regarded as the first step toward an execution, which may not take place on a Sabbath (J. *Sanhedrin* 4:7), or maybe because a trial involves writing, prohibited on Sabbaths, no criminal trials may be held on Sabbaths and holidays (Tossafot ad *Beitza* 36b and *Sanhedrin* 35a).

It has already been noted that the general criminal courts were composed of twenty-three judges (above, p. 200). They sat in the form of a half-circle, so that the judges could all see one another. Before them stood two court-scribes, one at the right and one at the left, who recorded the words of the judges—one the words of those in favor of conviction, and the other the words of those in favor of acquittal. Three rows of learned disciples sat before them, each knowing his place; when the seat of a judge became vacant, his place would be filled by a disciple from the first row (M. *Sanhedrin* 4:3–4). According to another version, both scribes record the words of all the judges, so that if one errs the other can correct him (Rashi ad *Sanhedrin* 36b). The public and the disciples would already be in court when the judges entered, the presiding judge last, and everyone present would rise and remain standing until the presiding judge gave them leave to sit down (T. *Sanhedrin* 8:8).

Only one capital case may be tried on any one day in any one court (M. *Sanhedrin* 6:4, T. *Sanhedrin* 7:2). An exception was made where there were several participants in one crime, provided they were all liable to the same penalty (B. *Sanhedrin* 46a). Where, however, participants in one crime were liable to be executed by different methods, as for instance in adultery, where the male adulterer was liable to strangulation and the adulteress, if a priest's daughter, to burning, they had to be tried separately on different days (Maimonides, op. cit. 14:10).

The arrest and detention of persons awaiting trial is reported in the Bible (Lev. 24:12, Num. 15:34), and the appointment of judges presupposed the concomitant appointment of police "officers" (Deut. 16:18). These officers (*shoterim*) are described by Maimonides as being equipped with sticks and whips. They would patrol the streets and marketplaces, and would bring any criminals they caught before the court; they would also be dispatched by the court to arrest any person against whom a complaint had been brought; in short, "they act upon the judges' orders in every matter" (Maimonides, op. cit. 1:1). In capital cases the accused would be detained pending trial (*Sifrei, Shelah* 114) if he had been caught *in flagranti delicto* or there was at least some *prima facie* evidence against him (J. *Sanhedrin* 7:8). However, the fact that available evidence was as yet insufficient to put a man on trial was no reason not to detain him until sufficient evidence was available (M. *Sanhedrin* 9:5, B. *Sanhedrin* 81b). Or, where death had not yet ensued but the victim was dangerously wounded, the assailant would be detained until the degree of his offense could be determined (B. *Sanhedrin* 78b, B. *Ketuvot* 33b).

Release on bail ("maybe he could bring sureties and walk around freely") is already mentioned in an early source (*Mekhilta, Mishpatim* 6), but the rule evolved that in capital cases no bail should be allowed (ibid.; *Beit Yossef* ad *Tur, Hoshen Mishpat* 388:12 and *Responsa Rivash* 236 quoted there). It may safely be inferred from this rule that in noncapital cases bail would be granted as a matter of course.

Criminal proceedings may never be conducted in the absence of the accused (B. *Sanhedrin* 79b; Maimonides, op. cit. 14:7 and *Rotzei'ah* 4:7).

There is good authority for the proposition that in cases of homicide the blood-avenger (i.e., next of kin: Maimonides, *Rotzei'ah* 1:2) acted as prosecutor (Ran ad *Sanhedrin* 45a). Where no blood-avenger was forthcoming, the court would appoint one for this purpose (B. *Sanhedrin* 45b). By analogy it may be assumed that in cases other than homicide the victim acted as complainant and prosecutor. In offenses of a public nature, the court initiated the proceedings and dispensed with prosecutors. Such proceedings were normally prompted by witnesses who came forward and notified the court that an offense had been committed; if they could name and identify the accused and satisfy the court that a *prima facie* case could be made out against him, the court would take action (Maimonides, *Sanhedrin* 12:1).

While incriminatory action was restricted to prosecutors or prosecuting witnesses only, any person who wished to plead or give evidence in favor of the accused was allowed and greatly encouraged to do so (M. *Sanhedrin* 4:1). If one of the disciples present in court wished to be heard in favor of the accused, he was raised to the bench and allowed to stay there until the end of the day (ibid. 5:4). In post-talmudic times we have records of defense attorneys being appointed by the court (*Responsa Rivash* 235).

Before the evidence of the witnesses was taken, they had to be warned by the court that the life of the accused might depend upon the truth and accuracy of their testimony (M. *Sanhedrin* 4:5, the text of the warning is given above, p. 151). There must be admissible evidence from at least two eyewitnesses (Deut. 17:6) to prove not only that the accused was seen to have committed the act constituting the offense (B. *Ketuvot* 26b, B. *Sanhedrin* 30a, B. *Gittin* 33b), but also that, immediately before committing it, he had been warned not to commit it because of its unlawfulness; and a difference of opinion as to whether the warning must or need not contain exact information as to what the penalty is which the law prescribes as sanction for that offense (B. *Sanhedrin* 80b) was resolved to the effect that the warning would be insufficient if the offender had not been advised beforehand which punishment, and which particular mode of execution in the case of capital punishment, was in store for him (Maimonides, op. cit. 5:2). No circumstantial evidence was ever sufficient to support a conviction (B. *Sanhedrin* 37b, T. *Sanhedrin* 8:3). The accused must be present during the examination of every witness testifying against him, and the witnesses must all be heard in the course of the same proceeding, *viva voce* and in open court (Maimonides, *Eidut* 4:1). Nor would it suffice if the witnesses had each seen the offender commit the offense from a different place of observation and without knowing of each other; they must have warned him together and observed him together when he committed the offense (ibid.).

The biblical injunction "thou shalt then inquire, and make search, and ask diligently" (Deut. 13:15) was literally interpreted to require witnesses to be subjected to three different kinds of examination: inquiry (*hakira*), investigation (*derisha*), and interrogation (*bedika*). *Hakira* is the examination relating to the time and place at which the event occurred (M. *Sanhedrin* 5:1, B. *Sanhedrin* 40b). Every examination starts with questions of this kind, which are indispensable (Ran ad *Sanhedrin* 40a). The particular legal significance of this part of the examination is due to its function as sole cause for allegations of perjury (Maimonides, op. cit. 1:5). *Derisha* is the examination relating to the substance of the facts in issue: who did it? what did he do? how did he do it? did you warn him beforehand? what did you say to him? (M. *Sanhedrin* 5:1, B. *Sanhedrin* 40b). As this line of examination is also indispensable, it is by some regarded as really forming part of *hakira* (Maimonides, op. cit. 1:4). *Bedika* is a sort of cross-examination relating to accompanying and surrounding circumstances and not directly touching upon the facts in issue (Maimonides, op. cit. 1:6). The more examinations of this kind a judge conducts, the better (M. *Sanhedrin* 5:2), because it leads to the discovery of the true facts (Deut. 13:15; *Sifrei, Re'ei* 93; B. *Sanhedrin* 41a). The conduct and amount of cross-examinations is at the discretion of the judges; they ought to insist on it whenever there is the least suspicion of an attempt to mislead the court, as where, for instance, several witnesses testify in exactly the same words—which would not normally happen unless they had learned their testimony by heart (J. *Sanhedrin* 3:8; Asheri ad *Sanhedrin* 3:32; *Hoshen Mishpat* 28:10). But cross-examination should concentrate on points on which suspicion arose and not be allowed to spread boundlessly (Ran ad *Sanhedrin* 32b, *Responsa Rivash* 266, Rema ad *Hoshen Mishpat* 15:3).

Where two sets of witnesses contradict each other on a material point, under either *hakira* or *derisha* as distinguished from *bedika*, the evidence of either set is insufficient in law to establish the facts in issue, because there is no knowing which of the two groups of witnesses is testifying truthfully and which is lying (Maimonides, op. cit. 18:2, 22:1; *Hoshen Mishpat* 31:1). Contradictions on matters not material to the issue will not normally affect the admissibility of the testimony (B. *Sanhedrin* 41a and Ran ad loc.), though the court may reject the testimony as unreliable (Maimonides, op. cit. 2:2). Where one witness positively testifies to a fact in issue, and the other testifies that that particular fact is unknown to him, the testimony of the former is deemed to be contradicted; only where the fact is not material to the issue does the ignorance of the second witness not amount to contradiction (Maimonides, op. cit. 2:1).

No man can be convicted of a criminal offense, even though two witnesses or more warned him beforehand and themselves observed him committing the criminal act, if the witnesses were not competent to testify. The following are incompetent witnesses: women (see above, p. 174); slaves, (see above, p. 58); minors below the age of thirteen (Maimonides, op. cit. 9:7–8); lunatics (ibid. 9:9–10); the deaf and dumb (ibid. 9:11); the blind (ibid. 9:12); the "wicked," including criminals, swindlers, perjurers, illiterates, and informers (ibid. 10, 11, 12, passim), who must, because of their record or reputation, be suspected of not being reliable and credible witnesses; relatives of the accused or of the victim or complainant (ibid. 13, 14, passim); and persons who have any interest in the outcome of the proceedings (ibid. 15, passim). Later authorities restricted the incompetency of relatives and interested parties to civil cases only, and in criminal cases allowed the kinsmen of a murdered man to testify against the murderer and even the victim of an offense to testify against the offender (Rema ad *Hoshen Mishpat* 33:16; Shah, ibid.).

But no person may be heard to say of himself that he is so "wicked" as to be incompetent to testify (B. *Sanhedrin* 9b; Maimonides, op. cit. 12:2). The incompetency of a witness because of "wickedness" has again to be proved by the testimony of at least two competent witnesses (Maimonides, op. cit. 12:1). The disqualification of a witness, even though because of "wickedness," is not regarded as a penalty, and hence no previous warning is required; but in cases of improper or contemptible conduct it has been suggested that a person should not be disqualified as a witness unless he was previously warned that this would happen if he persisted in his conduct (ibid.; *Hoshen Mishpat* 34:24). The disqualification of criminals to testify ceases after their punishment is completed (Maimonides, op. cit. 12:4; *Hoshen Mishpat* 34:29), and in the case of "wicked" persons not liable to punishment, when it is proved to the satisfaction of the court that they have repented and that their conduct is now irreproachable (ibid.).

Confessions of the accused himself are not admissible in evidence in criminal or quasi-criminal proceedings, for "no man calls himself a wrongdoer" (B. *Sanhedrin* 9b). This rule against self-incrimination developed from the notion that a wrongdoer is presumably untruthful and hence incompetent as a witness (cf. Exod. 23:1), and the idea underlying this rule is the same as that underlying the rule that no man may be heard to disqualify himself from testifying because of wickedness (see above). Moreover, no "matter being established" otherwise than "at the mouth of two witnesses, or at the mouth of three witnesses" (Deut. 17:6, 19:15), any other mode of proof, as by self-incrimination, is expressly excluded (T. *Sanhedrin* 11:1, 5). Maimonides adds the psychological consideration that melancholy and depressed persons are apt to confess to crimes which they have not committed, because they want to be put to death (*Sanhedrin* 18:6). Another theory was based on the prophet's words that all souls are God's (Ezek. 18:4), hence no man may be allowed to forfeit his life, as distinguished from his property, by his own admission, his life not being his own to dispose of but God's (Radbaz ad Maimonides, *Sanhedrin* 18:6).

The rule against self-incrimination dates only from talmudic times. Several instances of confessions are recorded in the Bible (Josh. 7:19–20, 1 Sam. 14:43, 2 Sam. 1:16), but these are dismissed by talmudic scholars either as made after trial and conviction for the purpose of expiating the sin before God (B. *Sanhedrin* 43b), or as exceptions to the general rule (Maimonides, Commentary ad M. *Sanhedrin* 6:2; Ralbag ad 2 Sam. 1:14). As all the instances recorded in the Bible related to proceedings before kings or rulers, it may well be that they did not regard themselves as bound by normal court procedures

(Maimonides, *Melakhim* 3:10); and in post-talmudic times some authorities, conscious of their overall responsibility for the maintenance of law and order, seized the ancient royal prerogatives in admitting confessions in noncapital cases where no other evidence was available (cf., e.g., *Responsa Asheri* 18:13; *Responsa Rashba* 4:311). In law, however, the rule against self-incrimination also extended to criminal cases involving only floggings, fines, or quasi-punishments (Rashi ad *Yevamot* 25b, *Responsa Asheri* 11:5).

While it is nowhere said in so many words, the reason for the exclusion of all self-incriminatory evidence may well have been the desire to prevent confessions being elicited by torture or other violent means. It is a fact that—unlike most contemporaneous law books—neither Bible nor Talmud provide for or know of any interrogation of the accused as part of the criminal proceedings, so that there was no room at all for attempts to extort confessions.

If and when the witnesses have been examined and their evidence has been found to be consistent, the judges start their deliberations (M. *Sanhedrin* 5:4). If the evidence was found to be inconsistent, the accused is acquitted and discharged there and then. The rule is that the youngest member of the court has the first say in the deliberations (ibid. 4:2), lest the junior members of the court be unduly impressed and influenced by what their elders say (Maimonides, *Sanhedrin* 11:1, 12:3; Rashi ad Exod. 23:2 and ad *Sanhedrin* 36a), but this rule is subject to the overriding rule that the deliberations must always start with a view propounded in favor of the accused (M. *Sanhedrin* 4:1, 5:4). The question was raised as to how anything could possibly be said in favor of the accused once the witnesses testifying against him had been found competent and credible and their testimonies consistent with each other; the problem was solved by suggesting that "opening in favor of the accused" really meant asking the accused whether he could adduce any evidence in rebuttal (B. *Sanhedrin* 32b, J. *Sanhedrin* 4:1), or it meant reassuring the accused that if he was innocent he had nothing to fear from the evidence adduced against him (ibid.; Maimonides, *Sanhedrin* 10:7). Deliberations were thus always held in the presence of the accused. At this stage he was given the opportunity to say in his defense anything he wished to say: "If he says, 'I wish to plead in favor of myself,' he is heard, provided there is some substance in what he says" (M. *Sanhedrin* 5:4). Maimonides says that the accused is even raised to the bench for this purpose, so that he may be better heard (ibid. 10:8). However, he is not allowed to say anything to his detriment; as soon as he opens his mouth to admit his guilt or otherwise prejudice himself, he is silenced and reprimanded by the court (T. *Sanhedrin* 9:4). Where the accused is not capable of speaking for himself, the court or a judge will do so for him (B. *Sanhedrin* 29a).

It appears that the probative weight of the evidence was, even though it had been found consistent and credible, an open issue for the deliberations of the judges, as was the question of law as to whether the act proven to have been committed by the accused constituted a punishable offense, and the determination of what punishment, and what mode of execution, was provided for it by law.

Once it is clear that a majority of the judges is in favor of an acquittal, the accused is forthwith discharged and released, without any formal judgment being rendered (M. *Sanhedrin* 5:5). The judgment of the court in a criminal case is, thus, always a sentence finding the accused guilty and specifying the punishment to be inflicted on him. Unlike in civil cases, where either party may ask the court to give its reasons (*Hoshen Mishpat* 14:4 and Rema ad loc.), in criminal cases the accused is aware of the views of each and all of the judges, since he had been present throughout their deliberations (though not at their nightly consultations); and hence no reasons are given in the judgment of the court.

Once a capital sentence is pronounced, it has been said that the accused is deemed as if he were already dead (B. *Sanhedrin* 71b). A person killing him would not be guilty of homicide (Maimonides, *Mamrim* 7:9), nor would a person wounding him be guilty of an offense or liable in damages (T. *Bava Kamma* 9:15). The only exception to this rule appears to be the criminal responsibility of children for hitting or cursing their parents, which subsists even after the parents were sentenced to death (B. *Sanhedrin* 85a; Maimonides, op. cit. 5:12; *Yorei Dei'a* 241:4). It is this legal fiction that the accused is deemed to be dead once the law is found to be that he has to die which enables the executioners to execute capital sentences without incurring the liability or the stigma of murderers.

On the other hand, as long as the sentence has not been carried out, the judgment is subject to revision in favor of the accused. On the way from the court to the place of execution a herald announces that A, son of B, is going to be executed for having committed the offense C, and witnesses D and E have testified against him; whoever may have anything to say in his defense should come forward and say it (M. *Sanhedrin* 6:1). The case is returned to the court for retrial not only if any such person is forthcoming, but even if the accused himself wishes to plead again in his own defense; if he wishes so to plead, the case is returned "even four and five times, provided there is some substance in what he says" (ibid.). In order to ascertain whether there is any substance in the pleas of the accused, two men learned in the law are seconded to accompany him on his way from the court to the place of execution, and if they are satisfied that there is some such substance, they will order that he be brought back into court (B. *Sanhedrin* 43a; Maimonides, *Sanhedrin* 13:1). If on retrial or redeliberation the accused is acquitted, the sentence is deemed to be annulled *ex tunc* as if it had never been pronounced.

Where the accused escapes after sentence and before execution and is then caught and brought before the court which sentenced him, he has no right to have the trial reopened (M. *Makkot* 1:10). But where he is brought before another court, that court may not order the sentence to be carried out unless two competent witnesses testify that the accused was indeed lawfully sentenced by a competent court (ibid.; Maimonides, op. cit. 13:7). If the sentence was a sentence of death, it was ruled that the latter court could not order it to be executed unless satisfied itself that the accused had indeed committed the crime, and a retrial had therefore to take place (Maimonides, loc. cit.). If the sentence had been passed by a court outside the land of Israel, a court in the land of Israel would not be bound to execute it (B. *Makkot* 7a; Maimonides, op. cit. 13:8).

Before a death sentence is executed, the accused is asked to confess before God in order that he may not lose his share in the world-to-come (M. *Sanhedrin* 6:2). If he does not know how to make confession, he is asked to repeat the formula, "May my death expiate all my sins" (ibid.).

25

TORTURE AND CRUEL PUNISHMENTS

The modern Hebrew word for "torture" or "torment" bears in biblical language the meaning of "afflict" or "oppress" (cf. Ps. 88:7: "Thy wrath lieth hard upon me, and Thou has afflicted me . . ."; Gen. 16:6: Hagar fled from her mistress because she had "dealt hardly with her"; and cf. Exod. 22:22–23: "Ye shall not afflict any widow, or fatherless child. If thou afflict them in any wise, and they cry at all unto Me, I will surely hear their cry"); and biblical Hebrew has no word for "torture" in the physical sense. Such physical tortures as were actually committed were called by their proper names (Judg. 1:6: cutting off thumbs and toes; 2 Sam. 4:12: cutting off hands and feet), as was the only such torture to be provided for as legal punishment: "When men strive together one with another, and the wife of the one draweth near for to deliver her husband out of the hand of him that smiteth him, and putteth forth her hand, and taketh him by the secrets: Then thou shalt cut off her hand, thine eye shall not pity her" (Deut. 25:11–12). There is no record of this law ever having been carried into effect; and in talmudical law monetary compensation was substituted for the loss of the woman's hand (B. *Bava Kamma* 28a; *Sifrei, Teitzei* 293). The talionic sanctions provided for in biblical law, "Eye for eye, tooth for tooth, hand for hand, foot for foot, burning for burning, wound for wound, stripe for stripe" (Exod. 21:24–25; and cf. Lev. 24:20, Deut. 19:21), were also replaced by monetary compensation in talmudical law (B. *Bava Kamma* 83b–84a; *Mekhilta, Nezikin* 8; *Sifra, Emor* 20; *Sifrei, Shoftim* 190), perhaps not so much because of the cruelty

217

as because of the injustice inherent in the talion: one man's eye may be larger, smaller, sharper, or weaker than another's, and by taking one for the other, you take something equal in name only but not in substance. Not only is the ratio of talion thus frustrated, but the biblical injunction that there should be one standard of law for all (Lev. 24:22) would also be violated. Nor can an eye or any other organ be extracted from a living man's body without causing further incidental injury, such as making him lose blood and even endangering his life: "and the Torah said, an eye for an eye, and not an eye and a soul for an eye" (B. *Bava Kamma*, loc. cit.). The substitution by the talmudists of monetary compensation for talion is the more remarkable as the talion is heavily reinforced by the divine command, "and thine eye shall not pity" (Deut. 19:21, 25:12), a warning which, in another context, was taken so seriously as to warrant the suspension of all procedural safeguards which might smack of "pity" for the accused (in the case of the inciter to idolatry: M. *Sanhedrin* 8:10; B. *Sanhedrin* 33b, 36b).

The modes of capital punishment which we find prescribed or described in the Bible are stoning (Lev. 24:14, 16; Deut. 17:5; et al.), burning (Lev. 20:14, 21:9), hanging (Josh. 8:29 et al.), and slaying (Deut. 20:13). For reasons into which we shall presently inquire, the talmudists dropped the hanging and added strangling (M. *Sanhedrin* 7:1). It is noteworthy that by talmudic law all jurisdiction to impose capital punishment ceased with the destruction of the Temple in 70 c.e. (B. *Sanhedrin* 52b, B. *Ketuvot* 30a), and the pronouncements made by talmudical jurists in respect of execution were never put into practice, but made *sub specie aeternitatis*, with the object of providing just laws for a rehabilitated society. They were, however, limited and handicapped not only by the restrictions and deficiencies inherent in the state of the general knowledge available at the time in which they lived, but, more particularly, by the constitutional framework of the divine will as expressed in scriptural law, within which they had to operate and which they could not in any way contradict or explicitly change. The more remarkable are the results which they actually achieved.

The form of capital punishment most frequently prescribed in the Bible is stoning. It is expressed in a number of slightly differing formulae, all to the effect that the convict is to be put to

death by being stoned by all the people (Lev. 20:2, 24:16; Num.
15:35–36; Deut. 13:11–12, 17:7, 21:21, 22:21). There are several
biblical accounts of such popular stonings having actually taken
place (Josh. 7:24–25; 1 Kings 12:18, 21:13; 2 Chron. 24:21; and
cf. Acts 7:58); all the people pelted the offender with stones until
he died, and the witnesses who had testified against him had to
throw the first stones (Deut. 17:7). In the Talmud there is no
mention any longer of this kind of execution. Instead there are
specific rules for an alternative mode, also called "stoning," but
having little in common with the stoning as divinely ordained. It
is submitted that the talmudists revolted against the notion of
having capital sentences executed by masses of people throwing
stones at the condemned man, and they looked for a more humane mode of "stoning." Whether they chose to adopt or imitate
for this purpose a mode of execution known to them from Roman
law (*Twelve Tables* VIII 23; Gellius XX 1, 53), or whether the
casting down of criminals or enemies from high rocks was known
to them from biblical records (2 Chron. 25:12), the reform they
introduced was to establish a "stoning-house" two floors high,
from the roof of which the convicted man would be thrown down
into the depth (M. *Sanhedrin* 6:4). The great penal reform which
was thus accomplished was the exclusion of the general public
from executions of capital sentences and the elimination therefrom of all traces of *vindicta publica*. The punishment of stoning,
whose main purpose (from a penological point of view) may have
been to absorb public vengeance and provide, even within the
framework of judicial organization and supervision, some outlet
to public fury and aggressiveness, reappears in an entirely new
shape, without public and devoid of fury. How deep-seated was
the apprehension of the sages that even this reformed stoning
might still appear aggressive or malicious is shown by the rule
that the stoning-house must be erected at some distance from the
courthouse, "so as not to let the court seem murderous" (B.
Sanhedrin 42b). Several other humane considerations underlie
the stoning reform: instead of being thrown as a hapless victim to
the anger of an uninhibited mob, the convict is now conducted in
an orderly and solemn manner to the stoning-house, while a
public crier asks for further witnesses who might come forward
in his defense (M. *Sanhedrin* 6:1); and while death by having
stones thrown at him might be slow and painful, and in the

process his body would be wounded and mutilated, the throwing down was calculated to cause a swift and relatively painless death (Rashi ad B. *Sanhedrin* 45a, s.v. *minval*). The overriding and fundamental "Love thy neighbor as thyself" (Lev. 19:18) was held to require "devising an easy death for him" (B. *Sanhedrin* 45b, 52a; B. *Ketuvot* 35b; B. *Pessahim* 75a), for it is not so much for your conduct toward a man in full command of his faculties, whom you may need as much as he needs you and where neighborly love is really based on reciprocal self-interest, that the divine injunction is needed, as rather for your conduct toward a man who is powerless, at your mercy, and on the threshold of death.

The punishment of burning is prescribed in respect of only two offenses (Lev. 20:14, 21:9; M. *Sanhedrin* 9:1), and there is no biblical record to indicate whether and how judicial executions were ever carried out by burning (the burning mentioned in Dan. 3:6 is a Persian, not a Jewish, mode of punishment). We find people threatened with being burned in their houses (Judg. 12:1, 14:15); and there is a much later talmudical report of bunches of vines having been ignited and put around a condemned woman until the flames consumed her (M. *Sanhedrin* 7:2). However burning may originally have been practiced, the talmudists discarded any burning proper, by which the body is consumed by fire, and replaced it by a method of "burning" which caused death by fire but left the body intact: the convict was to be strangled, and when he opened his mouth, a burning wick was to be thrown into his mouth to burn his intestines (M. *Sanhedrin* 7:2). The strangulation process is exactly the same as that prescribed for strangulation proper (ibid. 7:3); and it was not overlooked that in the "burning" process as prescribed, the convict might die of strangulation before any wick could be introduced into his mouth (ibid. 7:2), which appears, indeed, physiologically likelier than that he would obligingly open his mouth after strangulation and before death. This method of "burning," then, is a purely theoretical contrivance seeking to accomplish the impossible: to put to death by fire and still leave the body intact—for no man purporting to love his neighbor would apply a mode of execution which would make the body disappear and render burial impossible. (In contradistinction to the talmudic concept of burning while keeping the body intact, the burnings of the Inquisition had for their avowed purpose—following Matt. 13:42—the complete destruction of the body. In the words of a fourteenth-century Inquisitor, "The object of the Inquisition is the destruction of heresy. Heresy cannot be destroyed unless heretics are destroyed, and heretics are destroyed when they are corporally burnt": Lea 251.)

Many capital offenses are characterized as such in the Bible by words such as "he shall die" or "he shall be put to death," without indicating any particular mode of execution. In these cases the talmudic law provides that death shall be induced by strangulation—the reasons given for the rule being that this is the most humane mode of execution, or the one that most nearly resembles the divine mode of terminating man's life. Just as God leaves no outward mark on the body in taking human life, so man ought not to leave any outward mark when taking human life in obedience to God's command (B. *Sanhedrin* 52b–53a; *Sifra, Kedoshim* 9:11). Strangulation was effected by two men pulling in opposite directions on ties which were wrapped round the convict's neck, until suffocation ensued (M. *Sanhedrin* 8:3). Whether or not this kind of strangulation proved indeed to be the lightest and most humane mode of execution, nobody can say—for the simple reason, again, that it was never tested in practice. It was a *bona fide* device for a light and humane execution; its being considered lighter and more humane than stoning, burning, or slaying, even as modified by the talmudical law reforms, was its sole justification and the reason for its election as the residuary mode of execution. The astonishing fact is that, having once made the choice of execution by strangulation, the talmudic jurists did not adopt, or ever consider adopting, the form of strangulation by hanging which was widely practiced in other systems of law and widely reported in the Bible (Gen. 40:22, for Egypt; Esther 7:9–10, 9:25, and Ezra 6:11, for Persia; 2 Sam. 21:6–12, for the Philistines). We also hear of hangings practiced by Jews (Josh. 8:29), though not in the course of judicial process; and Shimon ben Shetah is reported to have ordered eighty witches to be hanged (M. *Sanhedrin* 6:4), and though this particular sentence was explained as an emergency measure from which no rule of law can be deduced (Maimonides and Ovadia of Bartenura, ad loc.), at any rate it shows that the jurists of the time were familiar with this mode of execution. We must therefore conclude that hanging was rejected for some well-considered reason, and the previously unknown and untested device of

strangulation preferred. The reason was that hanging was regarded as an affront to human dignity, if not to God.

Biblical law was that after execution, the condemned man was
to be hung on a tree, but his body must be taken down and buried
before nightfall, "for he that is hanged is accursed of God" (Deut.
21:22–23). The intimation that the impaled body is an affront to
God indicates God's own abhorrence of hanging; that God nevertheless ordained that executed convicts be hanged, albeit only
until nightfall, must have been a divine concession to the requirements of human law enforcement, including measures of deterrence. But these *post-mortem* hangings, while a necessary evil,
were bad enough: the talmudical law reformers reduced even
these hangings to the minimum, namely to the two offenses in
respect of which deterrence appeared to them indispensable,
blasphemy and idolatry (M. *Sanhedrin* 6:4, B. *Sanhedrin* 45b);
but they would on no account introduce hangings as a mode of
putting to death, which even Scripture had not prescribed. As
one commentator put it: "The accursed of all men and the most ill-
fated of all, is the one who is hanged. No death is more detestable
and more offensive; and the introduction of hangings would have
amounted to a defilement of the land for which a divine promise of
life and blessing was given to us" (Nahmanides, ad Deut. 21:23).
This is not to say that the strangulation which the talmudic
reformers introduced in preference to hanging was indeed more
humane; it was simply never put to the test. But there can be no
doubt that their sole purpose in introducing it was to substitute
for suffocation by hanging a mode of suffocation more compatible
with human dignity.

Slaying by the sword was the mode for executing murderers (M.
Sanhedrin 9:1). It was carried out by decapitating, "in the way
practiced by the Roman government" (M. *Sanhedrin* 7:3), and the
discussion as to whether this would not contravene the injunction "neither shall ye walk in their statutes" (Lev. 18:3) continued
for centuries (cf. Tossafot ad *Sanhedrin* 52b). Some thought it
would be less cruel and mutilating, and less Roman-like, to have
the convict lay his head on a block and decapitate him with a
hatchet, but the majority held that to be even worse (M. *Sanhedrin* 7:3). It is probable that a murderer was originally executed,
by way of talion, in the same manner in which the victim had
been killed (Philo, *De Specialibus Legibus* 3. 182; Josephus,

Antiquities 4. 279; Jub. 4:31); the talmudic reform equalized the law and made death instantaneous in all instances.

As for capital punishment in general, we find the dictum of two of the foremost talmudical jurists to the effect that were *they* still exercising capital jurisdiction, never would they pass sentence of death; others said that a Sanhedrin passing sentence of death once in seven years—or, according to another version, once in seventy years—ought to be called lethal (M. *Makkot* 1:10). When the question was raised as to how such great judges could have performed their judicial duties according to law without passing death sentences, the answer was proferred that they could have devised all sorts of cross-examining schemes to confuse the witnesses, make them contradict each other and themselves, and thus render their incriminating evidence untrustworthy (B. *Makkot* 7a). Rabban Shimon ben Gamliel, who in his early days presided over a Sanhedrin that still exercised capital jurisdiction, is reported to have accepted the neccessity of capital punishment for the sake of deterring potential murderers (M. *Makkot* 1:10); and Maimonides, not at all satisfied with humanitarian evasions of the law, wrote that while courts must at all times be very careful in weighing incriminating evidence, once they were satisfied that there was sufficient reliable evidence to support a conviction, it was their duty to pass sentence of death and "to execute even a thousand convicts on one day if that is what the law of the Torah requires them to do" (Commentary ad M. *Makkot* 1:10).

Offenses which were not punishable with death were under biblical law punishable by stripes; on conviction, the offender was to be beaten "according to his fault, by a certain number. Forty stripes he may give him, and not exceed; lest, if he should exceed, and beat him above these with many stripes, then thy brother should seem vile unto thee" (Deut. 25:2–3). The words "according to his fault, by a certain number" are better rendered as "by count, as his guilt warrants" (Jewish Publication Society translation, p. 369), meaning that the number of lashes to be administered shall be determined according to the guilt or blameworthiness of the offender. The maximum number of lashes, however, is limited to forty, and the explicit warning not to exceed that number was interpreted as meaning that any lesser amount of lashes may be administered if justified by diminished guilt (Ovadia of Bartenura ad M. *Makkot* 3:11). But the notion that any reduction in the number of lashes should reflect lesser guilt or mitigating circumstances was abandoned in favor of an entirely different concept, namely, that since flogging is a bodily punishment, it is the body of the particular offender rather than his guilt that should be the determining factor; and the biblical "according to his fault" gave way to the talmudical "according to his strength." In the language of Maimonides: "A man found liable to be flogged shall be flogged according to his strength, for so it is written, 'according to his guilt.' And that is why the maximum is forty, that even a man as strong and healthy as Samson shall not be liable to more than forty lashes, but a man less strong shall be liable to less" (Sanhedrin 17:1 and, to the same effect, in his Commentary ad M. Keritot 2:4). The substitution of strength for guilt, performed as it was with an air of utter innocence, reflects purely humanitarian considerations. The strength of the offender to suffer corporal punishment was determined by an estimate; the court would inspect and examine the offender and assess the number of lashes which he could safely endure (M. Makkot 3:11, B. Makkot 22b). If he was suspected of being incapable of enduring any lashes, he would be discharged forthwith (B. Makkot 23a). If after having been flogged to the extent ordered by the court, he was found quite capable of enduring more lashes (below the prescribed maximum), he would nonetheless be discharged, as he would be discharged if, notwithstanding the court's estimate to the contrary, he was, while being flogged, found incapable of standing any more lashes (B. Makkot 22b–23a). The lashes were administered by an officer of the court, about whose qualifications for this particular job opinions were divided. The majority held that he was to be great in knowledge and poor in strength; and the minority opinion, that he could very well be poor in knowledge so long as he was bodily strong enough to perform his task, was dismissed as smacking of cruelty (B. Makkot 23a).

Several offenses specified in the Bible carry divine punishment of death, the usual formula being that the soul who has committed them "shall be cut off from among the people" (Lev. 18:29, 20:3, 5, 18; et al.). The "inhumanity" involved in "divine" punishment such as this, and the bold measures taken by the talmudical-law reformers to mitigate it, have been described in Chapter 1, supra. Where the cruelty of punishment appeared to be manifest, even its divinity could not be allowed to stand in the way of its abolition.

26

LEGISLATIVE SAFEGUARDS

The revelation by God of His laws to the whole of the people from Mount Sinai (Exod. 20:18, 22; Deut. 5:4, 19) is already an indication of the recognition of a requirement of publicity. No law is binding unless and until publicized to all those to whom it is to apply (e.g., Exod. 12:3: "Speak ye unto all the congregation of Israel"; Exod. 35:1: "And Moses gathered all the congregation of the children of Israel together and said unto them, 'These are the words which the Lord hath commanded that ye should do them' "; et mult. al.). The ruler who had to administer and implement the laws was required to "read therein all the days of his life" (Deut. 17:19); and to refresh the memory of the people at large the laws were to be read to them in public at regular intervals (Deut. 31:11–12). One such public reading we find recorded from the time of King Josiah (2 Kings 23:2), another from the time of Ezra and Nehemiah (Neh. 8:1–3). It is uncertain whether the manner of promulgation of laws described in the Book of Ezra (1:1, 6:1), namely, putting the laws in writing and depositing them in the "house of rolls," and at the same time publicizing them by proclamation throughout the country, was peculiarly Persian, or whether it was commonly observed in the ancient world.

There are two instances of apparently retrospective criminal legislation in the Bible. A man "blasphemed the name of the Lord and cursed"; he was detained until inquiry could be made of God what the law was, and when God pronounced the law, it was then duly executed (Lev. 24:10–23). Another man was found gathering sticks on the Sabbath day; "and they put him in ward, because it was not declared what should be done to him"; God said, "The

man shall be surely put to death"; whereupon he was duly stoned
(Num. 15:32–36). As far as the second case is concerned, the
violation of the Sabbath was, of course, already known to be a
criminal offense; what had not yet been "declared" was the penalty
to be meted out to the offender. In the same vein it might be said
of blaspheming and cursing God that nobody would assume that
God's laws could permit or suffer such conduct; what needed
clarification here, too, was the kind of punishment this offense
would carry. Still, the fact that at the time the offenses were
committed, neither the offenders nor anybody else on earth knew
what their punishment would be, can on the face of the biblical
reports not be disputed. The notion of any injustice involved may
be mitigated by the consideration that what we are dealing with
in this context are the first origins of promulgated law, where
even in criminal law legislation still looks to judicial precedents
for signposts on its way.

With the evolution and development of criminal law the situation changed completely. Under talmudic law, no act is a criminal
offense and punishable as such unless laid down in express terms
in the Bible, i.e., the Written Law; but it is not sufficient that
there should be a provision in the Written Law imposing a specified penalty in respect of any given act (onesh), so long as the
commission of that act has not first distinctly been prohibited
(azhara). The law that the murderer shall be liable to the death
penalty (Num. 35:16–18), for instance, would not suffice to make
the offense of murder punishable, were it not for the preceding
prohibition, "thou shalt not kill" (Exod. 20:13, Deut. 5:17). Where
such prohibition is lacking, even the explicit statement of a penal
provision cannot warrant the imposition of any punishment (B.
Sanhedrin 54a–b, 60b, 66a; B. Makkot 5b; B. Avoda Zara 51b;
B. Yevamot 3b; B. Yoma 53a); the penal provision is nuda lex
which may be interpreted as a threat of divine punishment, in
respect of which no prior prohibition is required (B. Makkot 13b).

All biblical injunctions are either positive (mitzvot assei) or
negative (mitzvot lo ta'assei), that is, either to do or to abstain
from doing a certain thing. A negative injunction qualifies as a
prohibition for the purposes of criminal law (Maimonides, Commentary ad M. Makkot 3:1). But no prohibition may be inferred e
contrario from a positive injunction (B. Temura 4a). A prohibitory
provision is required not only for capital offenses (B. Sanhedrin

54a–b), but also for minor offenses, whether punishable with floggings (B. *Makkot* 4b, B. *Ketuvot* 46a) or with fines (*Sifra, Kedoshim* 2:1). A prohibition may not be inferred either by analogy or by any other form of logical deduction. The prohibition on intercourse with one's full sister, for instance, could not be inferred from the prohibition of intercourse with the daughter of one's father or one's mother (Lev. 18:9) but had to be stated expressly (ibid. 11).

Similarly, the penal provision must be explicit as applying to an offense constituted of certain factual elements, and may not be extended to cover other offenses, whether by way of analogy or by way of other logical deductions. Thus, for instance, malicious witnesses who commit perjury by testifying that an innocent man has committed a capital offense are to be executed themselves only so long as the accused on his part has not been executed yet; it is written, "Then shall ye do unto him as he had thought to have done unto his brother" (Deut. 19:19), and not as has been done to his brother already, and the latter may not be inferred *a fortiori* from the former (B. *Makkot* 5b). The reason underlying this seemingly hairsplitting precaution has been said to be that as the punishment laid down by divine law was the just and proper one for the lesser crime, it could not be the just and proper punishment for a graver one (Maharsha ad *Sanhedrin* 64b); and as the divine legislator has seen fit to penalize the lesser offense, no human legislator ought to presume to improve on or rectify divine legislation, least of all by human logic (*Korban Aharon* 2:13). The surprising result that the perjurers go scot-free if the accused against whom they testified has already been executed has been explained away by the consideration that God, whose judgment it was that the court has delivered (Deut. 1:17, Ps. 82:1), would never have allowed an innocent man to be executed; the fact that he was executed proves that God condemned him, and hence he must rightly have been executed (*Kessef Mishne* ad *Eidut* 20:2).

This strict legality gave rise to practical difficulties already in talmudic times. "Not in order to contravene the law, but in order to make fences around the law" (B. *Sanhedrin* 46a, B. *Yevamot* 90b), were courts empowered to impose punishments where the maintenance of law and order so required. In the language of Maimonides, "When the court sees that certain misconduct has become epidemic, it is its duty to check it at its best discretion, not as a matter of law which stands for generations, but as an emergency measure (hora'at sha'a). . . . The judges may exercise their discretion in these matters according to the needs of the hour, but must always direct their minds to heaven and hold human dignity (lit: 'the honor of men') in high esteem, taking great care not to infringe upon the dignity of men, sons of Abraham, Isaac, and Jacob, and bearers of the law of truth, but only to increase the glory of God." (Sanhedrin 24:4–10). Such extralegal punishments as are already reported in the Talmud (e.g., M. Sanhedrin 6:4, B. Sanhedrin 52b, 58b) are stated to be justified for upholding the authority and enforcing the observance of the law (B. Yevamot 90b, J. Hagiga 2:2).

The exercise of such emergency powers in criminal matters became indispensable when, under the law, capital jurisdiction ceased with the destruction of the Temple in 70 C.E. (B. Sanhedrin 37b, B. Ketuvot 30a). In many countries (e.g., in Muslim Spain) Jewish courts exercised criminal jurisdiction over Jews with powers conferred upon them by the local rulers; in other countries, internal jurisdiction was exercised under community regulations or by virtue of submission to factual authority. Everywhere were the courts responsible for the maintenance of law and order; and while they continued to administer the criminal law in those matters which were noncapital and thus left within their jurisdiction under the law, there arose in the course of time and with the change of conditions many matters of which the ancient law had taken no cognizance and which required, for the maintenance of public order, drastic action. By virtue of the talmudic authorization as further spelled out by Maimonides, courts assumed criminal jurisdiction in all these matters and even imposed capital punishment—not only for offenses declared capital in biblical law, but also for offenses considered particularly dangerous or obnoxious in the circumstances prevailing at the time (e.g., informers: Maimonides, Hoveil uMazik 8:11), or even for such offenses only as distinguished from those originally punishable under the law (Responsa Asheri 17:1). In order not to give the appearance of exercising jurisdiction under the law, the courts devised new punishments and new modes of execution unknown to the law (Me'iri ad Sanhedrin 52b, Responsa Rashba 238, Responsa Maharam Lublin 138), and also dispensed with formal requirements of the law of evidence and procedure (Responsa Rashba 4:311, Zikhron Yehuda 79). It comes to this: that in the exercise of these powers the courts were at pains to clarify that they were not administering the divine criminal law but acting, rather, in a quasi-administrative function to uphold the peace of the community and prevent its disturbance. (Needless to say that these emergency powers have now practically been obsolete for almost two centuries.)

Talmudical law is unique, however, in making previous knowledge of the law a condition precedent to criminal responsibility, and ignorance of the law an excuse. We have already noted (above, p. 210) that every offender must have been warned by two competent witnesses that the act he is about to commit is a criminal offense, and that if he commits it, he will be liable to the specific punishment provided for by law. This requirement is not only the most potent safeguard against retrospective criminal legislation, but also the most liberal measure to ensure that the *mens rea* of the accused do comprise, in addition to the intention to commit the act which constitutes the offense, an actual intention to break the law. It is true that any such requirement would nowadays— and possibly at all times and in all civilizations—prevent the vast majority of criminals from being convicted and punished; ordinary criminals commit their offenses without any such prior warning being administered to them. But then this rule of the talmudical law was first enunciated at a time when the capital jurisdiction of the Sanhedrin had already ceased, and was never put to the test of actual practice. In fact, it is but the expression of the procedural aspect of the fundamental principle of Jewish law that ignorance of the law provides a good defense to any criminal charge. A person who commits an offense "through ignorance" may expiate the sin by bringing a sacrifice to God (Lev. 4:27, 5:17; Num. 15:27); but he who acts deliberately ("presumptuously") deserves punishment as having "despised the word of the Lord and broken His commandment" (Num. 15:30–31). The antecedent warning of the offender was devised in order to enable the court to distinguish between the intentional ("presumptuous") and unintentional ("ignorant") offender (Maimonides, *Sanhedrin* 12:2 and *Issurei Bee'a* 1:3), the one being criminally responsible and the other not. Even if a man knowingly breaks the law as he understands it, but does so upon the advice or instruction of a court or other competent authority as to what the law is, he is not criminally answerable (B. *Horayot* 2b, 3b; *Sifra, Vayikra* 7).

CONCLUSION

Article 29.2 of the Universal Declaration of Human Rights provides that in the exercise of his rights and freedoms, everyone shall be subject only to such limitations as are determined by law solely for the purpose of securing due recognition and respect for the rights and freedoms of others and of meeting the just requirements of morality, public order, and the general welfare in a democratic society.

"Securing due recognition and respect for the rights and freedoms of others" is, indeed, the paramount duty incumbent upon any man who claims any right or freedom for himself. Of Hillel, a contemporary of Jesus, it is reported that a heathen once challenged him to teach him the whole of the law while he was standing on one foot. Hillel said, "Do not do to another what you would not like another to do to you: that is the whole of the law—and everything else is but comment and elaboration" (B. *Shabbat* 31a). These words were echoed in positive terms by Jesus in the Sermon on the Mount, "Therefore all things whatsoever ye would that men should do to you, do ye even so to them, for this is the law and the prophets" (Matt. 7:12). There is some deep meaning in the condensation of the whole of the law into this of all rules. On the one hand, it legitimizes the purely subjective and individualistic value judgment—what you want or what you do not want to be done to you—as the basis of legal norm-setting; but on the other hand, the only norm it puts on the pedestal of law is the purely prohibitive and altruistic one: do not do to others. All of the law is self-restraint, is practical recognition and implementation of the rights of others; though both the motivation and the justification of such self-restraint may be the ultimate recognition of and respect for your own rights. However motivated and justified, the fact remains that almost all normative Jewish law as between man and man is, in orientation and in effect, wholly altruistic. If "human rights" can be said to provide a basis or starting-point, or perhaps also the ultimate goal, of the norm-creating process, it is the duties, the do and the do-not, the care and respect for the other man, that make for true law.

231

ABBREVIATIONS
AND REFERENCES

ABRAHAMS. I. Abrahams, *Studies in Pharisaism and the Gospels* (reprint, New York, 1967).

ACTS. Acts of the Apostles, book of the New Testament.

AKIVA EGER. Responsa of Akiva Eger (19th cent., Germany).

AKKUM. *Akkum veHukoteihem*, chapter of *Mishne Tora.*

ALBO. *Sefer HaIkkarim* ("Book of Fundamentals") by Joseph Albo (15th cent., Spain).

ALFASSI. Abstract of the Talmud by Yitzhak Alfassi (Rif) (11th cent., Fez).

AMOS. Book of the Old Testament.

ARAKHIN. Tractate of the Talmud.

ARUKH. Talmudic dictionary by Nathan bar Yehiel of Rome (1035–1106).

ARUKH HASHULHAN. Synopsis of the law by Yehiel Mikhel Epstein (19th cent., Poland).

ASHERI. Novellae to the Talmud and Responsa by Asher ben Yehiel (Rosh) (13th cent., Germany and Spain).

ASSAF. S. Assaf, *Batei Din uSedareihem Aharei Hatimat HaTalmud* (Jerusalem, 1924), and *HaOnshin Aharei Hatimat HaTalmud* (Jerusalem, 1922).

AVADIM. Chapter of *Mishne Tora.*

AVODA ZARA. Tractate of the Talmud.

AVOT: Tractate of the Talmud (Mishna only).

AVOT DERABBI NATAN. Extracanonical tractate of the Talmud, the compilation of which is ascribed to Rabbi Natan (4th cent.).

B. Babylonian Talmud.

BAH. Abbreviation for *Bayit Hadash*, Commentary to *Tur* by Joel Sirkis (17th cent., Poland).

BAHYA IBN PAKUDA. *Hovot HaLevavot* ("Duties of the Hearts") by Bahya Ibn Pakuda (11th cent., Spain).

BA'EIR HAGOLA. Commentary to *Shulhan Arukh* by Moshe Ravkas (17th cent., Holland).

BA'EIR HEITEIV. Commentary to *Shulhan Arukh* by Zekharya Mendel (18th cent., Poland).

BAMIDBAR RABBA. *Midrash Rabba* on Numbers.

BARTENURA. *See* OVADIA OF BARTENURA.

BAVA BATRA. Tractate of the Talmud.

233

BAVA KAMMA. Tractate of the Talmud.
BAVA METZIA. Tractate of the Talmud.
BEHA'ALOTKHA. Section of Numbers.
BEHAR. Section of Leviticus.
BEHUKOTEI. Section of Leviticus.
BEIT YOSSEF. Commentary to *Tur* by Joseph Caro (16th cent., Palestine).
BEITZA. Tractate of the Talmud.
BEKHOROT. Tractate of the Talmud.
BEN SIRA. Apocryphal Book of the Old Testament.
BERAKHOT. Tractate of the Talmud.
BEREISHIT RABBA. *Midrash Rabba* on Genesis.
CARMILLY-WEINBERGER. Moshe Carmilly-Weinberger, *Censorship and Freedom of Expression in Jewish History* (New York, 1977).
CODEX HAMMURABI. Babylonian law code, dated at about 1700 B.C.E.
CODEX JUSTINIANUS. Roman law code, compiled in the 6th century.
CODEX THEODOSIANUS. Roman law code, compiled in the 5th century.
CHRON. Chronicles, two books of the Old Testament.
DAN. Daniel, Book of the Old Testament.
DARKEI MOSHE. Commentary to *Tur* by Moshe Isserles (16th cent., Poland).
DAUBE. D. Daube, *Collaboration with Tyranny in Rabbinic Law* (London, 1965).
DEI'OT. Chapter of *Mishne Tora*.
DEMAI. Tractate of the Talmud (Mishna only).
DEREKH ERETZ RABBA. Supplementary minor tractate of the Talmud.
DEUT. Deuteronomy, book of the Old Testament.
DEVARIM. Deuteronomy, and the first section thereof.
DEVARIM RABBA. *Midrash Rabba* on Deuteronomy.
ECCL. Ecclesiastes, book of the Old Testament.
EDUYOT. Tractate of the Talmud.
EGER. *See* AKIVA EGER.
EIDUT. Chapter of *Mishne Tora*.
EIVEL. Chapter of *Mishne Tora*.
ELIAHU RABBA. *See* TANNA DEBEI ELIAHU.
EMMUNOT VE DEI'OT. Philosophical treatise by R. Saadia Ga'on.
EMOR: Section of Leviticus.
ENOCH. Apocryphal book of the Old Testament.
ERUVIN. Tractate of the Talmud.
ESTHER. Book of the Old Testament.
EVEN HA'EZER. Third book of *Shulhan Arukh*, and title of a book by Eli'ezer ben Natan (12th cent., Germany).
EXOD. Exodus, book of the Old Testament.
EZEK. Ezekiel, book of the Old Testament.
EZRA. Book of the Old Testament.

FINKELSTEIN. Louis Finkelstein, *The Pharisees* (Philadelphia, 1962).

GEIRUSHIN. Chapter of *Mishne Tora.*

GELLIUS. Roman jurist (2d cent.).

GEN. Genesis, book of the old Testament.

GENEIVA. Chapter of *Mishne Tora.*

GERSHOM ME'OR HAGOLA. Responsa by Rabbenu Gershom Me'or HaGola (11th cent., Germany).

GEZEILA (VAAVEIDA). Chapter of *Mishne Tora.*

GITTIN. Tractate of the Talmud.

GORDIS. Robert Gordis, "The Right of Dissent and Intellectual Liberty," in *Judaism and Human Rights,* ed. M. Konvitz (New York, 1972).

HAB. Habakkuk, book of the Old Testament.

HABERAKHA. Section of Deuteronomy.

HAFETZ HAYIM. Treatise on the law of libel by Yisrael Me'ir Radin (20th cent., Lithuania).

HAG. Haggai, book of the Old Testament.

HAGIGA. Tractate of the Talmud.

HAVOT YA'IR. Responsa by Ya'ir Hayim Bacharach (17th cent., Poland).

HESCHEL. A. J. Heschel, *The Prophets* (Philadelphia, 1962).

HOKHMAT SHELOMO. Glosses to *Shulhan Arukh* by Shelomo Kluger (19th cent., Russia).

HORAYOT. Tractate of the Talmud.

HOS. Hosea, book of the Old Testament.

HOSHEN MISHPAT. Fourth Book of *Shulhan Arukh.*

HOVEIL UMAZIK. Chapter of *Mishne Tora.*

HULLIN. Tractate of the Talmud.

IBN EZRA. Commentary to the Bible by Avraham Ibn Ezra (12th cent., Spain).

ISA. Isaiah, book of the Old Testament.

ISHUT. Chapter of *Mishne Tora.*

ISSUREI BEE'A. Chapter of *Mishne Tora.*

J. Jerusalem (Palestinian) Talmud.

JER. Jeremiah, book of the Old Testament.

JOB. Book of the Old Testament.

JOEL. Book of the Old Testament.

JONAH. Book of the Old Testament.

JONES. J. W. Jones, *The Law and Legal Theory of the Greeks* (Oxford, 1956).

JOSH. Joshua, book of the Old Testament.

JOSEPHUS. Flavius Josephus, *Antiquities of the Jews* and *Contra Apionem* (1st cent. C.E.).

JUB. Book of Jubilees, pseudepigraphic work dating from the period of the Second Temple.

KASPA. Section of *Mekhilta.*

KEDOSHIM. Section of Leviticus.

KEILIM. Tractate of the Talmud.

KERITOT. Tractate of the Talmud.

KESSEF MISHNE. Commentary to *Mishne Tora* by Joseph Caro (16th cent., Palestine).

KETUVOT. Tractate of the Talmud.

KETZOT HAHOSHEN. Commentary on *Hoshen Mishpat* by Arieh Leib Shen (18th cent.).

KIDDUSHIN. Tractate of the Talmud.

KINGS. Two books of the Old Testament.

KI TISSA. Section of Exodus.

KLEI HAMIKDASH. Chapter of *Mishne Tora.*

KNESSET HAGEDOLA. Commentary to *Shulhan Arukh* by Yisrael Benbeneshet (17th cent., Turkey).

KOHELET RABBA. *Midrash Rabba* on Ecclesiastes.

KOHUT. Alexander Kohut, (ed.), *Arukh Hashalem* (Vienna, 1878).

KOLBO. Anonymous collection of legal and ritual rules (14th cent.).

KONVITZ. Milton Konvitz (ed.), *Judaism and Human Rights* (New York, 1972).

KORBAN AHARON. Commentary to *Sifra* by Aharon ben Avraham Ibn Hayim (16th cent., Morocco).

KROCHMAL. Nahman Krochmal, *Morei Nevukhei HaZeman* (2d ed. Lemberg, 1863).

LAM. Lamentations, book of the Old Testament.

LEA. H. C. Lea, *The Inquisition of the Middle Ages* (abridged ed., New York, 1961).

LEV. Leviticus, book of the Old Testament.

LUKE. Book of the New Testament.

M. Mishna.

MAHARAL. Rabbi Juda Loew of Prague (1525–1609).

MAHARAM ROTENBURG. Responsa by Me'ir ben Barukh of Rotenburg (13th cent., Germany).

MAHARIK. Responsa by Joseph Colon (15th cent., Italy).

MAHARSHA. Glosses to the Talmud by Shmuel Eli'ezer Edels (16th cent., Poland).

MAHARSHAL. Responsa by Shelomo Luria (16th cent., Poland).

MAHARYU. Responsa of Jacob Weil (15th cent., Germany).

MAIMONIDES. Moshe ben Maimon (Rambam) (12th cent., North Africa), author of *Moré Nevukhim, Mishne Tora* (or *Yad Hazaka),* and *Commentaries to the Mishna.*

MAL. Malachi, book of the Old Testament.

MALVÉ VELOVÉ. Chapter of *Mishne Tora.*

MAMRIM. Chapter of *Mishne Tora.*

MARK. Book of the New Testament.

MATNOT ANIYIM. Chapter of *Mishne Tora.*

MATT. Matthew, book of the New Testament.

MEGILLA. Tractate of the Talmud.

ME'IRI. Novellae to the Talmud by Menahem HaMe'iri (13th cent., Italy).

MEKHILTA. Exegetical Midrash to Exodus, ascribed to Shimon bar Yohai (2d cent.).

MELAKHIM. Chapter of *Mishne Tora*.

MENAHOT. Tractate of the Talmud.

MIC. Micah, book of the Old Testament.

MIDDOT. Tractate of the Talmud (Mishna only).

MIDRASH. Scriptural interpretation by homiletics, hermeneutics, parables, and textual exegesis.

MIDRASH RABBA. Collection of Midrashim, completed in the 6th century.

MISHNA. Collection of the rules of Oral Law, compiled by Yehuda HaNassi ("Rabbi") in the 2d century, and forming the basic part of the Talmud.

MISHNA BERURA. Commentary to *Orah Hayim* by Yisrael Me'ir Radin (20th cent., Lithuania).

MISHNE TORA. Code of law by Maimonides.

MISHPATIM. Section of Exodus.

MO'ED KATTAN. Tractate of the Talmud.

MOORE. G. F. Moore, *Judaism in the First Centuries of the Christian Era* (reprint, New York, 1971).

MORDEKHAI. Novellae to the Talmud by Mordekhai ben Hillel HaCohen (13th cent., Germany).

MORÉ NEVUKHIM. Philosophical treatise by Maimonides.

MUSSAFIA. Benjamin Mussafia (1606–1675), glossator to *Arukh*.

NAHMANIDES. Moshe ben Nahman (Ramban) (13th cent., Spain), author of Responsa, Commentary to the Bible, Novellae to the Talmud, and *Sefer HaMitzvot*.

NAH. Nahum, book of the Old Testament.

NAZIR. Tractate of the Talmud.

NEDARIM. Tractate of the Talmud.

NEH. Nehemiah, book of the Old Testament.

NEZIKIN. Section of *Mekhilta*.

NIDDA. Tractate of the Talmud.

NUM. Numbers (Numeri), book of the Old Testament.

OBAD. Obadiah, book of the Old Testament.

OVADIA OF BARTENURA. Commentator to the Mishna (15th cent., Italy).

ORAH HAYIM. First book of *Shulhan Arukh*.

PAINE. Thomas Paine, *The Rights of Man* (1776).

PEI'A. Tractate of the Talmud (Mishna only.).

PESSAHIM. Tractate of the Talmud.

PESSIKTA RABBATI. Early medieval collection of Midrashim.

PHILO. Philo Judaeus, *De Specialis Legibus* and *Vita Mosis* (1st cent. C.E., Egypt).

PINHAS. Section of Numbers.

PITHEI TESHUVA. Commentary to *Shulhan Arukh* by Avraham Zvi Hirsh Eisenstat (19th cent., Poland).

PROV. Proverbs, book of the Old Testament.

PS. Psalms, book of the Old Testament.

RADBAZ. Responsa by David Ibn Zimra (16th cent., Egypt).

RALBAG. Commentary to Bible by Levi ben Gershon (14th cent., France).

RAMBAM. *See* MAIMONIDES.

RAMBAN. *See* NAHMANIDES.

RAN. Novellae to the Talmud and Responsa by Nissim Gerondi (14th cent., Spain).

RASHBA. Novellae to the Talmud and Responsa by Shelomo Adrat (13th cent., Spain).

RASHBAM. Commentary to the Bible and to the Talmud by Shemu'el ben Me'ir (12th cent., France).

RASHI. Shelomo Yitzhaki, commentator to the Bible and Talmud (11th cent., France and Germany).

RAVAD. Glosses to *Mishne Tora* and Commentary to *Sifra* by Avraham ben David (12th cent., France).

RE'EI. Section of Deuteronomy.

REMA. Glosses to *Shulhan Arukh* and Responsa by Moshe Isserles (16th cent., Poland).

RESPONSUM. *Responsum by Maimonides on the Duration of Life*, translated into German by Weil (1953) and into Hebrew by Schwarz (1979).

RITBA. Novellae to the Talmud and Responsa by Yomtov Ibn Ashvili (14th cent., Spain).

RIVASH. Responsa by Yitzhak ben Sheshet (14th cent., Spain and North Africa).

ROSH HASHANA. Tractate of the Talmud.

ROTZEI'AH (USHEMIRAT NEFESH). Chapter of *Mishne Tora*.

RUTH. Book of the Old Testament.

RUTH RABBA. *Midrash Rabba* on Ruth.

SAADIA GA'ON. Greatest scholar of the Geonic period, author of *Emmunot ve Dei'ot* (882–942).

SAM. Samuel, two books of the Old Testament.

SANHEDRIN. Tractate of the Talmud, and chapter of *Mishne Tora*.

SCHULZ. F. Schulz, *History of Roman Legal Science* (Oxford, 1946).

SEDER OLAM RABBA. Midrashic chronology attributed to José ben Halafta (2d cent.) (cf. B. *Yevamot* 82b, B. *Nidda* 46b).

SEFER HAHINUKH. Treatise by an unidentified author (Spain, 13th cent.).

SEFER HASSIDIM. Treatise on ethics attributed to Yehuda HaHassid (12th cent., Germany).

SEMA. *Sefer Me'irat Einayim*, Commentary to *Shulhan Arukh* by Yehoshua Valk Catz (17th cent., Poland).

SEMAG. *Sefer HaMitzvot HaGadol* by Moshe Kouchi (France, 13th cent.).

SEMAHOT. Apocryphal tractate of the Talmud.

SHA'AREI ZEDEK. Collection of responsa from the Geonic period (up to 10th cent.).

SHA'AREI UZIEL. Treatise by Benzion Me'ir Hai Uziel (Jerusalem, 1944).

SHAKH. Siftei Cohen, commentary to *Shulhan Arukh* by Shabatai Cohen (17th cent., Lithuania).

SHEKALIM. Tractate of the Talmud, and chapter of *Mishne Tora*.

SHEKHEINIM. Chapter of *Mishne Tora*.

SHELAH. Section of Numbers.

SHELUHIN (VESHUTAFIN). Chapter of *Mishne Tora*.

SHEMITTA VEYOVEIL. Chapter of *Mishne Tora*.

SHEMOT RABBA. *Midrash Rabba* on Exodus.

SHEVI'IT. Tractate of the Talmud (Mishna only).

SHEVU'OT. Tractate of the Talmud.

SHOFTIM. Section of Deuteronomy.

SHULHAN ARUKH. Code of law by Joseph Caro (16th cent., Palestine).

SIFRA. Exegetical Midrash to Leviticus (completed about 4th cent.).

SIFREI. Exegetical Midrash to Numbers and Deuteronomy (completed about 4th cent.).

SOPHERIM. Apocryphal tractate of the Talmud.

SOTA. Tractate of the Talmud (Mishna only).

SUKKA. Tractate of the Talmud.

T. Tossefta.

TA'ANIT. Tractate of the Talmud.

TALMUD. Comprehensive designation for Mishna and all discussions and elaborations following upon it (Gemara), forming together the source of Oral Law (completed in the 6th cent.).

TALMUD TORA. Chapter of *Mishne Tora*.

TANHUMA. Midrash attributed to Tanhuma bar Abba (4th cent.).

TANNA DEBEI ELIAHU ZUTA (small) and RABBA (large). Midrashic compilation (completed 9th cent.).

TASHBATZ. Responsa by Shimon ben Zemah Duran (15th cent., North Africa).

TEITZEI. Section of Deuteronomy.

TEMURA. Tractate of the Talmud.

TERUMOT. Tractate of the Talmud (Mishna only.)

TESHUVA. Chapter of *Mishne Tora*.

TIM. Timothy, two books of the New Testament.

TOBIT. Apocryphal book of the Old Testament.

TOSSAFOT. Glosses to the Talmud by 11th- and 12th-century scholars (Tossafists) in France and Germany.

TOSSEFTA. Collection of rules of Oral Law allied to Mishna, contemporaneous to it and partly overlapping with it.

TUR. Code of law by Ya'acov ben Asheri (14th cent., Spain).

TUREI ZAHAV. Commentary to *Shulhan Arukh* by David HaLevi (17th cent., Poland).

VAUX. Roland de Vaux, *Ancient Israel* (paperback ed., New York, 1965).

VAYIKRA RABBA. *Midrash Rabba* on Leviticus.

YADAYIM. Tractate of Talmud (Mishna only.)

YALKUT SHIMONI. Anthology of Midrashim compiled by Shimon of Frankfort (13th cent., Germany).

YAM SHEL SHELOMO. Novellae to the Talmud by Shelomo Luria (16th cent., Poland).

YEVAMOT. Tractate of Talmud.

YESSODEI HATORA. Chapter of *Mishne Tora.*

YITRO. Section of Exodus.

YOMA. Tractate of the Talmud.

YONATAN BEN UZIEL. Translator and glossator of the Bible (1st cent.).

YOREI DEI'A. Second book of *Shulhan Arukh.*

ZECH. Zechariah, book of the Old Testament.

ZEKHIYA UMATANA. Chapter of *Mishne Tora.*

ZEPH. Zephaniah, book of the Old Testament.

ZEVAHIM. Tractate of the Talmud.

ZIKHRON YEHUDA. Responsa by Yehuda ben Asheri (14th cent., Spain).

INDEX

I. PASSAGES CITED

241

M. Hagiga
1:8	105
2:1	142
3	143

T. Hagiga
2:7	143

B. Hagiga
3b	27, 123
4b	41–42
5a	183
11b	142, 143
13a	132, 143
14b–15b	117
15b	117

J. Hagiga
1:7	139, 141
2:1	117, 118
2:2	30, 228

M. Horayot
3:7	176, 179
3:8	18, 141

T. Horayot
2:10	179

B. Horayot
2b	229
11a	134

M. Hullin
12:5	23

B. Hullin
13b	134, 159
60b	133
130b	140
135b	164
142a	41, 126

T. Keilim Metzia
1:6	176

M. Keritot
1:4	169
2:4	224

M. Ketuvot
2:5	10
2:6	175
4:12	9
7:6	171
9:1	173
13:10–11	74

T. Ketuvot
6:8	176
13:2	74

B. Ketuvot
15a	35
18b	10
22a	10
26b	210
28a	62
30a	164, 218, 228
32b	33
33a	189
33b	48, 209
35b	220
46a	68, 227
47b	170
50a	139
56a	170
67b	183
72a	168, 175
75b	168
77a	173
79a	174
97a	15
104a	12
105a	194
105a–b	202
105b	194
106a	102
110b	63, 74, 75
111a	75

J. Ketuvot
9:3	95
9:4	170

M. Kiddushin
1:1	170
1:7	167, 169
2:1	80
2:6	81
2:6–7	170
3:12	85, 161, 180
4:2	179

II. NAMES AND SUBJECTS

Aaron, 71, 109, 154
Abandoned property, 94
Abigail, 83
Abraham, 73
Abulafia, Meir Halevi, 135
"Acquisition," of wife, 80, 170
Adonijah, 79
Adultery, 173
Aequum et bonum, 12
Agents, 15, 164
Aggada, 10–11
Ahab, 78
Akavia b. Mahalalel, 118, 119, 121
Akiva, R., 31, 37, 66, 149, 150
Alfassi, Isaac b. Jacob, 5
Aliens, 56, 57, 58, 161–166. *See also* Non-Jews
Amalek, 155
"Ancient Jewish Equity" (Cohn), viii
Apostasy, 122, 159
Arab philosophy, 136. *See also* Islam
Aristotle, 135, 144
Asher b. Yehiel (Asheri), 7
Asylum, right of, 76–79
Attorneys, 191–192

Bail, 209
Bastardy. See *Mamzer*
Bathsheba, 83
Bedika (interrogation), 211
Beit Yosef (Caro), 7
Ben Azzai, 149, 150
Ben Pattura, 37, 38
Ben Sira, 131, 132
Bible, canonization of, 131
Bigamy, 172
Blasphemy, 47, 109
Blind people, 212

Blood-avenger, 44, 53, 54, 55, 76, 210
Boaz, 84
Book-burning, 129
Books, bans on, 144–145. *See also* Censorship
Bribery, 202
Burning, as mode of execution, 218, 220

Caleb, 110
Capital cases, 48, 49, 151, 162–164, 209, 228
Capital punishment, 30, 31, 39, 49, 159, 162, 202, 210, 215–216, 218, 223
Caro, Joseph, 6, 7
Censorship. *See* Information, freedom of
Chancery court (England), 95
Charity, 22, 176, 183
Christians, 115, 129, 130, 134, 159, 160
Circumcision, 58
Cities of refuge, 44, 53, 54, 76, 164
Coins, defective, 14
Communal councils, 9
Competition, unfair, 15
Confessions, 213–214
Conscience, freedom of, 107–128
Contempt of court, 51
Contracts, 15
Converts, 165
Corporal punishment. *See* Flogging
Courts, Jewish
    capital jurisdiction, 30, 163–164, 218, 223, 228
    civil penalties imposed by, 51, 93–94

omniscience of, 125, 127
as possessor of all, 87, 90
as source of justice and mercy,
  198–199
as source of law, 1, 2, 3, 4, 5, 14,
  19–23, 107, 121–123
Good manners, 66
Government officials, 29, 73, 87–
  95, 114–115, 175, 196–197
Great Sanhedrin, 9
Greek law, 10
Greek "wisdom," 135, 136,
  143–144
Guardians, 175

Habakkuk, 109
Hagar, 217
Halakha, 5–6, 11–12
Hakira (inquiry), 211, 212
Hamira books, 132, 133
Hammurabi, Code of, 58, 59
Hanging, 218, 221, 222
Hassidism, 136
Heber the Kenite, 83
Herem (ban), 8, 120–121, 171,
  172
Heretics, 130, 117, 159
Heschel, Abraham J., 110, 113
Hezekiah, 40, 155
Hillel, 124, 126, 231
Hiram (Tyrian craftsman), 83
Homer, 131, 132, 144, 145
Homicide, 28, 36, 37, 53, 54, 92,
  150, 162, 210
  unintentional, 76, 164. *See also*
  Cities of refuge
  See also Capital cases
Hora'at sha'a (emergency
  measures), 30, 31, 228
Human rights
  in Jewish law, vii, 5, 17–18, 19–
  20, 23, 231. *See also names
  of rights*
  See also Universal Declaration
  of Human Rights
Hygiene, 150

Idolatry, 36, 108, 157–159

Imprisonment. *See* Detention and
  imprisonment
Incest, 36, 227
Infants. *See* Minors
Information, freedom of, 129–136
Informers, 228
Inheritances and wills, 9, 14, 173,
  174, 181
Innuj din ("afflictions of justice"),
  207
Inquisition, Spanish, 220–221
Intent, 126–127
Interpretation, rules of, 3–4
Iscariot, Judas, 38
Islam, 159, 160
Israel, State of, 16–17
Isserles, Moses, 7
Issi b. Akiva, 163

Jacob, 168, 181
Jael, 83
Jeremiah, 45, 113, 114, 129
Jesus, 2, 38, 105, 117, 231
Jether the Ishmaelite, 83
Jewish law
  basic sources, 1–5
  change process in, 2, 3, 30, 228
  codes, 6, 7
  is color-blind, 154
  commentaries, 7–8
  defined, 1
  differing opinions and interpretations, 5, 6, 116, 122–124
  divinity of, 1, 2, 3, 4, 5, 14, 17,
  19–23, 107, 121–123
  equity in, 14, 15
  formalism of, 12–13
  as Halakha, 5–6, 11–12
  human rights in, vii, 5, 17–18,
  19–20, 23, 231
  immutability of, 1, 2
  and Israeli law, 16–17
  local customs and usages in, 8–
  9, 99, 103
  nature of prescriptions and prohibitions, 18, 22, 119, 226–
  227
  nonlegal sources of, 10–11

Naamah, 83
Naboth, 90
Naomi, 83, 84
Nathan, 114
Nehemiah, 84, 85, 90, 225
Niddui (expulsion), 118–120
Niebuhr, Reinhold, 22
Noachide laws, 161
Non-Jewish laws, 197
Non-Jews, 82–83, 84–85, 161, 162–163, 189. *See also* Aliens

Oaths, 51
Obadiah, 78
Oral Law, 1, 2, 3, 5, 6, 107, 115
Ownership, rights of, 87. *See also* Property, right of

Paine, Thomas, 149
Parental obligations, 9, 138, 140, 169
Peeping-toms, 66
Perjury, 109, 227
Persecution, 76, 77, 78
Pharisees, 2, 3, 115, 116, 118, 131
Philo Judaeus, 1
Police, 209
Polygamy, 170–171
Poor people, 22, 183–186, 190, 201
Praetorial courts (Rome), 95
Primogeniture, 181–182
Principles of Jewish Law, The (Elon), viii, 16
Prisoners, ransoming of, 52–53
Prisoners of war, 56–57
Prisons. *See* Detention and imprisonment
Privacy, right of, 64–67
Property, right of, 87–95
Prophecy/Prophets, 47, 108, 110–115, 176
Public works, 93
Punishments. *See* Rewards and punishments

Qumran sect, 115, 143

Racial discrimination, 154–156
Ransom, 52–53
Rape, 92
Rashi, 7
Rebellious elder, 48, 117
Rebellious son, 176
Recidivists, 49, 50
Religious discrimination, 157–160
Rema, 7
Reputation and good name, right of, 68–72. *See also* Libel and slander
Residence, freedom of, 73–75
Respecting of persons, 201
Responsa, 6–7, 8
Restitution, by thief, 93
Reuben, 181
Rewards and punishments, 21–23, 38, 42, 45, 76
Rich and poor, 184, 190, 201
"Right and good," 12–13
Righteous gentiles, 161
Robbery, 92–93
Roman law, 12, 95
Roth, Stephen J., vii
Royal officials. *See* Government officials
Ruth, 83, 84

Saadia Ga'on, 136
Sabbath, 58, 104, 105, 106, 117, 167, 168, 208, 225, 226
Sabbatical year, 87–88, 94
Sadducees, 2, 115, 116, 131, 133
Salome Alexandra, 176
Samuel, 30, 93
Sanctuary, right of, 79
Saul, King, 58, 155
Schools, 139. *See also* Education, right to
Sectarians, 159. See also *Minim*
Self-incrimination, 213–214
Self-preservation, 37
"Seven nations," of Canaan, 81, 158
Sexual offenses, 36, 51, 92, 142, 227